THE
ROOSTER
HOUSE

THE

ROOSTER HOUSE

A

UKRAINIAN

FAMILY

STORY

VICTORIA BELIM

ABRAMS PRESS, NEW YORK

Library of Congress Control Number: 2023934102

ISBN: 978-1-4197-6785-2
eISBN: 979-8-88707-018-6

Printed and bound in the United States
10 9 8 7 6 5 4 3 2 1

Abrams books are available at special discounts when purchased in quantity for premiums and
promotions as well as fundraising or educational use. Special editions can also be created to
specification. For details, contact specialsales@abramsbooks.com or the address below.

Abrams Press® is a registered trademark of Harry N. Abrams, Inc.

ABRAMS The Art of Books
195 Broadway, New York, NY 10007
abramsbooks.com

In memory of my grandmother
Valentina (1934–2021)

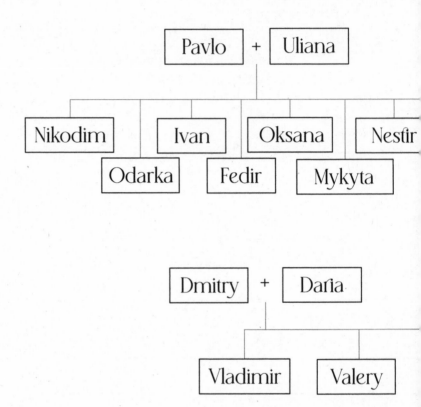

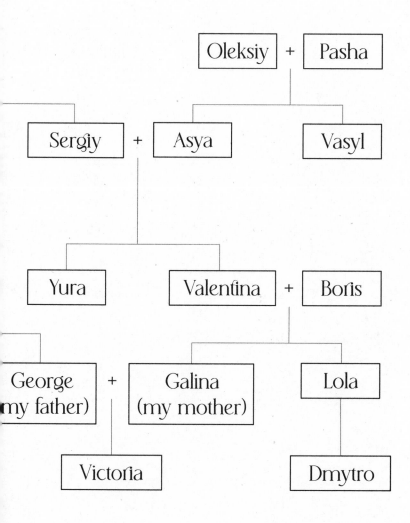

Places in Ukraine mentioned in the book

Who are we? Of what fathers born?

TARAS SHEVCHENKO

It's so clear, you see, that if we're to begin
living in the present, we must first of all
redeem our past and then be done with
it forever.

ANTON CHEKHOV,
The Cherry Orchard

Prologue

I made the final revisions to *The Rooster House* in August 2022, and when re-reading the manuscript against the backdrop of recent news from Ukraine, I was struck anew by the urgency I felt in writing this book. My portrait of Ukraine is personal, tracing my own story against the tidal wave of Ukrainian history. At the same time the book reveals the complicated nature of Ukrainian identity and the country's difficult relationship with its Soviet past. As such, *The Rooster House* explains the context in which the current war takes place.

The year 2014 was a life-changing one for me, and its events made me realise the intensity of my connection to the place where I was born, even though I hadn't lived there for years. The annexation of Crimea showed how easily the world order could be reversed and how fragile were the agreements made by nation-states. It also revealed to me the complexity of Ukraine's history, influenced by its geography as a 'Borderland'. Situated between Russia and the European Union, Ukraine cannot help but be pulled either in one or the other direction. Sometimes this oscillation means a vibrant exchange of ideas. Sometimes it turns into a catastrophe, as happened in 2014.

That year I returned to the country where I had lived for the first fifteen years of my life to spend time with my grandmother Valentina and to rediscover Ukraine. The trips I made between then and 2019 provided the inspiration for *The Rooster House*.

Reading *The Rooster House* at this time, I find an echo between old wars and the one still ongoing, one that I hope, despite its sad note, will resound even more powerfully for readers who wish to understand the country I call home. While the future remains uncertain, Ukraine's resilience makes me hopeful that it will emerge out of this war victorious.

I chose to write *The Rooster House* under my great-grandmother Asya's last name, Belim, using the spelling she preferred, to honour one of the most influential women in my life and the one who inspired me to write down our stories. While the names of my family members are real, the first names of some people in the book have been changed for privacy reasons, in light of the current situation in Ukraine.

PART 1

To the Ukrainian Shore

One

Uncle Vladimir and I fell out a month after his namesake annexed Crimea. At three a.m. Tel Aviv time, he sent me his last message saying that our family should be grateful to the Soviet Union. When I read my uncle's email at eight a.m. in Brussels, I hardly noticed that his Skype avatar had turned lifelessly grey and that his Viber profile no longer displayed a photo of him in the lotus pose.

My attention was riveted by Vladimir's message. He wrote many outrageous things: America had brainwashed me; American capitalism had killed my father; but what struck a nerve was that we, meaning our family, owed the Soviet Union a debt of gratitude. The thought that anyone should long for a regime whose name was synonymous with totalitarianism struck me as obscene. I couldn't believe that my uncle, an avid practitioner of yoga and a keen photographer, had turned apologist for the atrocities of the Soviet Union. The USSR had hacked so ruthlessly at my family tree, decimating us in wars, famines and purges, that we had paid dearly for the seven decades of Soviet socialism. The more I sifted through the memories from my Soviet childhood in Ukraine and recalled the squalor of our lives in the eighties, the more my throat clenched and my temples throbbed. I closed my laptop, stepped over to the window and pressed my forehead against the cold glass.

The gabled buildings of Brussels glistened after recent rain and heavy clouds still hung over a dark line of trees in the distance that marked the outer limits of the city. I exhaled slowly onto the glass, watching the red roofs fade to pale orange. A few seconds later, however, the mist from my breath cleared and everything sprung back to life, more vivid than before. But my thoughts remained in disarray.

Vladimir was my father's older brother. I had lost my father three years before, and Vladimir remained the only link to that side of my family. We were born in the same country, Ukraine. We spoke the same language, Russian. We each now lived in places where nobody knew us as children, as Vladimir liked to say. Yet, when we argued, we might as well have been from two different planets. I emigrated from Ukraine at the age of fifteen to Chicago and Vladimir at the age of fifty-five to Tel Aviv, but he remained in his own Soviet galaxy. His Soviet Union bore no resemblance to the one I knew. For me, the Soviet Union was deprivation and empty store shelves. His was nuclear might and a strong army. My Soviet Union was the collapse of the eighties and the disaster of Chernobyl. His was the boom of the fifties and the flight of Yuri Gagarin, the first man in space. That Vladimir expected me to feel grateful to any of those Soviet Unions astonished me.

We had had several card-carrying Communists in the family and my maternal great-grandfather had proudly called himself a Bolshevik. However, those same Communists had voted for

Ukraine's independence in 1991, as had my Bolshevik great-grandfather. Nobody had longed for the Soviet Union. I always thought of nostalgia as an illness and of Soviet nostalgia as a special pathology, and Vladimir's case disturbed me. Normal people shouldn't miss the lines for food, the blackouts and constant shortages. Sane people shouldn't long for a regime that overthrew all humanistic values and killed and jailed millions of its subjects. Vladimir himself was imprisoned for making copies of Beatles tapes, so if anyone was brainwashed, it was him.

Had my conversation with Vladimir happened at another time, I would have ignored his comments. He was in his late seventies and many people from my grandparents' generation had opinions and ideas that I couldn't fathom. I resented his anti-American diatribes, but Russian television made him look at the world in terms of fifth columns and devious conspiracies. Usually I deflected the conversations from politics to yoga, an interest we shared. Or I would ask him to play the silent films he had recorded as a young man and was gradually digitising. His latest restoration featured me, existing but not yet born. Vladimir had shot the film during a family camping vacation: my pregnant mother with her hand on her belly, dipping her toes in the river and glancing coyly at the camera; my father pulling a large, glistening fish out of the water. The camera panning from my father to my mother as he handed her the fish to be cleaned. The camera zooming in on my mother's pale face framed by a black bob and showing us her grimace. Vladimir was working on the second part of the footage that tracked my childhood until 1986, the year Chernobyl exploded and my parents divorced.

However, while Vladimir was propagating his brand of Soviet nostalgia, Ukraine was being torn apart in the name of rebuilding the Iron Curtain. Another thing Vladimir had in common with Putin was his conviction that the demise of the Soviet Union was 'the greatest catastrophe of the century'.

If my uncle weren't so fixated on the United States as the source of all evil, he could have blamed my new home, Brussels, because everything had started with a document concocted at the EU headquarters down the street from my apartment. He could have traced the tragedy to an agreement that set out the terms of collaboration and trade between the EU and Ukraine. The agreement detailed an economic and political association, with the EU promising to provide financial support, preferential access to markets, and eventual convergence of legal standards and defence policy. Ukraine's rich agricultural resources and its strategic position on the EU's eastern frontier made it an attractive partner. However, for Russia, its neighbour's turn towards the West looked menacing and provocative, as it meant the loss of influence and control over Ukraine, an important territory in Russian politics since the days of the tsars. Had the association agreement been signed, perhaps not much would have changed, least of all for Ukraine, as only the most optimistic could hope that this piece of paper would unlock the doors of EU membership to a dysfunctional post-Soviet country.

However, the agreement wasn't signed. The then Ukrainian president Viktor Yanukovych simpered at the meetings with EU officials and made noncommittal noises about freedom and democracy. Then in November 2013 he latched on to a Russian loan bailout and handed the EU an unsigned agreement. When the news broke out, many Ukrainians were outraged. Despite the insignificance of the agreement, it represented a turn towards the West and a dream of life without rampant corruption and Russia's constant pressure. 'Now nothing will ever change,' my mother said on the telephone from Chicago, swallowing hard and sniffling. We watched TV reports showing students gathering on Maidan Nezalezhnosti, Kyiv's central square, to protest Yanukovych's sudden volte-face. 'Nothing ever changes in Ukraine,' my mother repeated whenever we talked, the despair making her voice brittle. Christmas came, and students continued their vigil in Maidan during the coldest days of the Ukrainian winter. 'Where will this lead?' my mother asked me, but I didn't know.

The start of the Maidan protests reminded me of the Orange Revolution of 2004, which contested the election fraud committed by Yanukovych. That revolution petered out amid the same allegations of corruption that plagued all Ukrainian presidencies. I couldn't invest myself in another revolution that was likely to end the same way, and Vladimir and I agreed that making sense of Ukrainian politics was a thankless affair. I had studied political science and had even written a thesis on the patterns of corruption in the post-Communist world, but Ukraine still puzzled me. The place where I was born remained a distant, unknown land.

But whether or not I could figure out Ukraine, the Maidan events ended up absorbing me. When government forces attacked the protesters, the gathering grew, drawing people of all classes and backgrounds. The government response became brutal and culminated with the shooting of protesters by snipers.

I watched the news footage in a state of shock. The surreally graphic images of red puddles on the pavement, bullet holes and burning car tyres didn't register in my mind as Maidan. My Maidan was a different place.

'Let's meet on Maidan.' Though my schoolfriend Alyona and I lived within a short walking distance of each other, we crossed the city to go to Khreshchatyk, a mile-long street in the centre of Kyiv, where Maidan stood. We sat on the warm stone steps of the square and watched the colourful crowd of students, families and tourists rush past us. We imagined ourselves part of that energy, gaiety and glamour. The day before I left for the United States in 1994 – three years after Ukraine became independent – Alyona and I went to Maidan, bought chocolate ice cream from a street kiosk, and ate it strolling around the square. Alyona was wearing a cobalt-blue dress with a velvet collar that made her look like the femme fatale she wished she were. I was wearing cranberry lipstick that bled into the corners of my mouth and made me look like the awkward teenager I wished I weren't. The chestnut trees bloomed darkly pink, the way they did only on Khreshchatyk, and it seemed as if spring would never end.

In 2014, it seemed that spring never came. The figures on screen lurched and hurtled into each other. The camera ran after them, slicing through black smoke, and then grabbed the shadows of the shooters. The sound of gunfire ricocheted and echoed in my room in Brussels. My heartbeat deafened me. When something of ours, something we took for granted as being ours, is destroyed before our eyes, we are destroyed along with it. Witnessing the shooting on Maidan, I latched onto my memories of Ukraine in an attempt to restore what was mine and part of me.

Was Alyona protesting on Maidan, I wondered? We had kept in touch for a few years after I left Ukraine, but then our letters became shorter and finally stopped. I remembered where Alyona lived in Kyiv but I didn't know what had become of her.

As relations grew tense between Ukraine and Russia, I nevertheless assumed that the conflict would never affect my family. Even after the shooting on Maidan, I didn't imagine that war would be instigated by Russia. And even if I allowed for the improbable event of war, I was sure that a conflict between Russia and Ukraine couldn't splinter my family's intertwined roots. The Ukrainian branch of my family had

Roma and possibly Jewish origins, and the Russian one took the Communist slogan 'the friendship of the peoples' to heart, because through various marriages a good half of the Union's republics appeared in the human mosaic of my family.

We spoke Russian at home, except for my maternal great-grandparents Asya and Sergiy, who spoke Ukrainian. I didn't take it as a sign of ethnic difference, because Asya and Sergiy lived in a village and the rest of us in Kyiv; in the Soviet Union, the cities spoke Russian and the villages the local languages of the republics. Both my ethnically Russian father and Vladimir knew Ukrainian and could recite the verses of the national bard Taras Shevchenko better than my ethnically Ukrainian mother. Some of our relatives spoke Azeri, Armenian, Yiddish, Polish and Belarusian. New customs and traditions appeared as new marriages and friendships brought even more colours and cultures to our variegated household. I was so confused as to what I should put in the nationality column on the mandatory forms we filled out at school that I left it blank, much to my teacher's consternation. I wasn't taught to think of people in terms of their ethnicity, language or race and I wasn't raised to identify myself with any particular group. It took me years to learn that it wasn't the norm, but I never lost my belief that it should be.

When we moved to Chicago, my self-identity remained as vague as ever. I missed my friends and my grandparents in Ukraine. I missed Kyiv and the juxtaposition of its Soviet rawness with medieval, gold-domed splendour. I grew depressed and wrote poems about death and the futility of life. My mother and stepfather were busy adjusting to their new life, and I was left to my own devices to survive this period of transition from one country to another, from childhood to adulthood. But before long I found much to love about my new country. Growing up in the suburbs of Chicago in the nineties, I absorbed the American idea of a melting pot and multifaceted identity. I didn't feel the need to define myself. When people asked where I was from, I replied, 'Russia'. Most Americans I had encountered could patch together the rudiments of a Soviet story, but Ukraine was a blank. My mother was Ukrainian, my father Russian, and since in the USSR ethnicity was passed down from the father's side, I might well have been Russian.

None of it mattered within our family. Neither the collapse of the Soviet Union nor emigration altered my family's open-minded, tolerant approach to diversity, and I wasn't expecting that yet another political crisis in Ukraine would.

But when the Russian army appeared in Crimea, tensions flared between Vladimir and me. The more I read the news – and I read it hourly – the less my body felt like it belonged to me. I couldn't stop myself from watching the grim footage, searching for hope of something, anything, that would stop events from spiralling out of control. But the tanks rolled in, men in unmarked green uniforms held their positions, and panic filled me.

'Don't take it so hard. The peninsula was gifted to Ukraine by Khrushchev,' Vladimir said. It was his attempt to comfort me. When Vladimir and I connected on Skype, Crimea was very much on our minds, and he referred to the act of 1954 when the General Secretary made the peninsula part of the Ukrainian Soviet Republic. 'The Crimeans are Russian, like us.'

I wanted to add that I was half-Ukrainian, but I didn't, because the war wasn't about ethnicity, despite attempts to make it otherwise, and I still resisted the labels.

'You're forgetting about the original residents, the Tatars,' I said.

'The original residents were the Greeks,' Vladimir replied.

'Well, Stalin deported both the Greeks and Tatars after the Second World War,' I said, impatiently.

'And when Ukraine broke off from the Soviet Union, it took

Crimea with it and didn't ask the people what they wanted. Did you think of that?' Vladimir raised his voice and no longer cared about consoling me. I again disagreed with my uncle's reading of history, because in 1991, Ukraine held a referendum on independence, and all regions, including Crimea, voted to leave the USSR. To be fair, in Crimea the proportion was smaller than anywhere else, but I didn't mention that to Vladimir since he wasn't listening to me anyway.

'Do you blame the Crimeans for supporting Putin?' he continued.

'Why are you supporting Putin?' I asked. 'In Tel Aviv, of all places!'

'I'm Russian.'

'You became more Russian once you left Ukraine, it seems. But where were you born? Where did you spend most of your life? In Ukraine!'

Vladimir was looking down into the left corner of his screen. He was all sharp joints, bald head, and sunken cheeks. Ascetically thin, he looked like a stylite monk, but when I said something that flustered him, like now, he twisted his mouth into a crooked smile that made him resemble a bad-tempered elf.

'When I listen to the speeches of American and European politicians, I'm amazed by their ignorance of Ukraine's history,' Vladimir said at last. 'Their talk is nothing more than childish babbling.'

'Even Ukrainians hardly know their history, so what can you expect of others?' I said. Vladimir nodded, and relieved that we could still agree on something, we switched to talking about film and how the camera saw more than the eye.

The extent to which the war became a personal tragedy dawned on me that day. The conflict in Ukraine was about control, not ethnicity or language. However, labels like pro-Russian, pro-Ukrainian, Russian-speaking, Ukrainian-speaking or pro-European became shorthand for a political position. For the first time in my life, I was expected to take sides and define myself with a tag, and yet I couldn't pull the Ukrainian or Russian threads out of the tapestry of my identity. I also wasn't sure about my political position, except that I categorically didn't want a return to the USSR.

Yet I wasn't sure then if I wanted to return to Ukraine. My mother had visited every year since we moved to the US, spending the summer with Valentina, her mother and my grandmother, but we couldn't always afford a transatlantic airfare for the two of us. On the rare occasions when I joined her I felt more foreign in Kyiv than I ever did in Chicago. The Soviet Union where I lived for the first thirteen years of my life had vanished and the Ukraine that took its place struck me as unfamiliar. After twenty years in the US, I moved with my husband to Belgium and retraced my steps to the old world that my family had left with few regrets. I thought that I would travel to Ukraine more often. I didn't. 'Leaving is hard, and so is returning,' Valentina said. I didn't understand what she meant. All I knew was that it was complicated enough to arrive, much less to reckon with what had been left behind.

In the end, I had no choice in the matter, because Ukraine returned to me. Time reset itself, rewinding past the years spent in Belgium and America as if they had never happened. The Ukraine I never claimed took hold of me and filled my thoughts and voids with its memories. The familiar landmarks from my childhood – our old apartment in Kyiv, the chestnuts of Khreshchatyk, and my great-grandparents' peach-coloured house in Bereh – appeared more lucid to me than the buildings outside my window in Brussels. These bright memories flickering against the news of carnage in Ukraine were excruciating, but I sought them, conjuring up the minutest of details, the way one pressed a throbbing bruise to see how much pain one could bear. The Maidan shooting dispelled my illusion that Ukraine was distant. Then Putin's decision to use military power in Ukraine, sanctioned by the Russian parliament on 1 March 2014, shattered my misconceptions about the war. The war was coming.

Like most Soviet children, I grew up with my grandparents' memories of the Second World War. 'If only there was no war,' was a mantra they repeated. Every other catastrophe could be overcome, they said, but living through war was worse than death.

The Soviet–Afghan war gave me the first intimation of what my grandparents meant. Distant though the battles were, the veterans returning from the mountains of Afghanistan brought the war back with them. Sometimes we saw them, scowling, limbs missing, playing an accordion in the street or talking loudly on the bus, saying garbled phrases that frightened me. The most terrifying, however, were people like my father's friend Danil. He was drafted in 1984 and discharged a year later. Tall, dark-haired and strikingly handsome, he sat at our dining table with his wife Masha and cracked jokes, rushing through the punchlines and laughing so hard that he didn't notice our silence. Then he cut himself off mid-sentence and clutched the side of the table, the knuckles of his fingers turning white. Masha's hands and eyes couldn't find a place to rest. My mother glanced at my father, who stared imploringly at Danil. After a few seconds that lasted an eternity, Danil recomposed his face and laughed, baring his teeth, but his wife still replied in non-sequiturs and my mother told me to go and play outside. We didn't say words like depression, anxiety or post-traumatic stress disorder. We just said one word, war, and it explained everything.

One day Danil and Masha invited us to have dinner with them. When we reached their house, we were blocked by a large crowd and an ambulance. 'Such a handsome man,' said someone next to us.

'Former soldiers always have guns.'

'Many of them return troubled.'

'No, it was his hunting rifle.'

'He did it in the bathtub.'

'War ...'

My father pushed the people aside and hastened towards the house. My mother covered my ears and pressed my face into her skirt. Her hands were shaking so violently that her little pearl ring painfully yanked my hair. I freed myself from her grip. Two doctors were carrying a stretcher covered with a white sheet. A ragdoll's arm swayed to the rhythm of their steps. Masha stood rigid at the entrance of the house, but when she saw my father, she crumpled to the ground and howled. My mother grabbed my hand and ran out of the courtyard, dragging me behind her. Masha's harrowing animal cry followed us for the rest of our way home.

I must have been only seven when Danil died by suicide, but in 2014, reading about the war in Ukraine, I still shivered from the memory. Masha's howl lived in me, and the more real the war became, the more I felt it in my throat. The war became real even before any shots were fired, but soon that happened too and people died. After Russia annexed Crimea, several cities in eastern Ukraine declared independence from Kyiv's government and sought Russian support. New republics appeared overnight, as did new battlefields. The front pages of newspapers were splashed with the names of towns where people stormed government buildings and battered each other – Kharkiv, Donetsk, Odesa, Mariupol.

Seeing the landmarks of my personal geography plunged into tumult, I lost my sense of time. My mother was born in Kharkiv, the easternmost metropolis in Ukraine, where my grandmother Valentina studied geography. My father once brought a lump of raw coal from Donetsk where he worked briefly after an unsuccessful gold-mining stint in Siberia. He said that it was a meteorite; my mother said that it was an ordinary rock, but the rough, shimmering form captivated me anyway. In Odesa, I lost my favourite teddy bear running down the famous Potemkin Stairs and was inconsolable until later at the beach my father showed me how hermit crabs changed their shells. In Mariupol, a town famous for its fruit, my mother and I bought a slender cherry seedling for my great-grandmother Asya's garden. Current events in Ukraine muted all sensations in me apart from fear and panic. The place where I was born, where I grew up, and where my grandmother lived, suffered and I suffered too. Each new bout of violence convulsing Ukraine reverberated in me, releasing a flood of images and memories.

Vladimir also struggled with his own anxieties. On good days, he emailed me photos from his youth accompanied by stories about travelling across Ukraine on the back of his friend's motorbike or building sound-recording devices with his brothers. More often, however, he bombarded me with links from Russian websites that described the events in Ukraine as the work of neo-Nazis and nationalists. When separatists in Donetsk and Lugansk established their breakaway republics, Russian propaganda went into overdrive and kept its viewers feverish with a litany of conspiracy theories, great power posturing and paranoia. Once Vladimir grabbed onto the theory that events in Ukraine were the work of the CIA in collaboration with Ukrainian nationalists, our conversations became haunted by their spectres. Another target of his ire was the US. 'Why did America have to meddle? Why do they always meddle?' Vladimir pointed his bony finger into the camera.

I may have left the US, but it was the place that had nurtured me, and I felt a strong affection for it. Moreover, I saw the US support of Ukraine as crucial to stop Russia from encroaching on its territory. I was losing my patience and I grew more defensive with each conversation.

'When your father decided to move to America, I told him what I thought,' Vladimir continued. 'I told him that he was making a big mistake. If only your father had listened to me . . .'

My jaw twitched. 'Leave my dad out of it, OK?' I said, and invented a postman at the door as an excuse to cut our conversation short.

As time went on, Ukraine and politics dominated our discussions. Despite our increasingly tense exchanges, Vladimir was the only link to my father's family. I thought that he needed my company because he was in his seventies and lived with his daughter who was busy working two jobs. His frail health meant that most of his social life was online, and for my part, I longed for family ties in a place where I had none. Yet, as Vladimir's opinions became more radical, I could neither predict nor control my reactions to them.

'Europe should be grateful to Stalin,' Vladimir said. 'If it weren't for him, we would all have been destroyed by Hitler.'

I had already heard Vladimir praising Putin and decrying democracy as a permission to accumulate wealth, but his veneration of Stalin came as a surprise.

'Stalin was like Hitler,' I said, raising my voice higher than I intended.

'But he won the war,' Vladimir parried. The war explained everything, as it always did.

'At what cost! The Soviet Union lost nine million lives because of its disregard for people. Out of Grandmother Daria's twelve siblings, your uncles and aunts, only two survived the war! And how many people did Stalin's regime kill? Twenty million, if not more!' A cold spring breeze blew through an open window and made the papers on my desk quiver, but the air around me felt hot and electric.

'I survived the war,' Vladimir said gloomily. I didn't say anything and we shuffled in front of our screens, fidgeting with camera angles.

'But as I said, Stalin had a war to fight and he had to be tough. There are always consequences.' Vladimir was calm and collected again.

'What war did he fight in the 1930s when he starved millions of peasants in Ukraine?'

'Are you talking about the so-called Holodomor?' Vladimir said, putting a sarcastic inflection on the word the Ukrainians used to refer to the Great Famine. 'The harvest failed. People starved in many other places, not just Ukraine.'

'But Stalin forced the disastrous collectivisation and the Communist Party withheld aid to the famine-stricken areas. There are documents to prove that the famine was created deliberately to break the Ukrainian peasantry that was resisting Soviet policies.'

'Is that what they teach you in American schools?'

I had laid out evidence and facts in my mind, but now my arguments unravelled into agitation.

'I grew up with people who remembered it. Asya and Sergiy lived through it and told me stories about it,' I said, my voice cracking.

'We all tell stories, but they don't always mean what you think they do.'

Later, Vladimir emailed me an article from a Russian

nationalist website titled 'The Real History of the Ukrainian Famine'. I shouldn't have opened it, but I couldn't resist inflicting more pain upon myself. The article claimed that the famine of the 1930s was invented by Ukrainian nationalists in Canada and that Ukrainians latched onto the idea to exploit their victimhood. I scanned the text with dry eyes, feeling every muscle in my body tightening.

The famine affected other regions in the Soviet Union, but Ukraine suffered the worst of all. Four million Ukrainians starved to death in the Holodomor of 1932 and 1933. It left deep scars in the memories of my maternal great-grandparents who lived through it. My great-grandmother Asya, on my mother's side – whom Vladimir had met at my parents' wedding – worked as a teacher at a small village school near Poltava and watched her students die one by one. Her daily lessons started after she dug graves for the dead children who had nobody else left to bury them. Crops were confiscated and sent to other regions of the USSR or for export, and borders were closed to prevent people from leaving their villages. Asya was only eighteen then and the fear of hunger obsessed her for the rest of her life. Once I threw away a jar of mouldy jam, and when my great-grandmother discovered it, she was livid. She screamed that I was a spoiled brat who wasted food, that I didn't know what hunger was like. She crouched by the garbage can and scraped the jam out of it into a little tin. She then ate it.

I closed the computer. My ears were ringing and my cheeks burned. Vladimir's denial of my family's experience was like a slap in the face.

I didn't answer the next time he called, but I sent him a message saying that I didn't understand how he could praise a Soviet Union that destroyed so many lives in our family.

Vladimir replied, arguing at length that the USSR defended

the world from fascism. The USSR sent the first man into space. The USSR was a great power. Of course, there were problems too. Any system had flaws. US capitalism was far worse, for example.

'The rotten ideology of democracy is filling Ukraine with its stink,' he said, when he called the next time. 'Putin is standing up to America. It's about time someone did.'

'If you like Putin so much, why are you living in Israel?' I replied.

'And you, the Ukrainian patriot, why are you in Brussels and not in "your country" with "your people"?'

It was then that I brought up Vladimir's imprisonment over something as trivial as The Beatles. He was the one who had suffered from Soviet repressions by being condemned for selling music records. Did the judges take such offence to 'I'm back in the U.S.S.R. You don't know how lucky you are' that they put Vladimir behind bars for three years?

Vladimir hung up. I felt guilty and berated myself, but I was still angry with his comments about the Holodomor. For the next few days, I saw his Skype profile light up occasionally, but he neither called nor emailed me. He responded at the end of the week and his message was brief.

He wrote that he had been imprisoned in the Soviet Union, but that he had no regrets. 'We must be grateful to the Soviet Union for all the opportunities it gave us,' he added at the end of his message. 'Nothing else I can tell you will sink in, because America brainwashed you as surely as American capitalism killed your father.'

A whistling sound pierced my ears as if I were falling from a great height. I breathed in, trying to fill my lungs despite the tightness in my throat. Once my initial anger receded, I spent the whole day thinking of a reply. I wrote that my experience of the Soviet Union left me unable to feel grateful to it. If our family achieved anything, it was in spite of the system, not because of it. I re-read the message and deleted it. I wrote reminding Vladimir that however long I had been away from Ukraine, it was still the place where I was born and grew up. I deleted that too. I then wrote asking him not to engage in ridiculous theorising on the role of American capitalism in my father's death. I thought for a moment and moved the message to the trash.

The email I sent Vladimir in the end consisted of one line, 'Did you forget about the pact we made three years ago?'

As I wrote, I could see my father's face clearly – his bushy moustaches touched with grey, his gold-rimmed glasses and curly chestnut hair. The last time I saw him was in San Francisco. He and my stepmother Karina had already been living in the Bay Area for more than ten years, and I made a surprise visit after a work-related trip to California. My father picked me up at the train station, loaded my small suitcase into the trunk of his car and looked at me with unexpected tenderness. Our relationship was often strained, and I didn't know how to react. I gave him a hug and caught a familiar whiff of cigarette smoke and cologne that made me feel comforted.

'You're an adult now,' he said. I wanted to tell him that at thirty-two I certainly was, but a note of sadness in my father's voice made my heart lurch. Did he regret being absent from my life for years at a time? Did he want to make amends?

We had a good time together during the visit, watching singing contests and cooking crab with my stepmother. My father seemed to be in good spirits, talking about a new business venture and even showing me a few houses he wanted to buy. We discussed my work as a freelance writer focusing on olfaction and how I described scents and the memories they evoked. It was only a long weekend, but I still recalled it vividly, down to the batik pattern of my father's yellow shirt and the sweet taste of boiled crab.

After his death Vladimir and I made a pact. Vladimir offered it himself; that we would talk about my father and whatever happened when I was ready. As my father's older brother, he was the closest person in my life to know my dad so well. Vladimir shared many memories of them growing up together, but I wasn't ready to examine the causes behind his death. It was too raw and too painful. Now, in all our arguments about the Soviet Union, Vladimir had broken his promise. Denying the history of Ukraine was upsetting to me; raising the ghost of my father was painful. If Vladimir thought that capitalism had truly killed him, I could not bear to know why.

Vladimir never received my message. My note bounced back with a curt comment that the user wasn't found. Being robbed of a chance to reply so infuriated me that I blocked Vladimir's inanimate Skype avatar and marked his email address as spam.

Two

Mourning a place is even more difficult than mourning a person. Losing a loved one is a tragic but inevitable part of human experience, but war is not. Seeing our familiar landmarks sink into violence, we grieve for ourselves as we once were and we question what we have become. Grief squeezed me to the point that I could no longer articulate any thought coherently. Sometimes, sharing a glass of wine with friends, I thought, what if the Russian army invades beyond Crimea? Grey images borrowed from the Second World War films of my childhood sped through my mind: tanks rolling through my great-grandparents' village, men in fatigues chopping down our cherry orchard, bombs falling onto our old apartment in Kyiv. Someone would then ask me if I was OK, and I would take a sip of my wine and nod. I didn't know how to explain to my sympathetic friends for whom war existed in faraway places and on the pages of newspapers, that every day of that undeclared war something shattered inside of me. Asking for compassion in such circumstances forced people to make moral judgments and pick sides, and I struggled to make sense of the events myself.

On many nights I lay in bed and the only way I could relieve my pain was to imagine a sharp knife cutting through my diaphragm, breaking through my bones and tearing my flesh. Imagining a pain worse than I felt soothed me momentarily before revealing the true depth of my agony. Then I suffered even more. Or I stayed awake and sat on the windowsill in the living room, pressing my face to the cold glass and letting my tears stream over Brussels shivering in the silvery halo of lights.

My family mourned and panicked, each in their own way. My mother imagined worst-case scenarios and drew on examples from the Balkan Wars to explain the situation in Ukraine. My aunt shared her arguments with people whose views were similar to Vladimir. She complained about a former classmate's captivation with the president of Russia. 'He even bought a jacket similar to Putin's. You know, all black and with a small hard collar,' she said. 'Every year he travels to Russia "to breathe the air of freedom". That's what he writes in his Facebook status updates. He lives in Canada.' After these conversations, I wanted to either weep or punch the walls.

The person I spoke to the most was my grandmother Valentina, because she didn't want to talk about the war. She said that every TV channel and every conversation was filled with it and she was tired. She talked mostly about the orchard and spring planting. When I asked her if she had a travel passport in case we had to evacuate her out of Ukraine, she told me that she didn't need one. When I insisted, she repeated, enunciating every word, that she didn't want to go anywhere, come what may. And so with Valentina, I didn't have to worry about stumbling into a topic that left us upset with each other.

Talking to my grandmother about pruning cherry trees and

planting tomatoes distracted me, but when I hung up, I reverted to my anxious, despondent state. I also obsessed over my conflict with Vladimir. I ran various arguments through my mind to convince him that the greatest catastrophe was not the collapse of the Soviet Union but its existence. I imagined telling him that Ukraine, with its key position between Russia and Western Europe, was always going to be a battleground for Russian imperial ambitions and that Russia would do anything to keep this strip of land under its control, but that Ukrainians had a right to choose who governed them and how they lived. Then I recalled his unfair accusations and my anger returned redoubled.

I nevertheless found one thing I could do. It was to buy a ticket and go to Ukraine. Vladimir taunted me with the idea, and I decided to take him up on the challenge. And just like that, one morning I vowed to return to Bereh.

~

Bereh, or more properly Krutyy Bereh, was our name for a village near the city of Poltava in Central Ukraine. Once, Krutyy Bereh determined the strategy of the Battle of Poltava, a watershed moment in European history, and thrived on silk weaving, but those glorious events were long past it. Krutyy Bereh means 'steep shore', denoting its location on the Vorskla River, but unadorned with adjectives, Bereh signifies 'our shore' to the maternal side of my family.

None of my mother's family was born here, not even the patriarchs, my great-grandparents Asya and Sergiy. Their roots were in the Poltava region, but Bereh was the closest thing to an ancestral home that they had. They had no jewels passed down from illustrious forebears and no books of family trees. They knew of their distant ancestors only by virtue of their own existence. They left few traces. It was hard to accumulate belongings and uninterrupted history when one lived in a place referred to as 'the bloodlands', 'the borderland', or 'the frontier'. Asya and Sergiy lived through many upheavals in the twentieth century and their way of life was swept away by one tsunami of events after another. In the end, anything that survived was valued simply because it had emerged out of the chaos. My mother and aunt disputed ownership of Asya's chipped cups from the 1930s with the passion of Greeks talking about the repatriation of the Parthenon marbles. A translucent bit of porcelain was the opposite of a *memento mori*, a reminder of mortality. It became a *vivere memento*, a precious testament to life and resilience. As the place where my mother's family landed after the tumult of the war and survived, Bereh became our most important *vivere memento*.

I was born in Kyiv, but the first fifteen summers of my life unfolded in this hamlet on the Vorskla River. Bereh was my second home, and Asya and Sergiy were my second set of parents. I keep their wedding photograph on my bookshelf in Brussels – two young people with serious expressions on their faces. They look ready for battle, rather than marriage, but theirs was an ideal partnership in our family. They also gave all of us a sense of home. When I was eight, my parents divorced, and Bereh became my haven.

Sergiy was the head teacher of a middle school in Bereh and a war veteran who had lost his leg during the infamous Battle of Kursk in 1943. In his retirement, he tended to the garden and his great-grandchildren. He assumed the responsibilities of a father when mine was absent after the divorce. A soft-spoken and mild-mannered man, he rarely raised his voice or lost his patience, and yet he projected strength and resolve. The only time I remember him becoming angry with me was when after reading voraciously through his library, I swallowed a tome of

Lenin's writings and decided that the best insult for my six-year-old cousin would be a 'bourgeois'. 'Nobody in our family is a bourgeois! That's not a good word!' Sergiy thundered when he overheard me. He embraced the Communist movement while still a teenager and never wavered in his loyalties. The offensive nature of being called a 'bourgeois' was the whole point, of course, but I held my tongue, while Sergiy pondered whether a twelve-year-old's reading list should receive more supervision. Asya laughed heartily when she heard the story.

Asya once worked at the same school as Sergiy, but by the time I was born, she had long retired from teaching and poured her passion into her orchard, collecting different varieties of flowers and fruit trees. Ever the entrepreneur, she took a chance and as soon as the government allowed small-scale private commerce, she started a business selling flowers and fruit at Poltava's central market. Called 'the city' in Bereh, Poltava was a quiet provincial place of white neoclassical buildings, mint-green churches and monuments to Nikolai Gogol, a local boy. It took a fifteen-minute bus ride to reach it from Bereh, a trip Asya made every day, save for Monday when the Poltava market was closed. Asya invested her earnings into gold and when the Soviet Union collapsed along with its economy, she and her savings emerged unscathed. Her cherry orchard fed and clothed us and helped us survive the chaos of the early nineties. Asya saw nothing wrong with being called a bourgeois.

Unlike my strait-laced great-grandfather, Asya had a sharp tongue and a bawdy sense of humour. She could be counted on to say unexpected and bewildering things. One day, when I was old enough to have crushes on boys at school, I wondered how Asya and Sergiy had met. The afternoon sun slipped into the room through the narrow, mullioned window and draped its amber rays over the heavy oak furniture and a table set for tea.

Asya was resting after a day at the market, for which she woke up at four a.m.

'Grandmother, why did you marry Grandpa?' I addressed Asya in Russian, while she replied in Ukrainian, a typical pattern in mixed Soviet families like ours.

'Why? I was a fool,' she said, unaware that her reply confused me. I had expected guitar serenades and other courtship rituals that I had glimpsed in films and books.

'I was beautiful,' she added, gesticulating with both hands to conjure up her erstwhile hourglass figure. This I could believe, because even in her late seventies Asya was a striking woman, tall, majestic, with Rubenesque curves.

'Your great-grandpa was in love with me.' This too I could believe, because Sergiy was still putty in her hands. He served in a tank division in the Second World War, but at home it was Asya who called the shots. We were so silent that we could hear doves fluttering their wings under the eaves of the house.

'He had a ration card,' she said. Sergiy walked in at that moment, carrying a basket of cherries. 'Asya, what on earth are you talking about!' he said, and his face flushed as red as the fruit in his hands. Asya looked up with a mischievous glint in her blue eyes and broke into a melodious laugh that no doubt still made Sergiy swoon. He shook his head and walked out of the room.

At the time I didn't understand what Asya's story meant. It seemed impossible that her marriage was based on cold, mercantile calculations. When Sergiy looked at her, the deep frown between his eyebrows softened and his face lit up. 'May you find someone who loves you as much as Sergiy loves Asya,' my mother would say, not quite believing that it was possible. My great-grandparents' marriage had lasted sixty years, my mother's only eight. Yet my great-grandparents met while working as village teachers and in 1932 the famine started. During those years, ration cards were the main means of survival, and as a senior teacher, Sergiy had one. He was infatuated with Asya, and when he proposed, she accepted. She didn't pretend that she married him for love.

Asya's stories were like the tales of the Arabian Nights – intricate narratives containing other parables that only the initiated could follow. I was too young and too steeped in Soviet propaganda to grasp Asya's hints. At school in the eighties and nineties we were taught that peasants and workers were the foundation of society, the main beneficiaries of Communist rule. The Soviet government wouldn't have starved people to death, the same people they had 'freed from the yoke of evil landowners'. Stalinism was discredited by Khrushchev in the sixties, but Lenin was still a good guy, and on my school uniform I wore a Young Pioneer star emblazoned with the profile of the leader of the Bolshevik Revolution and looked forward to the day when I could sport a red scarf. Lenin himself said, 'The intellectual forces of the workers and peasants are growing and getting stronger in their fight to overthrow the bourgeoisie.' I read it in one of Sergiy's books. I only began to put the puzzle together much later, as I grew older.

Asya was the centre of our household, and I liked it when my aunt and her family came to stay in Bereh, because I had to give up my bedroom to them and could sleep next to Asya. My great-grandparents occupied separate beds – he in a narrow Spartan cot and she in an enormous spring-frame confection covered with embroidered pillows and colourful quilts. I curled up next to her, between her soft belly and the scratchy Turkmen carpet on the wall. Sergiy woke up often during the night – his amputated leg bothered him, sending spasms of dull pain through his whole body, and in the morning, he had an elaborate ritual of putting on his prosthetic leg. I watched him wrapping the pale pink stump in layers of flannel with the same fascination as when I observed Asya's false teeth floating in a glass of water. The Second World War cut through the family with a scythe, leaving scars, but to me they were part of ordinary life.

'Tell me a story from your past,' I whispered to Asya, once I heard Sergiy's breathing become even and slow. She rarely told her stories in front of him. These riddle-like tales baffled me, lingering in my memory, and I prompted Asya to tell me more.

'An old woman's talk, that's what my stories are. Don't fill your head with such nonsense. The past is behind us,' Asya retorted, closing her book and rubbing a pungent-smelling ointment into hands scratched by rose thorns. Sometimes, however, she obliged me and talked.

When I was fifteen, my mother, stepfather, brother and I moved to Chicago, and Asya and Sergiy passed away a few years later. In my twenty years in the US, I visited Bereh only twice, and both times the reminders of their absence were so stark that the place depressed me. I saw overgrown flower beds and cobwebs on Asya's gardening tools. Sergiy's prosthesis, unnaturally shiny among the dust-shrouded furniture in the house, stood next to his empty bed. Since my grandmother Valentina still lived in Kyiv at that point and returned to Bereh only in the summer, the house and orchard bore signs of neglect. My mother and her sister returned without fail every year, unable to give up the *vivere memento* of Bereh. But for me it lost its meaning without Asya and Sergiy. I sealed it in the amber of memories and set it aside, following the counsel ingrained into me by Asya to think of the past as behind me. I became an expert at forgetting, shuffling anything uncomfortable or painful to the folder called 'the past'.

Now, though, I had to return there, because my grandmother Valentina had sold her Kyiv apartment and lived permanently in Bereh.

As apprehensive as I was about Bereh, I was thrilled to see Valentina again. I was never as close to her as I was to Asya, but I admired and emulated my grandmother. During my childhood, Valentina was a busy career woman, a geography teacher and later a director of a human resources department. Once, when I was eleven, she arrived in Bereh for the weekend, and even the elegant way she stepped out of my grandfather Boris's white Volga made her seem intimidatingly glamorous. Gaping at her lacquered, flipped bob, pistachio-green suit and white pumps, I noticed a grass stain on my overalls and dirt on my bony knees. After Valentina changed into a house dress and slippers, she still exuded sophistication. She gave me one look and launched into action, scrubbing the house from top to bottom, marching me off to change my clothes, and cooking a multi-course feast. She told me stories about famous artists and painters and left me with lists of books to read, films to watch, and museums to visit. After I moved to the US, we talked weekly over the phone, discussing Tolstoy's belief in redemption or Picasso's treatment of women.

'Good, you'll help me in the cherry orchard,' Valentina said, when I told her that I wanted to come to Ukraine for Orthodox Easter. 'Did you know that I plan to expand it this year?' She didn't say that she would be happy to see me after so long or that she had been waiting for me to come. She only talked about the orchard, but since gardening filled all our recent conversations, it didn't strike me as odd. We compared airfares, discussed dates and made lists of gifts for different neighbours in Bereh. I had a few projects in Brussels, but since most of my work consisted of freelance writing, I could be away from home for long stretches at a time. I decided to stay for three weeks. My husband was worried about me travelling to Ukraine, but he recognised the importance of this journey and supported my choice. The preparations so distracted me that I ruminated less and less on Vladimir's hurtful missive and no longer checked to see if he logged into Skype.

~

As a child, I kept diaries in imitation of the memoirs and auto-biographies that Valentina liked to read. I asked my mother to post them to me in Brussels, because I had written the most while in Bereh and I was curious to see what I had captured so many years ago. My mother used my request as an excuse to clear out the attic and sent me two boxes filled with my childhood books, drawings and journals. I leafed through musty volumes of Pushkin's poetry, fairy tales from around the world, Japanese haiku in Russian translation, and my school papers. When I reached the bottom of the box, I found a little blue notebook. 'Our native village of Maiachka in the Poltava Governorate was a Cossack settlement, and that's why we sup-ported the Bolshevik Revolution,' was written on the first page, and I recognised my great-grandfather Sergiy's hand.

At first glance, the journal contained nothing I hadn't heard from Sergiy himself. In my great-grandfather's meticulous style, it was organised by topic: 'our village of Maiachka, my parents, our farm, our daily life, the First World War, my brothers and sisters.' Each sibling had his or her own entry. The shortest and the final one drew my attention. It said, 'Brother Nikodim, van-ished in the 1930s fighting for a free Ukraine.' It was underlined.

Sergiy was the youngest of eight siblings. Oksana died of typhus fever during the Civil War of 1918. Mykyta worked for the Tsar's secret police and was killed during the Bolshevik Revolution. Fedir perished on the Eastern Front in 1942. Nestir and Odarka survived two world wars. Ivan was born with a short leg, so he avoided the draft and toiled on a collective farm.

And then there was Nikodim. In Old Greek, his name meant 'victory of the people'. He vanished.

The absence of Nikodim in our family stories was striking. I didn't remember Sergiy talking about him either. As I sat leafing through the notebook, I realised how elusive Sergiy's voice was in my recollections. I tried to grasp hold of a memory, but it dissolved before I could piece together any narrative. He, like Asya, told us many stories, but apart from the Second World War, in which he fought heroically, I remembered little else. War defined Sergiy and his life experience for me. Nikodim wasn't part of it.

I called my mother to ask about the journal.

'Don't you remember that summer when Sergiy came to Kyiv to have an operation on his leg?' my mother said. 'But no, you don't. You were in Chicago then.'

Sergiy kept a journal while recuperating in our Kyiv apartment, but he never took it back with him to Bereh and a year later he passed away. I asked my mother if she had heard of Nikodim.

'One of Sergiy's brothers lived in a village near Bereh, but Asya didn't like that family,' my mother said.

'Why was that?'

'She said that they were not right,' she said, searching for a word. 'Like they were not well-adjusted or something.'

'Did Sergiy ever mention Nikodim?' I asked again.

'He often talked about World War II . . .'

'Mum, did Sergiy ever mention Nikodim?' I interrupted her.

'He didn't talk much about his family.'

I leafed through the notebook in my lap, puzzled by my mother's evasive replies.

'But in the journal Sergiy wrote about his family,' I said, trying again, 'he wrote, "Brother Nikodim, vanished in the 1930s fighting for a free Ukraine".'

'If this Nikodim fought for Ukrainian independence, as you say, then it would have been dangerous to talk about him.'

'Even after the fall of the Soviet Union?'

'Maybe. I don't know. Old fears linger. Anyway, why are you interrogating me?'

Who was Nikodim? What had he done? How did he vanish? I asked my Aunt Lola, my mother's younger sister, but she confirmed what my mother had told me. Sergiy didn't much talk about his family and Asya didn't like visiting them. Meanwhile, Nikodim's name was written in dark blue ink in the notebook. 'A spoken word can't be taken back; a written word can't be erased,' was Sergiy's favourite Ukrainian folk saying. I rubbed my finger over the line. The pen was wielded with such force in writing 'Nikodim' that it left an imprint on the following page.

I thought of asking Valentina about Nikodim when we spoke on the phone, but finally decided against it. If the topic was as sensitive as my mother and Lola suggested, then it would be best to raise it when we saw each other in person.

However, I couldn't stop thinking of Nikodim. In the spring of 2014, people were dying for a free Ukraine and disappearing without a trace. My grief over my country and my falling out with Vladimir formed into one dark shape, and I sat on the floor in my room and stared at Sergiy's notebook, willing the written word to speak. Nikodim disappeared in the 1930s. One night – when? – he was taken away from his home – by whom? – and never returned. What happened?

The mystery of Nikodim's disappearance and subsequent amnesia on the part of my family disturbed me. Many of my great-grandparents' stories had omissions, and now Vladimir's sarcastic words about stories and the deception of memory sounded ominous. What else that I took as truth had the foundation of a sandcastle? The stories that I sought for comfort fell apart in my hands.

My mother said that old fears lingered, and there was one place that embodied them, in brick and mortar. Out loud, Asya called it the Rooster House. Under her breath, she called it the Rooster Trap.

The Rooster House didn't look horrifying. It was in fact the most beautiful building in Poltava. 'House' wasn't a proper word for it either, because it was an elegant mansion built at the turn of the twentieth century to house a bank. Two voluptuous red sirens, 'roosters' in colloquial speech, flanked its portal, while elaborate mosaics of firebirds rising from ashes shimmered on its crimson facade. The firebird's symbolism as a creature that burns up before being reborn was ironically appropriate for the organisation that occupied the Rooster House during Soviet times. At first, it was known as the Extraordinary Committee (Cheka), then as the State Political Directorate (GPU), later as the Soviet Security and Secret Police Apparatus (NKVD), and finally, it became the Committee for State Security (KGB). By any name, the secret police.

Poltavans used to joke darkly that the Rooster House was the tallest building in town, because even down in its basement, one could see all the way to Siberia. The lower floors served as Cheka torture chambers, and at the height of the Great Terror in 1937–38 people living nearby could hear muffled screams emanating from below the earth. Or so Asya said. My great-grandmother preferred to take a long detour instead of walking down the elegant boulevard over which the red sirens presided. By the way her right cheek twitched and her voice fell to a whisper, I knew that the Rooster House was a place to avoid. I also knew that I was not to ask her questions about it.

To read Ukrainian history one must take a bromide, quipped

Volodymyr Vynnychenko, a novelist and a premier in the first independent Ukrainian government of 1917. Asya and Sergiy had survived the Bolshevik Revolution, the Civil War, the Red Terror, forced collectivisation, the Holodomor of 1932–33, the Great Purges of 1937–39, the Second World War, the famine of 1946, the decay of the seventies and the collapse of the eighties and early nineties. 'Speech is silver, silence is golden,' Asya used to say. Despite the fact that the Soviet Union of my childhood was not the violent Stalinist state, the Rooster House instilled dread in me too. If the legacy of the past century in Ukraine was traumatic for someone who had not experienced the worst of it and who had lived most of her life abroad, how dark of a shadow did it cast on the present? Wasn't it the best illustration of how awful the USSR had been, I imagined telling Vladimir.

I became obsessed with discovering the truth about Nikodim. I thought of this uncle who had fought for a free Ukraine and who had paid the highest price as a kindred spirit, and I wanted to restore him to his rightful place in the family story.

The next day, as Russia deployed troops along the border with Ukraine, I bought a ticket from Brussels to Kyiv. 'Are you sure you want to go now?' my mother worried aloud on the phone. 'Why not wait a little?' The newspapers were already guessing how many hours it would take for the Russian army to reach Ukraine's capital. I didn't want to delay my trip. The more I resolved to plunge into an unknown past to find Nikodim, the more my fears about the present faded.

Three

I opened my eyes and stared in confusion at the paisley-patterned wallpaper and then let my eyes travel to a painting of two stags in a wintry landscape. It took me a few moments to remember that I was in Kyiv in my Aunt Lola's apartment. She kept it after she emigrated to Canada, hoping that two bedrooms in Kyiv would assuage her anxiety in the face of the unknown across the ocean. Lola never returned to live in Ukraine but my cousin Dmytro did. One summer he came to Ukraine and stayed, a year of 'studies abroad' turning into another and then into another ten. When I had spotted him at the arrivals hall of Boryspil airport, I could hardly believe that the man holding a large bouquet of roses was the same little cousin I had taught to swim. After Dmytro and I kissed three times on the cheek, the Ukrainian way, he took my suitcase and handed me the bouquet and the phone. Valentina was on the line.

'Dmytro, what on earth is this? Why is the plane so late?' she was saying, as though my cousin controlled the air traffic.

'Babushka, I've arrived safely,' I said and heard her sigh in relief. Valentina always worried too much when we travelled, and nothing had changed, despite me being in my late thirties. Though I lived far away and though there were long gaps between my visits, her protectiveness never wavered.

We exchanged a few words. Mostly it was my grandmother who talked, while I stood in a daze by the terminal entrance holding my roses, listening to Valentina and smiling blissfully.

～

Dmytro's steps echoed in the hallway and approached the door. 'Are you awake already?' he asked, his broad-shouldered silhouette pixelated by the patterned glass of the door. 'Sorry about the sun, I didn't have time to buy curtains. I spend little time in Kyiv these days.' The sun was beating down on me with an alarming intensity, making my eyes water, but I could still see that the apartment looked as if its residents had never finished moving out. Cardboard boxes towered in one corner, next to a bench press. A maroon wall unit, a hot trend circa 1989, was empty, apart from Czech crystal glasses, two empty liqueur bottles displayed like souvenirs, and a bronze Buddha figurine. A shelf next to my bed was full of Soviet editions of classics that looked intellectual in their identical grey bindings.

'I'm awake,' I said. I looked at my phone and saw that it was only six a.m. Dmytro went for a run, and I got out of bed. I walked down the long corridor, the linoleum flooring sticking to my bare feet. I found two towels and a soap bar that Dmytro had left for me on a chair in the hallway and stepped into the shower. The icy cold water pouring from the rusty shower head sent me into hypothermic shock – I noticed too late that Dmytro had stuck a Post-it note on the mirror: 'Sorry, no hot water. Welcome to Ukraine!'

The cupboards in the kitchen were empty, apart from a box of buckwheat groats, sugar and rock salt. The fridge let out a whine when I opened it to reveal its void. I filled a glass with water from the tap and peered out the window. The curtain in the kitchen had coquettish bows and folds that clashed with the austere landscape outside. The boxy outlines of the buildings, the bare poplar branches and the electricity pylons looked like a minimalist painting, stripped of all excess and of some bare necessities, too.

The entrance door swung open and Dmytro appeared on the threshold balancing a tray with two paper cups. 'Your delivery of morning coffee,' he said, putting the tray on the kitchen table and handing me one of the cups.

I swallowed a bitter mouthful and sighed with pleasure. It was delicious, in addition to being coffee. 'I needed it,' I said. 'Though there is only one hour difference between Kyiv and Brussels, I feel like I've travelled halfway around the world. And is it me, or is this coffee really good?'

'Everyone is obsessed with coffee here. Even in Bereh, you can get a nice shot of espresso at the store on the hill,' Dmytro said, sipping his Americano. Bereh had only one grocery store and only one hill, but everyone still insisted on specifying the location.

'Do you want to go to Puzata Hata for breakfast?' Dmytro asked. I had no idea what Puzata Hata was, but I nodded; I longed to get out of the house.

Outside the air was crisp, bright, and buoyant. We crossed the yard, saying good morning to an elderly gentleman in a patched grey suit reading a leather-bound book. 'Remind me to buy food for Petr Ivanovich,' Dmytro said. 'He spends his pension feeding the local cats and goes hungry.' I pointed to a bottle of beer by the gentleman's side. Dmytro grinned at me. 'I said hungry, not thirsty!'

'Things were at least stable before all of this started,' he said, as we crossed the street to a shopping mall that was part of the now-defunct arms factory. 'Who knows what will happen next?' It was as close as we had come to discussing politics, but after my confrontation with Vladimir, I had become wary of probing others, especially family, on their viewpoints. Dmytro's cynical tone as he said 'all of this' set off my internal alarm.

Puzata Hata, meaning 'Potbellied Hut', was a chain restaurant serving popular Ukrainian dishes like borsch, dumplings, stuffed cabbage leaves and crepes. I ordered a plate of varenyky, crescent-shaped dumplings with potatoes, and asked for extra soured cream. Dmytro selected cabbage and cucumber salad, black bread and tefteli, meatballs in tomato sauce. He insisted on paying for our meals and carried our tray to a table by a large bay window. As we ate, I peered into the faces of people around me, as though I could find the meaning of the Ukrainian revolution in a cafeteria. The place was full of students drinking coffee and eating varenyky, all the while checking messages on their phones.

'What do you want to do today?' asked Dmytro, pushing his plate aside. 'I have to work on my new PR campaign, but we can go out together later.' In Bereh, he ran a small metalwork business making sports equipment and he spent hours online looking for new clients.

Dmytro was six years younger than me and we had grown up together. We were more like siblings than cousins, sharing the same memories of Bereh. He was only four years old when he emigrated, much younger than I had been when I left. Yet he was the one who returned. I once asked Dmytro what made him select Ukraine over Canada, but he shrugged, at a loss for an answer. As I now knew from my own experience, latent yearnings evade logic.

I fished around in my bag for my phone and saw that it was already past nine o'clock. The morning was dashing away from me, and I wanted to run and catch up with it. 'Don't worry about me,' I said. 'I will take the metro to the city centre and wander around. I feel like I need to introduce myself to Kyiv again. Are you ready to go?'

'I need to stay for a few days in Kyiv to meet some people about work,' Dmytro said when we stepped into the street. 'After living in Bereh, I find Kyiv exhausting. I don't like coming here more often than I have to. When are you going to Bereh?'

'Tomorrow,' I said, squinting into the freezing sun. 'Or the day after. Anyway, I need to go ...' My voice trailed off. I wanted to prepare myself to return to a place that held so many memories that it had stopped being part of real-world geography.

'I'll walk you to the metro station,' Dmytro said, seeing that I wasn't returning to the apartment. He assumed the serious, protective air that I had already noticed in Ukrainian men and found sweet and exasperating in equal measure.

Kyiv's metro was modelled on Moscow's, with splendid underground palaces and mosaics. Lola's apartment was close to a newer station that didn't have the magnificence of central locations like Khreshchatyk or Maidan, but as I descended an interminably long escalator into the cool underbelly of the city, I savoured every detail. Even the distinctive smell of metal dust and the yellowish glow of the matted-glass lamps in the metro thrilled me. I checked these fleeting impressions against my recollections – and found myself back, truly back, in Kyiv.

I emerged from the metro a few blocks from Maidan and saw that I was on Khreshchatyk. Kyiv, a city with many distinctive neighbourhoods and enclaves, has one indisputable centre – a mile-long street joining the Upper Town to the busy lanes around the Besarabsky Market. Once Khreshchatyk used to be a ravine in the shape of a cross, but its only reminder is the Slavic word 'khrest' at the root of its name. When the city expanded by virtue of sugar and wheat profits at the end of the nineteenth century, the cross-shaped ravine was filled in and made into Kyiv's Champs-Élysées. In September 1941, the entire length of Khreshchatyk was demolished by the retreating Red Army, and when it was rebuilt in the 1950s, the neoclassical mansions gave way to Stalinist rococo. In the twenty-first century, new glass and chrome buildings built to suit the tastes of the new elites obscured the familiar view, confirming to me that Khreshchatyk retained its central status.

I grew up in the capital of Ukraine, but the Kyiv of my childhood years was confined to a three-bedroom apartment that belonged to my father's family and a neighbourhood of grey cement boxes from the Khrushchev era. These so-called khrushchevki apartments were filled with other families like ours, living in cramped, ill-designed quarters. They stood in the same lines, squeezed into the same white and red trams and sent their children to the same schools named after the same Soviet heroes. Outside the window of our bedroom, I could see the courtyard, dominated by a dumpster and a row of identical apartment blocks. If I walked into Vladimir's bedroom, ignoring his downward dog pose and jars of fermenting carrots, I could admire the poplars standing like rows of soldiers on a military parade, the zigzags of the tram lines and the yellow eyes of windows in a similar set of apartment blocks across the street. Still, I liked that Kyiv. It was familiar, it was mine.

The Old City, with its ancient monasteries and Italian baroque palaces, might as well have been on another planet. Yet it was also my Kyiv, because I discovered it with my father. While my parents were still living together, he took me on long walks around the Kyivo-Pecherska Lavra, a medieval Orthodox sanctuary on the Dnieper River. We strolled around the monastery complex and admired the ornate frescoes inside the dark churches. I wanted to head straight to the lavra, but I first needed to see Maidan. I looked for signs of what the city had suffered only weeks prior, but I saw only the springtime Kyiv I remembered from my childhood. The golden domes of the churches glowed in the cold spring sun. Near the metro entrances, grandmothers sold violets and green onions wrapped in damp newspapers. Girls in vertiginous heels glided down the winding streets of the Old City. The famous Khreshchatyk chestnut trees stretched their branches decisively towards the sky. I turned in the direction of Maidan.

The wind blew into my face, bringing the humid freshness of the Dnieper River and the acrid smell of smouldering rubber. I walked as if pushing against a strong current, but I neither slowed down nor held my breath. I let the smell fill my lungs until I was choking. When I finally glimpsed Maidan's round square and the victory column, the back of my throat was so dry that it hurt.

I saw blackened buildings, torn-up cobblestone streets, towering piles of car tyres, and rough-hewn encampments. But none of these mementoes of violence startled me as much as the eerie calm. Rows of photographs, candles and flowers lined the sidewalks. Some people kneeled on the ground praying. A young woman in a white jacket cleaned one of the portraits and rearranged the stiff garlands of red carnations around the black frame. The face looking out was that of a young man with large wide-set eyes and a gap-toothed smile. It was no longer a city square; it was a graveyard.

I leaned on the wall of the nearest building and steadied myself with one hand. My fingers slipped down the smooth surface of the wall and felt a round hole surrounded by a star-shaped jagged indentation. 'Why would you face bullets for some boring EU agreement?' people kept asking me back in Brussels, looking for a simple explanation of things that were fiendishly complex. I sometimes wondered myself. On Maidan, however, that question appeared absurd and irrelevant. The convictions that drove people to face their fears went beyond any one fact, one occurrence, one unsigned agreement – or one line in my great-grandfather's journal. Then I asked myself whether I would have been on Maidan if I were in Ukraine during the protests, and I didn't know the answer. I probably wouldn't have been. I was forced to take part in so many parades and demonstrations in the Soviet Union that I hated anything that made people chant slogans and lose their individuality, even if the slogans were ones I believed in. The only thing I knew was that I had to be here now.

I wandered through Kyiv for the rest of the day. Outside of Maidan, life went on as before, defying all expectations, including my own. I waited for the city to reveal something dark and grim, but Kyiv was lively. I expected people to be morose, but they smiled when our eyes met. 'Divchynka, little girl, don't be sad, all will be well,' I heard someone call out. A woman selling bluebells at the bus stop waved to me. Her bright turquoise headkerchief matched the colour of the tightly closed buds. I didn't initially realise that she was addressing me, because I had long passed the age when anyone could call me a little girl. Another thing I forgot about Ukraine was the warm familiarity that strangers expressed towards each other by using words like 'mother' or 'grandmother', or diminutives like 'little girl'. I smiled back at the woman.

'If little flowers can survive a long harsh winter, so can we,' said the woman. I also forgot about the Ukrainian propensity to speak in parables. Without bargaining, a grave sin according to Valentina, I bought three bunches of blue flowers and buried my face in their cool petals.

The phone in my bag vibrated impatiently. 'Where are you?' asked Valentina. 'When will you be here?'

'Tomorrow,' I said.

'Good. Then I need to start cooking,' she replied.

When I returned home, Dmytro was watching *Friends* dubbed in Russian on his laptop while doing crunches. 'Puzata Hata?' he asked and I nodded. Tomorrow I would be going to Bereh. I would see Valentina. It would all be all right.

Our neighbour Petr Ivanovich was still sitting with his book outside in the courtyard under the only working street lamp. Several cats milled around him, rubbing their heads against his legs. 'These days I feel like Prince Andrei,' Petr Ivanovich said, looking up from the book and staring at the bruised, cloudy sky above us. He was reading Tolstoy's *War and Peace*. I felt more like Pierre Bezukhov, the outsider returning.

~

Arriving on the overnight train from Kyiv to Poltava, I had always loved my first glimpse of the bend of the river from the train window. The train would chug and hiss, and then suddenly the river would jump into view, with its voluptuous curves overgrown with willows and dotted with matchbox houses drowning in cherry and apricot orchards. I would always anticipate this moment. I knew that beyond the river, shrouded in mist, stood our peach-coloured house with grey shutters.

However, at Kyiv's Central Station, I discovered that the overnight journey I used to make as a child had been reduced to a couple of hours via a new commuter line. 'There is a sleeper train, but it takes a very long time,' a ticket seller said, amused by my insistence. 'Do you really want to travel for more than twelve hours?' The practical and impatient side of me prevailed, and I booked a seat on a high-speed Hyundai train for the same evening. I only had time to make another run to Puzata Hata with Dmytro and repack my suitcase.

The journey was so short that before I knew it, the modern Korean-made train had disgorged me onto a platform in Poltava swarming with other travellers. The shrill whistle of the traffic controllers died down, the crowd dispersed, but I remained standing on the platform, clutching my suitcase. Evening fog descended on the station, obscuring the rows of white brick warehouses, rusting boxcars and the green sentry boxes for the traffic ladies – the job of controlling the rail crossings in Ukraine was an exclusively female domain. Puddles of spring rain reflected the cold blue lights of the station hall and the flickering red letters of the running announcement under its roof, 'Welcome to Poltava'.

I walked up to a group of taxi drivers all wearing identical black puffy jackets and tracksuit bottoms. 'How much to Krutyy Bereh?' I asked them in Ukrainian. One of the men looked me up and down and quoted a price. I suspected that he was over-charging me, so I frowned and pursed my lips in the same way that I remembered Asya doing when bargaining at the market. The man chuckled and quoted a slightly lower price. I nodded, and feeling proud of myself for grasping the ways of Poltava with such ease, I loaded my suitcase and myself into his beige Lada car, a Soviet copy of Fiat.

We drove through darkening Poltava and zoomed past the river with its magnificent steep banks. The taxi driver tried to make small talk, but because I was too focused on the famil-iar contours appearing and disappearing in the dusk, the conversation didn't gel. He turned on the radio and started humming alongside a hoarse-voiced singer, who complained about the burdens of criminal life. 'Listen to Radio Chanson,' the announcer screeched as each song ended. I wasn't sure how a French chanson had become a Russian ballad about the criminal underworld, but the genre had been popular among Ukrainian bus and taxi drivers in the past. This too remained the same.

We crossed the railroad track that officially marked Bereh's border. My first glimpse of our village was a scattering of lights and the outlines of tree branches against the dark grey sky. I recognised the football stadium and then spotted the store 'on the hill'. The store had a new flashing sign advertising European-quality products. Did it still sell the dusty caramels that the saleswoman, our neighbour down the street, had once weighed out with a jeweller's precision?

Though I could only make out its shape in the murky darkness, I knew that next to the store on the hill stood Dom Kultury, the House of Culture, a village club with a faux-Greek portico and a tin roof. As we reached it, I indicated to the taxi driver to take the second turn, and he drove carefully into the residential section. The road was unpaved and the slower we drove, sinking into the soft mud, the more my heart raced.

'Please stop here,' I said to the driver, indicating a spot just up ahead. I sat on the edge of the seat and my hand was already on the door handle. I couldn't see anything in the darkness, but I knew – I sensed – that the house was there. The car came to a standstill at last, and I jumped out. The driver opened the trunk and handed me my suitcase. 'Came to visit your folks from abroad?' he asked. I was puzzled how he knew. Putting a wad of money into his hand, I grabbed my suitcase and rushed towards the house. My fingers, encoded with muscle memory, undid the latch on the heavy wooden gate. It let out a lusty screech and swung open. I stepped into a darkness that smelled of bitter almonds and rice powder – the apricots were in bloom.

I could see the dancing lights in the house. The closer I approached the louder the voices on the television grew. I pushed the door and the lights and sounds rushed towards me. Valentina was sitting in a chair, with one of her arms resting on the plastic tablecloth of the dining table and the other holding a remote control. She turned to me, gasped and leaned forwards. She wore a white flannel nightgown and a fur-lined jacket on top of it. Her short mahogany hair, damp from the bath, was breaking into tight curls along her forehead. Her cheeks were flushed crimson and her mouth was twisted between a smile and a sob.

'Babushka, I'm here,' I called out. Valentina went to turn the TV off but instead turned up the volume. I moved towards her. The woven rug on the threshold got caught on the buckle of my left boot. 'You're here,' Valentina said. She remained awkwardly on the end of her chair and extended her arms to me. Dragging the rug into the living room, I stumbled into her embrace. She hugged me with all of her might, squeezing me as if to ensure that I was real. My grandmother was taller and more heavy-set than I was, but in my arms she felt fragile, like a baby bird, and the pounding of her heart pulsated through me.

'Why didn't you return together with Dmytro?' my grandmother asked as I turned off the TV, removed my shoes and sat down in front of her. 'He was worried that it wouldn't be safe for you to arrive so late.' I said that Dmytro still had some unfinished business in Kyiv and would be joining us in a few days.

'How much did you pay for the taxi?' Valentina asked. Her smooth face with soft cheeks and a rounded chin hardly betrayed her age, but it was her large hazel eyes that made her look especially youthful. All of her emotions could be read in them – her excitement, impatience, relief.

Hearing the price, she narrowed her eyes and slapped the table. 'He ripped you off! He charged you at least double what you should have paid. That's why I should have insisted that you and Dmytro travel together.' She berated the taxi driver for being wily, me for being naive and herself for not having foreseen it. Being scolded Ukrainian grandmother-style as soon as I crossed the threshold delighted me so much that I laughed.

'Money is not a joke here,' Valentina said. 'What seems trivial to you in euros is exorbitant in hryvnias.'

'I even bargained with him and patted myself on the back for getting the hang of the local ways fresh off the boat.'

'He could figure out that you were from abroad just by looking at you.' Then my grandmother dropped her arms and laughed. Her laugh was bright and unrestrained.

'You're here, that's all that matters,' she said. 'Let me make you something to eat.'

I wasn't hungry, but Valentina reheated a bowl of borsch. She talked about the garden and the neighbours, and she only mentioned the war once, when complaining about rising prices. 'I wanted to make roast pork for Easter, but meat costs double what it used to,' she said. 'Do you mind if we make chicken instead?' I said that I didn't mind at all and privately decided to buy the best pork roast for our Easter Sunday meal.

Valentina and I went to bed after midnight. 'I've set up everything in Asya's bedroom. Nobody uses it any more, but I've cleaned and heated it for you,' she said, giving me a set of towels and a white flannel nightgown that matched her own. She headed towards her bedroom and then turned around to take a look at me. 'You're back,' she said softly, and put a sign of the cross over me from a distance. 'Thank heavens.'

Wrapped in linens smelling of linden water and dampness, I pressed my cheek against the Turkmen carpet on the wall, its familiar roughness reassuring. 'I am back,' I said out loud to solidify the idea, then fell asleep.

~

I woke up in the morning to the sound of voices. My grand-mother was talking to someone about the price of water. The woman with the lilting Poltava accent complained about the difficulty of watering the orchard because the pump of her well was broken. Though she could always use the government water supply, she explained, she was afraid of the police. 'They have special planes that fly over Bereh and check who's using the government water illegally. Special planes!' she kept repeating. The cheerful barking of dogs and a hissing kettle lulled me back to sleep.

When I finally got up, Valentina was setting the table for breakfast. She was wearing a dark blue tracksuit accessorised with Asya's pink shawl. 'I've never seen you wearing trousers, much less such a sporty outfit,' I exclaimed, pointing to the Nike logo on her sweatshirt. My eighty-year-old grandmother looked just as stylish in sportswear as she did in tailored suits and cocktail dresses.

'Your mum sent it to me, and it's the most comfortable thing I've worn. It's perfect for garden work. I can bend any which way and I don't have to worry about scandalising the neighbours,' said Valentina. 'And then I don't fit into any of my old clothes. Do you see how overweight I've got?' She patted her ample thighs and laughed, unconcerned about her extra pounds.

My grandmother stomped off into the kitchen and returned with a big plate of golden syrnyky, small pancakes made of fresh white cheese, then vanished again. I heard the popping sound of a jar being opened.

'I hope that Sasha and I didn't wake you up,' Valentina said, as she returned with a tea tray. 'She showed up to discuss a rumour about special planes that fly and check on those who misuse the government water supply.'

Valentina dropped heavily onto the chair, slathered a piece of bread with butter and sprinkled it with coarse salt. 'If Ukrainian aviation had such prowess, we wouldn't have this war, but I didn't argue with Sasha,' my grandmother said, biting into her tartine and not caring that breadcrumbs fell on her sweatshirt. 'When I first came to Bereh, I used to think that the people were mad to believe all of these rumours, but these days when I water the garden, I look up to check if a plane is flying overhead.' She laughed and brushed the crumbs off her ample chest. 'And I never use the government water for gardening!'

'Aren't you eating breakfast with me?' I asked, observing the single plate on the table.

'I just ate,' Valentina said, swallowing the rest of her tartine. 'I'm going to see our neighbours about extra seed potatoes for planting.'

My grandmother left the table and lingered near the coat rack. 'I was so happy that you decided to come,' she said, rummaging through the winter clothes. 'Where is my hat?

'You're visiting just in time to help me with planting,' she continued, tying a woollen hat with a bright red pompom under her chin. 'There is so much work to do around here. Later I'll show you my new garden designs.'

Valentina zipped up her thick jacket and patted her pockets. 'Money, eyeglasses, a list, a pen . . . See you later. I won't be long, but when you get hungry, reheat the borsch,' she said.

'You probably don't know, but we have a gas line and a proper stove now!' she yelled from the corridor. For many years Bereh

50

had no gas supply, despite sitting next to the gas fields of the Poltava plain, and we had to use portable fuel tanks. I followed Valentina into the corridor, wanting to say that I hadn't been away that long and I knew about the gas line, but she was already out of the house, walking briskly across the yard.

I returned to the living room and slumped at the table. The house enveloped me in such eerie silence that it hung over me, heavy and oppressive. I piled my plate with syrnyky and drowned them with apricot jam and soured cream. I took a bite. The jam filled my mouth with the bitterness of apricot stones. I wondered why the seed potatoes were so important that my grandmother didn't stay to have breakfast with me on my first day of being back. I swallowed hard and my throat tightened. I suddenly felt alone and lost. The rusty ticking of the clock in Asya's bedroom measured out the minutes parsimoniously.

I took my cup of tea and stepped into the yard. The sun appeared from behind a cloud and threw handfuls of golden dust in my face. Dazzled by the sunshine, I could barely make out a wide yard surrounded by sheds, overgrown with curly grass and embraced by a cherry orchard on both sides. The laundry on the clothesline struggled to free itself and flapped excitedly in the wind. I forgot how exhilarating spring was in places that knew real winter, and how delirious. I remembered my plans to find Nikodim, and the promise of new adventures thrilled me despite my misgivings. It will all be all right, I told myself. Why wouldn't it be?

PART 2

The Cherry Orchard

Four

The next few days unfolded in the same fashion. Valentina often left before I awoke to tend her orchard or to visit neighbours to discuss their gardening projects. When she returned in the evening, she was too busy planning the spring planting to talk about her day, much less about events that happened almost a century ago. I became used to having my breakfast in the company of the ticking clock and the morning sunshine.

The house appeared as I remembered it, and even the doors creaked in the same high-pitched register. The floors still sagged and the wall clock still chimed the hour fifteen minutes late. The furniture was the same – cupboards and a fridge from the fifties, and an oakwood table of such solidity that it appeared to be growing from the foundations. The house was built by Red Army soldiers in 1945. An engineering division working on a new railway network selected a meadow between the train station and the river and built a squat dwelling, with frilly brick decorations over the windows, charmingly out of place on the austere facade. Once the engineering division left, the army command assigned the house and land around it to my recently demobilised great-grandfather. The haste of construction haunted us decades later – the single bedroom was tiny and narrow, the kitchen was freezing in the winter and sweltering in the summer, and the flooring was uneven. When I looked at photos from the fifties, the building didn't appear very different from its present state. We eventually adapted to the house, rather than the other way around.

A photograph of Pasha, Asya's mother and my great-great-grandmother, loomed over the dining table. She wore a white headscarf pulled low over her forehead and a long black robe that made her look like a nun. According to Valentina, during the German occupation, she prowled around her village freeing the requisitioned livestock and erasing the chalk markings from the houses to be appropriated by the German army. When the Germans retreated in 1943, she stayed behind to 'defend her home', while the rest of the family fled. When they returned, she was safe and sound and wearing a pair of sturdy German boots. Pasha was known to be bad-tempered, sulky and prone to violent outbursts. 'No wonder the Germans left her alone,' said Valentina. Whenever we gathered for dinner, Pasha's portrait glared at us disapprovingly from its high vantage point on the wall.

The room where I slept once served as Asya and Sergiy's bedroom and library. My great-grandparents were resting under a tall pine tree at the Bereh cemetery, but to us remained their slender carved bookcases, stuffed three rows deep with leatherbound volumes of Gogol, Dostoyevsky and Lermontov. Before I first learned to read, I used to pry open the stubborn glass doors and sit down on the floor, inhaling the musky scent of old books. The lower shelf once contained Sergiy's collection of Lenin's writings and a gilt-covered edition of the Soviet

Constitution. The thick tomes were perfect for drying flowers that I had pillaged from Asya's garden. Now Lenin was banished and Valentina's books on agriculture took his place.

I wandered from room to room, opening the bookcases and photo albums as if looking for clues. I continued outside, following the garden path and peering into the storage sheds along the way. In Bereh, these constructions were called 'sarai', which in original Turkish meant 'palace'. I choked on the musty odour of petrified wood and mildew and brushed off a cobweb that had fallen on my face. Dust danced in the air shot through with pale rays of sunshine. How a Turkish palace became a Ukrainian garden shed was a mystery to me, but ours could be called a memory palace. Valentina threw nothing away. At the top of the piles, I saw my old school jacket and my cousin's worn-out jeans. I then found my mother's dresses and magazines from the 1970s. At the bottom of the pile, I recognised the flounces of my grandmother's ball gowns that she wore to dances at the officers' club. Valentina and my grandfather Boris made for a glamorous couple at those evenings – she in her full lace skirts and red lipstick and he in military uniform, every crease knife-sharp, every star brilliant. He was an engineer and director at an airplane factory, and he received awards at work but no proper medical treatment. A man who practised ice swimming and ran marathons, one day he complained of stomach pains and some months later he was dead. 'Infectious appendicitis,' the doctor said. Later Valentina learned that he died of cancer. Boris's engineering textbooks and stacks of newspapers spilled out of the boxes in the sarai. I flipped through the crumbling issues of *Pravda*, the main Communist Party newspaper, whose name meant 'truth'. 'The decadent West is on the brink of collapse,' a headline from 1988 augured.

One of my favourite spots in Bereh had always been a small hut on the edge of the cherry orchard. We called it the summer kitchen even though nobody ever used it for cooking. It was a traditional dwelling made of reeds and clay, whitewashed and covered with a terracotta roof, the kind that was vanishing in Ukraine's shrinking villages. Ours consisted of one square room with a tiny window draped in lace and spiderwebs, a wood-burning stove and earthen floors covered with straw mats. Painted bright pink, the room was furnished with a carpet on the wall, a spring-frame bed, a large round table and an antique wardrobe. My reflection in a pockmarked mirror hanging on the wall appeared sepia-toned, like a vintage photograph. In early spring, the unheated summer kitchen was still too cold, but I lingered and sat on the bed inhaling the scent of damp clay and walnut shells.

The melancholy filling this neglected room overwhelmed me. 'Every corner of this house is filled with reminders of lives cruelly squandered by a negligent state,' I composed an email to Vladimir in my mind, before realising that I couldn't send it to him. I stretched out on the macramé bedspread and closed my eyes, recalling a poem I wrote at the age of ten, sitting on this bed: 'Who am I? Where am I? A grain of sand in the vast universe. Where is hell? Where is heaven? Who could tell me?'

'What are you doing here?'

Valentina's voice made me bolt up.

'That blanket hasn't been washed since last autumn. It's filthy. Aren't you hungry?' Valentina was standing in the doorway holding a bunch of spring onions. She had no interest in existential angst. When my Aunt Lola turned fifty and reached out to her mother for words of wisdom, asking what she wished she had learned earlier in life, Valentina didn't pause before replying, 'Growing big tomatoes.'

~

Dmytro returned from Kyiv on Wednesday before the Easter weekend, and though he lived in Poltava proper, renting a small apartment with his friend, he came straight to Bereh. Valentina called him several times to verify the exact time he would be arriving and cooked a large pot of chicken soup with dumplings. She was fluttering like a butterfly from room to room, unfolding futons and ironing towels. After a few days of lonely breakfasts and aimless strolls around Bereh, I was also happy to see Dmytro. The hubbub of excitement, unwrapping of gifts and fussing over food reminded me of our childhood vacations.

'Are you sure that you aren't hungry?' Valentina asked. 'Vika, please reheat the soup for Dmytro.' She called me by the diminutive version of Victoria, as my family usually did. I lit the stove and hoisted the heavy pot onto the fire.

'Babushka, I already told you that I'm not hungry,' Dmytro said, sitting down with a cup of tea.

'Maybe, a few potatoes?'

'I'm not hungry.'

'Or do you want something else?'

'I'm not hungry right now. I will have a snack later. I've lived here long enough to know where the fridge is.'

'You don't live here now,' Valentina said through a sniffle and went into the kitchen, slamming the door behind her. I stood with a soup ladle in the middle of the living room unsure what was being said or who had accused whom of what.

'Babushka didn't want me to move out, and even though it's already been two years since I rented my own place in Poltava she brings up the topic whenever she can,' Dmytro said, glancing guiltily at the door. He began to explain why he moved out and why it was better both for him and Valentina.

If Valentina thought that Dmytro had abandoned her by

moving to the neighbouring town, what must she think of her daughters moving across the ocean? What must she think of me? I knew that my mother and Lola wanted Valentina to emigrate with them, and that every year, they entreated her to sell the house and move to either the US or Canada, but she refused. She didn't want to give up her house, her orchard or her freedom. It was their choice to leave, but it was her choice to stay. Still, our absence must have pained her.

Dmytro paced up and down the room and then went into the kitchen to look for Valentina. Through the thin wall, I heard their agitated voices, more sniffles and then soft murmurs. A few moments later, Dmytro returned to the living room and announced that he would stay with us for the entire Easter break. Valentina stood behind him, clasping her hands and radiating happiness.

The next morning, which was Maundy Thursday, the three of us cleaned the house for Easter. Dmytro scoured the floors in the living room, while I hung the rugs on the washing line in the yard and slapped them with a broom. They gave up satisfyingly large clouds of dust.

'Hello!'

I spun on my heels to see our next-door neighbour Sasha unlocking the gate separating our properties and walking into our yard. She was an attractive woman of about fifty, with burgundy-coloured hair and russet cheeks. Her printed cotton dress, woollen vest and house slippers were the Bereh version of leisurewear. 'I've been wanting to drop by to chat with you, but business keeps me busy these days,' she said. Like my grandmother, Sasha and our other Bereh neighbours spoke to me in Russian, but among themselves they used Ukrainian. Since my Ukrainian came out accented with English, our neighbours found it charming but strange. I wondered what it meant for my Ukrainian identity, worrying that I might not belong to the place where I was born, but I enjoyed the mellifluous sounds of the language so much that I kept speaking it. Valentina looked proud when I spoke Ukrainian, and while she corrected me in a soft whisper, she showed me off like a star student. Whenever I had the chance, I switched to Ukrainian and she delighted at the new words and phrases that I had learned.

'Good morning, Sasha,' I replied in Russian. Ever since I was a child, it was the only language I had spoken with her, so it felt natural to continue in it.

Sasha's business was a stall in the Poltava central market where she sold vegetable seedlings and cut flowers.

'Little Sasha was looking for work abroad, but I'm glad that in the end he stayed at home,' she said. Little Sasha was Sasha's nineteen-year-old son – her family solved the naming dilemma by calling all of their offspring, male or female, Sasha.

Sasha was smiling widely, but her sharp green eyes were scrutinising me from top to bottom. The spring sun in Ukraine was deceptive, and I had piled on all of my sweaters and topped them off with Sergiy's sheepskin jacket. It made me look like a shepherd, but I was comfortable and warm.

Valentina warned me that whatever I told Sasha would become village gossip, but I suspected that would happen whether or not I said anything, so I smiled in a manner that I hoped looked natural and said that home was the best place of all. It came out so fake that I cringed, but Sasha didn't notice, because she was frowning at Valentina's rubber boots on my feet.

'Do you and your husband earn good money there?' Sasha asked.

I shifted from foot to foot in my clunky rubber boots. 'It's enough for the two of us.'

Unconvinced, Sasha glanced one more time at my jacket and wellies. 'What exactly do you do there?'

Valentina came out of the house at that moment, and I slipped behind her into the corridor and left my grandmother to talk about a new tomato variety she wanted to plant.

On Easter Saturday, I woke up to the sound of gunfire. With my heart pounding, I sat up in bed and strained my ears to hear where it was coming from. I jumped up and ran barefoot into the yard. I stood on the grass, which was cold enough to make my skin burn, but each popping sound nailed me firmer in place.

'It's just the army recruits training. Their base camp is over by the river,' Valentina said, walking out of the sarai with a large pot. She noticed my bare feet and flung her hands to her face, dropping the pot. 'Good heavens, are you trying to give me a heart attack? Go inside now!'

I wiped my feet on the rug, my cheeks crimson. As I was making the bed, I could hear Sasha entering the house and greeting Valentina.

'What ruckus they are making,' she said.

'They don't have a holy bone in their body. To do such a thing on the Easter weekend,' Valentina said, her voice high pitched with indignation.

'I told them not to start so early, but Igor said that they need to finish the fence by the end of this week.'

The drilling noise coming from our other next-door neighbour's plot muted the gunfire and my grandmother's response. The army fire practice didn't trouble either my grandmother or Sasha as much as Igor's fence.

We cooked for Easter with the soundtrack of gunshots and electric drills. Since the oven was on, we left the door between the veranda kitchen and the living room open, and the sounds from the outside entered more distinctly. I peeled potatoes and tried not to flinch every time the shots reverberated, though after a few hours they merged into the usual cacophony of Bereh sounds – roosters, dogs, children, neighbours shouting greetings at each other. The ease with which we all accepted the abnormal unsettled me, but I didn't know if there existed another way of living through a calamity.

'The way we prepare for holidays is more eventful than the holiday itself,' Dmytro said, arriving from the store on the hill with two loaves of bread. 'We spend two days cooking and then everyone is too tired to enjoy the meal. I'm sure that babushka will also wake us up before dawn to get the eggs and Easter bread blessed at church.'

'Of course I will. You act as if you've never celebrated Easter before,' Valentina said. 'Why did you get the wholewheat bread?' She poked the bread we called kirpichik, little brick, for its rectangular shape. 'It tastes too sour!'

'It looks exactly like the white kirpichik,' Dmytro said. He tore off a piece of bread and popped it in his mouth. 'And it doesn't taste sour.'

'Hey, don't eat all of the crusts,' I said, waving the potato peeler. Both of us loved the crunchy, caramelised edges and still fought over them the way we had as children.

'We have too much to do,' Valentina said, pressing handfuls of onion peels into a big pot. 'Vika, you need to peel more potatoes.'

'I already peeled at least a dozen. How many people are coming to dinner?' I protested, reaching for another tuber. Unlike the potatoes sold in Brussels, yielding and oval, these ones were hard and shaped like miniature surrealist sculptures. Yet they tasted decadently sweet and buttery.

'The three of us,' Valentina affirmed as she put six more potatoes into a bowl for me to peel. 'Dmytro and I like potatoes.'

'Valentina and the US army share the same motto – be all you can be,' Dmytro said loud enough for Valentina to hear. 'From my own experience, it's better to submit to General Valentina and follow orders.'

'I resent being compared to an army general,' Valentina said, looking nevertheless pleased.

She took the bowl of potatoes from me and gave me a list of ingredients for the paska, an Easter brioche baked in a tall cylindrical mould. 'Are you sure that we need two kilograms of flour?' I asked Valentina, calculating that it would make enough paska for the entire village. She was in the corridor instructing Dmytro, who was leaving for yet another shopping expedition, and didn't hear me. I measured out the flour, milk and yeast into a large wooden basin Valentina had left on the dining table and plunged my hands into the lumpy mixture. The creamy scent of wheat enveloped me. Even when we didn't celebrate Easter because of my great-grandfather's objections to all religious rites, we made paska every spring to enjoy the rich taste of the buttery brioche full of rum-soaked raisins and candied orange peel. The dough turned elastic in my hands, and the more I pushed it, twisting it into the series of folds the way Valentina taught me, the more it fought back. I covered it with a bowl and sat down, wiping flour from my forearms.

Valentina returned to the kitchen and started making the natural dye for Easter eggs. She covered the onion peels with water and set them to boil. Their sweetish smell wafting into the living room reminded me of overripe mango. Writing about perfume, I grew to notice scents around me and associate them with other aromas that evoked memories. Only a few months earlier I had been in India with my husband visiting his relatives in Mumbai. Though it wasn't mango season, the scents of tropical fruit with their distinctive pungent notes danced in air saturated with the smells of spices, cooking oil and bonfires. We visited a spice plantation in Goa where the farmers showed me how they harvested black pepper, cardamom and vanilla pods. I sent Vladimir photos of the village, green vines and jasmine garlands. Vladimir replied saying that the farmers' huts reminded him of his grandparents' village in Russia. The memory floated and vanished like a half-remembered tune.

The squares of sunlight coming through a small window slipped from the table to the floor behind me; it was past noon. Valentina strained the oily liquid of boiled onion peels and slipped eggs into it. They simmered until the pale colour of their shells deepened to dark mahogany.

Valentina and I took turns pampering the paska dough, adding eggs, sugar, butter and more flour in increments. The dough glistened and expanded, filling the room with the scent of nutmeg and cream. Valentina kneaded the dough vigorously, pushing her whole body against the table and making it tap dance and shimmy. She leaned in, pushing the dough forwards and then suddenly froze mid-motion and gasped. With her hand covered in butter and flour, she grabbed her lower back.

'Babushka, what is it?' I ran over to her.

'Nothing really,' she said, drawing in her breath sharply. Her face was contorted by a grimace of excruciating pain.

I grabbed the chair and helped her to sit down.

'You probably pulled your back. Leave the dough, I will do it.'

Valentina looked at me, annoyed. 'The last thing I need is a back problem,' she said, wiping her hands on a towel I gave her, but she remained sitting.

Dmytro came back from the market and Valentina got up with difficulty and went into the kitchen. I followed her.

'Do we have pain medication at home?' I asked Dmytro. 'Babushka pulled her back.'

Valentina turned around and glared at me. 'I told you, I'm fine,' she snapped. My mother warned me that Valentina was sensitive about her health and afraid of doctors, and even if she complained, she refused to have her ailments treated. I returned to the living room.

'I don't like this brand of ham,' I heard Valentina say to Dmytro.

'It's the one we always get.'

'How much was the sliced cheese? So expensive! Why did you buy so much of it?'

The snippets of their voices darted back and forth in the spiced air. I punched the dough.

Dmytro peeked into the living room and saw me standing at the table with my arms elbow-deep in flour.

'What kind of a bread is it that takes the whole day to make?' he asked with a gentle mockery that didn't amuse me. I turned away.

He came up closer and searched my eyes. 'Do you need my help? I can do the dishes.' He picked up the leaning tower of plates and bowls from the table and carried them into the kitchen.

'You can't wash the dishes! I will do it myself or Vika can do it after she's done with paska,' Valentina said, intercepting him. 'Let me make you tea. Are you hungry?'

'Why can't Dmytro wash the dishes?' I asked, watching Dmytro drop the sponge into the sink and step outside. I was kneading the dough again, folding the last portion of butter into it. Thick and slippery, the dough resisted the butter and my hands.

'That's not a man's job,' Valentina said, squeezing dishwashing liquid onto a tattered sponge.

'At home, my husband washes the dishes,' I said stubbornly.

66

'Men in the West are different.'

'But Dmytro grew up in Canada.' My arms throbbed from fighting with the dough. Fatigue and irritation were wearing me down, and I couldn't hold my words back even though I knew that each remark set me firmer on a collision course with Valentina.

'My husband never washed the dishes at home. I wouldn't let him do such menial women's work,' Valentina said, dropping forks and knives into soapy water. She said 'my husband' and not 'your grandfather', and despite the rattle of dishes in the sink and the slaps of dough against the table, an icy silence fell between us. The dough briefly escaped from my grip.

'Here in Bereh, we have our own ways, and Dmytro is one of us,' Valentina said as she ran the cold water to rinse the dishes. I punched the dough again, slamming my fist against the table and releasing a jolt of pain into my arm. I didn't say that Sergiy, her own father, washed the dishes, made tea for Asya and cooked breakfast for me. I didn't ask if she included me as one of 'us' too. I was afraid she would say no.

~

Dmytro woke me up at dawn. Bereh didn't have its own church but the village across the railroad tracks did, and the priest drove in from Poltava to perform the ritual blessing. I rummaged through the closet in the bedroom for suitable clothes, recalling that some Orthodox churches had a strict dress code for women. I put on a long pleated blue skirt, a black wool overcoat, and a grey scarf that kept slipping down my hair.

'You look like Asya when she was young,' Valentina said when I walked out of the bedroom. After our spat the previous night, we both treated each other with unnatural reserve and politeness. Both of us knew that I looked nothing like tall and blonde

Asya and that my dark hair and petite build were all from my father's side, but I understood what Valentina wanted to say and it comforted me.

In the main room, the table was covered with paska. Their tall cylindrical forms glistened under a layer of white meringue and sugared violet petals. We selected the prettiest loaf and put it in the basket, along with several eggs and salt wrapped in a handkerchief. Easter dinner started with an egg dipped in blessed salt and a slice of paska. I hadn't eaten much the day before and my hunger made every colour, every texture and every scent sharper.

Valentina put a sign of the cross over us as we walked out of the gate. She decorated her vanity table with icons and marked religious holidays in the calendar to remind herself not to do gardening work on those days, but she rarely went to church. She said that she didn't know how to behave there, but that she liked the idea of blessed bread.

We walked past sleeping houses and awakening orchards. The white clouds of blooming apricots suffused the village with the refinement of a Japanese painting. As Dmytro and I turned towards the river, vegetable plots delineated by portable greenhouses floated into view. Seen from the steep point of the river shore, Bereh resembled an antique daguerreotype of whitewashed huts with wooden shutters, weeping willows and tangled grape vines. The riverbanks were deserted, and the current flowed swiftly, carrying with it trees turned upside down, houses standing on their roofs and our blurry shadows.

'Where is the army training camp?' I asked Dmytro. He pointed in the direction of the forests that stood transparent and bright against the clear morning sky yet appeared dark and foreboding to me.

The church was a small white building with a blue metal roof decorated with golden crosses. We joined the crowd of people in the courtyard waiting for their eggs and paskas to be blessed. Two women in jeans and leather jackets glanced at my long skirt and overcoat and whispered something to each other, snickering. I noticed that I was the only woman under seventy wearing a skirt. The door of the church opened, and a young priest with a wispy black beard that made his face appear even more boyish emerged into the yard carrying a small broom and a tin bucket like the kind Valentina used to store potatoes. He dipped the broom into the bucket, intoned 'Khristos Voskres' and splashed us with water. The broom became a holy water sprinkler, the tin bucket turned into a sacred receptacle, and the sleepy crowd looked exalted as it replied in a harmonious chorus, 'Voistinu Voskres'. The morning sun climbed higher and set the crosses on the church roof ablaze. The priest walked around the circle blessing us with holy water three times and disappeared inside the church. Still under the spell of the blessings, people greeted each other, embraced and kissed. We didn't see anyone we knew, but at that moment everyone seemed familiar and dear, even the women who mocked my old-fashioned outfit.

'Are you two Asya Berezko's?' Near the church gate, a stooped woman holding an enormous basket and a walking stick motioned for us to come closer. Dmytro nodded, but I stared at her in confusion. It had been a long time since I had lived in a place where people knew my family, and I forgot that in Bereh we were defined by our elders, dead or alive. The woman studied our faces in silence. 'Yes, we are Asya's great-grandchildren,' Dmytro said.

'Our young folk are trying to get away, and you keep returning,' she said, putting her basket on the ground.

Under the embroidered towel covering her basket, I noticed Easter breads, eggs and a bunch of red tulips, their crimson heads clasped by rubber bands. When Asya sold flowers at the market, she entrusted me to slice toy balloons into thin bands and slip them over the cool buds. Red balloons for red tulips, white balloons for white. The trick kept the flowers from opening and losing their freshness. Without waiting for my response, the woman rubbed her lips with the back of her hand and said, 'But why shouldn't you return here? Home remains home.'

When we reached the house, I fell asleep on the sofa and woke up when it was dusk. The Easter service incantations still echoed around me. My eyes were wet and my breathing heavy. I felt someone's hand on my forehead and saw that Valentina was standing over me.

'We couldn't wake you up. Dmytro went to take blessed Easter breads to Sasha and our other neighbours. You seem a little warm. Should I make you a cup of tea with raspberry jam?'

'I'm fine, I really am,' I said sitting up and shaking off my daze. 'But I want tea with raspberry jam.' Our family's favourite remedy for colds was a cup of black tea with a spoonful of raspberry jam swirled into it.

'It's all my fault,' Valentina mumbled, walking out of the bedroom. 'I should have prepared better. I made you work too hard.'

Valentina reheated the pork roast and potatoes and sliced the blessed paska. We knocked our eggs together to see who would have better luck in the coming year. My egg cracked; Valentina won. The next day I woke up early and joined her to tend the cherry orchard.

Five

I anxiously waited for the Easter holidays to end so that I could call the national archives in Kyiv. I had studied the history and politics of the Socialist Bloc long enough to know that if a person disappeared in the 1930s in the Soviet Union, the most likely culprit was the secret police. I had to find a way into the Rooster House.

'How do you expect me to find records of your relative when you have no information about him?' the voice on the other end of the line asked me. 'Did you just fall from the sky?'

The gratuitous insult reminded me of my visceral distaste for Soviet-style bureaucracy and for some reason I thought of Vladimir and grew angrier. However, since I bet high stakes on this conversation, I swallowed my sharp repartee and pleaded for help.

'Leave us your coordinates and we will call you back,' the voice said, placated but bored.

Nobody called me.

Valentina's dashing off to do garden work on my first day back in Bereh should have been a sign that teas around the samovar and long leisurely chats would languish in my imagination. She pretended not to hear my questions about Nikodim and had no interest in reliving days long gone. People often assume that those older than themselves live in the past and delight in shuffling through their memories like a stack of photographs, but Valentina was no Vladimir. She expressed little nostalgia for the Soviet Union and the days of her youth. She smiled whenever she saw me looking at the photographs of a tall, slender woman posing coquettishly for the camera, her younger self, that were scattered around the house. 'Yes, definitely beautiful,' she pronounced as if appraising a stranger.

She then pushed the photos aside and grabbed one of her favourite farming almanacs. 'But that was in the past. Now we must think about the future,' she would say, making notes in the margins and drawing complicated vegetable bed designs.

Miffed as I was in the beginning, I couldn't help finding Valentina's pursuit of a perfect garden touching as a reminder of Asya's obsessive quest. Soon I stopped expecting my grandmother to change her routine for me and instead changed mine – I joined her in the orchard.

'Who taught you to whitewash the orchard this way!' Valentina said. I looked up. My grandmother stood next to me, arms akimbo, and her round face wore an exasperated look. 'You aren't applying the whitewash thickly enough,' she said.

I had never whitewashed an orchard before. For me it used to be a place for devouring the novels of Jules Verne under the spreading branches of the cherry trees, the soft rustle of their leaves accompanying me on my journey to the centre of the Earth. Later, when I left Ukraine for the United States, my memories of the orchard became romantic fantasies of afternoon teas under the blooming boughs. I envisioned our orchard when I read Taras Shevchenko's renowned poem: 'A cherry orchard by the house. Above the cherries beetles hum.' Even Ukrainians like my mother who weren't fluent in their native language could recite the poem's romantic coda, 'And nightingales their vigil keep'.

As I began writing about scents, the orchard provided the fragrant canvas, and I drew on my memories of flowers and trees in bloom to add layers to my descriptions of aromas. Bereh's garden became my endless reservoir of scents and their nuances. Whitewashing the orchard was never part of my reveries. However, Valentina's idea of a perfect cherry orchard included trees with white bands of lime solution painted on their trunks.

'What do you mean not applying enough?' I asked. 'How much is enough?'

'Enough is when the bands look white, not streaky grey,' Valentina said. I started whitewashing all over again, painting the lower half of the trees as carefully as I could and filling in every crack with the thick paste. After a couple of hours, the orchard stood white and gleaming, and I had peeling red patches on my fingers from the caustic solution seeping through my gloves. Wearing my grandfather's old tracksuit and my great-grandmother's apron, I looked like a tramp from Gogol's city nightmares – and not the country manor lady of my Chekhovian fantasies.

Valentina came out to inspect the work. 'Looks nice,' she said, circling the trees. Then she paused and frowned. 'But can't you see that it's now uneven? Some bands are thicker than others. You also missed the tree over by the well.'

My lime-splattered hands smarted. 'I studied political science, not agriculture,' I grumbled, as Valentina demonstrated the proper technique.

'And how much good did that do?' she retorted. When I first told Valentina about my field of choice for graduate work, she pronounced it 'impractical'.

I pressed my brush against the tree trunk, watching the milky solution seep into the grooves. Its chalky scent reminded me of school blackboards and old crayons. 'I still don't understand what's so impractical about political science?' I ventured.

Valentina ran her hand over the cherry branches and caressed the sticky buds with her fingers. 'Studying politics is the most useless thing in the world. Either you enter politics and play the field or you leave them alone and hope they won't mess up your life,' she said at last. 'Though it's hard to avoid being messed up by politics here. Now because of the situation with Russia, the prices of everything are shooting up. Even this lime that you can't apply properly costs twice what it did a few months ago.'

I stared at the opaque liquid dripping from the end of my brush.

'I wanted to study political science because of what we lived through when the Soviet Union collapsed. I wanted to understand this place,' I said. 'And I thought I would enjoy teaching. Didn't you like being a teacher?'

'I liked teaching,' Valentina said. 'However, I chose my field by accident. Asya insisted that I become a meat technologist – a glorified butcher – because it meant that we would always have meat on our table. The moment I stepped inside an abattoir, I fainted from the stink of rotten flesh and the sight of entrails oozing onto the cement floor. I decided to become a geographer. The field was then called economic geography, because it was about making nature comply with the five-year plans,' Valentina shook her head. 'I foolishly assumed that you don't have to deal with blood when you're handling numbers and maps.'

It was the frankest conversation Valentina and I had had since my arrival, and I wanted it to continue. 'You were a wonderful teacher, whatever you taught,' I said. 'I loved listening to your lectures as a child, even if I understood nothing of what you were saying. I also enjoyed when people crowded around us at museums to eavesdrop on your explanations of art. I wanted to emulate you by becoming a professor myself.'

However, Valentina's face regained its neutral expression and she crouched near a cherry tree with a brush. My grandmother was more preoccupied with the tree than my life choices. So I didn't tell her that she had influenced me in another way by giving me the confidence to try something new. When studying political science didn't measure up to my expectations, I didn't hesitate to change careers. I put game theory models away, joined a perfumery school and learned organic chemistry. I wrote about scents and flavours, translating the intangible into words. One thing that never frightened me was plunging into the unknown.

I recalled my last visit to California to see my father. He too was ready to start something new and I remembered how elated he sounded. I wanted to tell Valentina about it. She knew my father well, but she rarely brought him up herself.

'Why does whitewashing have to be so mathematically precise, if the only point is to protect the bark from insects?' I asked instead. A fear I couldn't identify held me back from asking Valentina about my father.

My grandmother cocked her head to the side and extended her hand towards me. 'Give me that large brush,' she said.

She fixed the crooked line of lime solution on an old cherry tree. 'The whitewash protects the bark from sun-scald in winter and from insects, but it should look beautiful too,' she said. My grandmother's standards remained high.

Part of our cherry orchard abutted Sasha's vegetable patch,

and whenever Valentina's perfectionism and my stubbornness collided, I could see our neighbour peering at us through the flimsy wire fence that separated our properties. The wind carried conversations back and forth between our gardens, and I was certain that Sasha was as privy to the details of our small dramas as we were to her fights with her son.

'I see that you decided to whitewash today,' Sasha said, pushing the gate open and stepping inside. 'Valentina Sergiyvna, how much did you pay for the lime powder?'

Valentina and Sasha discussed the cost of lime, while I painted.

'Little Sasha invited a cucumber whisperer to come this afternoon. I need to prepare the seeds,' Sasha said, about to retreat to her garden.

I stopped painting and turned around to look at her. 'A cucumber whisperer?'

'Yes, a cucumber whisperer. She's a true professional, not like the quacks that advertise their services in the *Dawn of Poltava*,' Sasha said, sounding offended for some reason. 'Never get a cucumber whisperer from a newspaper. They're all scammers.'

'What does a cucumber whisperer do?' I asked. It never occurred to me that such a service existed, much less that people placed classified ads for it.

'A cucumber whisperer casts a spell to ensure a plentiful harvest,' Sasha said, rolling her eyes. While I stood dumbfounded, wondering if Valentina also hired cucumber whisperers, Sasha glanced at the trees I had whitewashed and gave me a pinched smile. 'I didn't know that city ladies could whitewash so well.'

Sasha always complimented me to my face, but she did so in such an exaggeratedly saccharine way that it sounded phony. I also knew that she said harsher things about me behind my back.

'Sasha says that you always wear ugly shoes,' Valentina said the next day, as we were about to start our daily round of gardening. 'She says that your shoes are more appropriate for a kolkhoznitsa, a collective farm worker, than an amerikanka. An amerikanka who lives in Europe, no less!' Valentina laughed out loud and wiped her eyes.

I didn't find it nearly as amusing.

'But what am I supposed to wear? It's been raining and the dirt road in front of the house is impassable!' I glanced at my rubber boots standing near the entrance. Sturdy and rough-hewn, they were not high fashion, but considering that Sasha herself preferred torn house slippers, I didn't understand why my shoes bothered her.

'It doesn't matter,' Valentina said, waving her hand in front of her face as if chasing away flies. 'Sasha is just a chatterbox.'

My irritation with Sasha's passive-aggressive comments coalesced into anger that I couldn't hold back. 'She spreads rumours about me,' I said. 'Someone asked me the other day whether I got divorced, because why else would I return here?'

'This is just idle talk. Sasha talks nonsense, but she means well. When none of you are around, she helps me,' my grandmother said. I didn't understand how Valentina remained undisturbed by the gossip about my marriage.

'Then why are you telling me what she said about my shoes? And why are you always defending her?'

'Why are you getting upset? The fact is that the rubber boots are ugly. Wear them if you want, but don't get annoyed if you hear people making comments,' Valentina said, raising her eyebrows.

'But you were the one who gave them to me and told me that they were better than sneakers,' I said, pointing to the faux-fur-lined booties that apparently caused so much drama in Bereh.

Valentina exhaled sharply and stood up. 'Wear whatever

you want. I'm off to the garden.' She put on her jacket without looking at me.

'People here will hold you to a different standard, because you live abroad. They appreciate that you return. You can say that they feel proud of you for coming back. But they will judge you anyway,' she said, throwing a scarf around her neck. 'Can you imagine what they said when Dmytro returned from Canada to live here?' Her face softened and she stepped outside.

I dusted the rubber boots off with my sleeve and resolved to wear no other style of footwear when Sasha was around.

Later I called my husband and mentioned the conversation with Valentina. He consoled me by saying that in small places people knew everything about each other and needed to discuss it. We missed each other, but we agreed that I would stay in Ukraine for as long as I needed to. At that point I recognised that my one-month stay would have to be extended. I had to make a trip to the south of France for the rose harvest, but otherwise my writing assignments didn't require me to return to Brussels right away.

In the end, it wasn't Sasha's talk that really troubled me. I could shrug it off. But I couldn't ignore the tension between my grandmother and me. I found her unpredictable and unreadable, and I saw that getting close to her would take more than buying a ticket to Ukraine or whitewashing a cherry orchard.

∽

I also had to acknowledge that I was getting nowhere in my search for Nikodim. Having given up on the national archives, I explored Poltava's regional resources. I checked the archival division's official website for visitor information, and having satisfied myself that no appointment was required, I changed out of my rubber boots into city-appropriate footwear and took the bus into Poltava.

The town baffled and delighted me. In Ukraine, where geography often determined destiny, Poltava defied easy classifications. It was neither the east nor the west. It was the centre, but also the periphery. In the main square, the imposing neo-classical buildings, like many replicas of the Parthenon, encircled a large park with a monument to Peter the Great's victory over Sweden in 1709. A Ukrainian flag fluttered above it, affixed to the Russian imperial eagle at the top of the column. On the hills above the city, the golden domes of the Holy Cross Exaltation Monastery shimmered darkly. The monastery was funded by the Cossacks, many of whom fought on the Swedish side in that distant but still vividly remembered eighteenth-century war. Lenin Street ran parallel to Old Monastery Street. Engels nudged Gorky. Pushkin Street stumbled over Gogol and Rosa Luxemburg before halting in the quiet of Linden Alley where the Russian poet cast a bronze eye over grandfathers playing dominos and cats napping on empty benches. The street names were in the process of being changed, but the signs still bore Soviet-era designations and people arranged to meet near the absent Lenin monument. I was certain that a town whose psyche was imprinted so deeply with memories should provide clues to Nikodim's fate.

Yet my confidence wavered as I entered the Regional Archive Bureau. The grey cement block had all the hallmarks of a Soviet-type bureaucratic institution and projected faceless might. It assaulted me with the smell of dust and unfulfilled five-year plans and transformed me into yet another number in a line of people.

Though 'line' wasn't the right word for the impatient crowd that surged towards the reception desk. 'Go to the second floor,' I heard a young receptionist say to an elderly lady with a hearing aid and a vintage felt hat.

'Seventh floor? What am I supposed to do? This building doesn't have seven floors,' the lady said, trying to adjust her hearing aid but instead dropping it on the floor.

'Second floor. Second floor!' The receptionist's voice was hoarse from straining. Others searched for pieces of the hearing aid on the floor and guided the lady to the right place, screaming instructions of their own. The line recomposed itself, and I found myself at the tail end. Two elderly men in tweed jackets hung with war medals brandished yellowing sheets of paper as proof for some official document whose acronym I didn't recognise. Certificates, permits and attestations were sought and denied; inquiries were lodged and pronounced impossible. The archives remained unassailable.

A middle-aged woman wearing a long red coat wanted proof of her Jewish heritage.

'Were you born in Poltava? Did you contact the synagogue?' a receptionist asked.

'Which synagogue? The synagogue was turned into an opera house. The opera house burned down and now stands shuttered,' the woman replied.

'You say it as if I closed the synagogue and burned down the opera house,' the receptionist said, shoving a piece of paper at her. 'Here is the list of all synagogues in Poltava. There is more than one, you know.'

'And what do you want?' the receptionist glanced at me and then returned to her computer screen.

I explained that I was tracing my family tree and needed the archival information from my great-grandparents' villages. Recalling my experience with the national archives, I decided not to bring up Nikodim at this point.

'Devushka, you need to make an appointment with the chief archivist, but she's busy today. Next person in line!'

Being called a young lady for some reason irritated me even more. 'You have no appointment system. I checked your website for instruction,' I said, feeling the crowd pressing on my back.

'I had no idea anyone used our website,' the receptionist said.

'I came from another town,' I said, meaning Bereh.

'I don't care if you came from Paris. Do you understand? Next person in line!'

'I didn't come from Paris . . . ' I started saying, but the receptionist interrupted me.

'Yes, I can see that,' she said, looking at my simple black coat accessorised with Asya's rose-patterned shawl.

I involuntarily pulled back and someone elbowed me out of the way to take my place. I stepped aside and felt another elbow jabbing me in the ribs. The pain, unearned and unexpected, infuriated me and I plunged into the crowd, making my way back to the reception desk.

'I understand that this is an archives bureau and that your job is to help, not insult your visitors,' I said. Once I had made a decision to stand my ground, my anger evaporated and my voice rang out crisp and clear above the suddenly silent crowd. 'I live in another country – close to Paris, if that matters – and I came here to trace my family history. If I need to make an appointment, I'd like to know how I should do it.'

The receptionist gawked at me and so did the people in line. I now wished I had worn my village rubber boots in addition to Sergiy's Soviet-issue jacket. 'But why didn't you say from the beginning that you were from abroad?' the receptionist murmured. 'You need to see Oksana Vasylivna, the chief archivist. Her office is around the corner.'

I stepped aside, dusted off my coat, and straightened my shawl, feeling as if I had emerged from a brawl. The ease with which the doors had opened at the mere mention of the land beyond the border made my victory seem cheap. Still, I accepted it and walked down the hall to the chief archivist's office, with the receptionist at my heels. She entered Oksana Vasylivna's office with me and explained that I was a foreigner looking for my family in Poltava. I nodded ruefully. The chief archivist reached for a voluminous book of records, and my heart raced – I took her gesture to be a good sign.

'Let me check what we might have in our database. Yes, we are so high-tech here.' Oksana Vasylivna rolled her eyes and opened a page with a handwritten glossary.

I recited the names of the villages where different branches of my Poltava clan originated: 'Mykhailivka, Maiachka ...' But Oksana Vasylivna closed the book and put it back on the shelf. 'Then I can't help you. None of the archives for these villages survived. They were either burned during the Civil War, destroyed during the Stalinist repressions, or lost after the German occupation. Wiped out.'

She turned to the receptionist, who listened to our conversation leaning on the door. 'Isn't it the case? It's as if they never existed.'

The women spread their hands as if to say that even the mighty bureaucracy was helpless against Ukrainian history.

'As if they never existed.' Lost records were a common story in a country that changed government dozens of times in 1919 alone, but before I went to the archives, I hadn't imagined that the traces of an entire family in an area the size of Belgium could be wiped out.

'I also have an uncle who disappeared in the 1930s,' I started tentatively. 'Do you think that I should make an inquiry at the Rooster House? I mean, the Security Service of Ukraine.' The two women smiled at me with motherly pity and shook their heads.

'The criminal archives are still classified. Plus, with our situation these days, do you really think anyone at that organisation would help you look for some uncle who disappeared who knows when?' Oksana Vasylivna said.

'And then you're not a direct relative,' the receptionist said. 'The only way to make an inquiry is to ask the nearest of kin to do so.' I doubted that Valentina would be interested in doing so, busy as she was in the orchard. I couldn't even persuade her to share anything about Nikodim.

I walked out of the archives building, avoiding eye contact with the crowd of seniors at the reception, who whispered to each other as they watched me scuttle past. At the bus stop, oblivious to people shoving me, I stood under the metal awning plastered with advertisements for second-hand furniture and farm tools and reflected on my findings. If the archives were wiped out, and if Valentina didn't want to talk about the past, I had to give up my search.

I didn't wait for the bus and headed down the street where the central paved avenues of Poltava gave way to cobblestones and cherry orchards. I turned right and saw a white building topped with a simple green dome. 'Saint Nicolas Ukrainian Orthodox Church', read a newly minted plaque at the gate. The small church consisted of a covered portico and two protruding wings, and since it hovered precariously at the edge of a ravine, it seemed like a bird ready to take flight – or to plunge into the abyss.

I knew more about Judaism through my father's side of the family than about Orthodox Christianity. My great-grandfather Sergiy grew up in a religious family, but he held the church responsible for fostering fatalism and fear and he despised anything reminiscent of its creed and rituals. He even cringed when people used common phrases like 'God willing' or 'for

God's sake'. The first person in the family to receive a university degree, he taught history and literature, and called himself an atheist whose only sacred mission was to spread education.

Nevertheless, the mysticism of the Orthodox church that repelled Sergiy attracted me, and I found its rites and rituals enigmatic and soothing. I liked stepping inside churches and finding myself enveloped in incense smoke and incantations – the mystery awakened my curiosity. I lingered in front of Saint Nicolas and then pushed open its heavy wooden doors, not knowing what to expect and not wanting to know.

The bright sunshine was roughly pulled away and replaced with murky shadows. The hall was narrow and dark, full of gold-trimmed banners and garlands. I stumbled, passed through a small door, and though the church was empty, I felt as if I had disturbed a large gathering. Hundreds of Byzantine eyes surveyed me, the lone mortal in this celestial realm. The plain white walls of the church were covered with icons of saints, martyrs and the Virgin Mary. Ornate embroideries swathed the icons, and the light falling through the lancet windows glittered on the baroque frames and golden halos. A silence redolent of flowers and myrrh amplified the sounds of my footsteps. I lit a candle below the icon of Saint Barbara, who was beheaded for refusing to give up her faith. I noticed that her altar had the most candles and offerings.

I felt someone watching me – a warm human stare – and I turned around so swiftly that I nearly bumped into a short woman of about sixty, with a round flushed face and a thick blonde braid wrapped around her head.

'Can I take a photo?' I asked.

'Sure, go ahead,' she replied. 'I'm Pani Olga.'

I wondered if I had misheard her. People rarely used 'pani', an old-fashioned word for lady, in our town of Lenin streets and Engels squares. Pani Olga meanwhile was eyeing my Canon.

'I have an archive that needs to be photographed,' she said without any preamble. 'Would you be able to come once or twice a week and take photos?'

She noticed my hesitation and added, 'I will pray for you.' I said yes without fully understanding what I had accepted to do.

If Sergiy left the church to follow Lenin, that spring I reversed the course. I still helped Valentina in the orchard, but at the weekends I took a bus to Poltava and photographed Pani Olga's archive.

I wasn't mistaken in feeling that Saint Nicolas sat on the brink of destruction. The Poltava Communist Party blew it up in the 1950s, at a time of peace and plenty, when it seemed that God would no longer be of service. The only part that had survived was a narthex, the hall connecting the sacred and the mortal worlds. The church raised money to rebuild the ruins and turn them into a functioning parish, but funds were lacking to fill the ravine and reconstruct the rest of the building. Still, the church lived its own vibrant life. It enfolded me too, and the scent of incense permeated my skin and hair. After a few visits Father Oleksiy, the cherubic priest with a jet-black beard, ignored my presence and conducted his rites and confessions against the sharp clicks of my camera. Leaving me to my photography, Pani Olga dispensed candles before the icons, cleaned up the dripping wax from the floor, and wrote down names to be read during the mass, for health or for eternal repose. 'She's curating our history,' she explained, though most people passing through Saint Nicolas had enough of their own concerns and problems to give much thought to me. The doors of the church were open to all, and like many of them, I was flotsam brought in by the current.

What Pani Olga called 'the archive' was a bundle of cloth. Even before Saint Nicolas had re-opened its doors for service after the collapse of the Soviet Union, people brought icons, crosses, incense burners and other religious paraphernalia that they had kept hidden. It was the start of Pani Olga's collection of unburied treasures, the most precious among them being the rushnyky. At first glance, a rushnyk looks like a fancy hand towel with two thick bands of embroideries, but as Pani Olga explained, surprised at my ignorance, they served as talismans, which was why they draped icons whether at home or at the church. Asya and Valentina embroidered rushnyky, but they were used as ordinary towels, and while Sergiy was alive, I hadn't seen a single icon in our house, rushnyk-adorned or not. These days Valentina kept a few icons, but they were mostly the flimsy paper prints, souvenirs she received from friends and neighbours returning from pilgrimages to important Orthodox sanctuaries.

'A rushnyk holds a new-born baby,' Pani Olga continued. 'It binds newlyweds to symbolise an unending union. The size of a rushnyk depends on its function. The longest rushnyk is that one that lowers a coffin into the ground . . .'

In Bereh, when Sasha or other neighbours dropped by, they talked about Russian sanctions, the threat of invasion, the weather and the dangers of tomato blight, treating each subject with the same level of importance. They weren't blind to reality or ignorant of the consequences, but they accepted that they had no control over events, and so they tended to their orchards and carried on as they always did. At Saint Nicolas, however, the war was a constant presence. It was in the crumpled face of a woman who hadn't slept for days and enquired if the church had any jobs for a refugee. It was in the uniformed, heartbreakingly young soldiers who came to receive a blessing. It was in the distraught relatives asking for funeral services. It was in conversations, in prayers, in thoughts. To make sense of it, people talked about 'this war' as different from 'the war'. Even without definite articles in the Ukrainian language, they need not have specified that they meant the Second World War. It was the war that had left scars in families, and even as the generation that experienced it passed away, the idea of the Second World War as the Holy War, the Just War, the war of heroism and sacrifice remained as one of the most lasting Soviet legacies. The current war appeared cowardly and ugly against it. It wasn't even called war. In Western newspapers it came under the bland name of 'the Ukrainian crisis', while in the domestic media it was confusingly referred to as the Anti-Terrorist Operation, ATO for short. 'How could it be war?' I heard time and again. Whatever it was, people died all the same.

The evening mass was about to start when a man walked in and asked me if he could see the priest. Father Oleksiy arrived, closing his cassock and smoothing his long black beard.

'My son vanished in Donetsk ...' the man said. 'They can't even find his body.' Tears streamed down his stubble-covered cheeks and he didn't bother wiping them off. He bent his baseball cap in his callused hands and stared at the large crucifixion decorated by Pani Olga with a red rushnyk. Father Oleksiy opened the missal. 'We place ourselves into God's hands ...'

The prayers echoed against the white walls and faded, leaving behind the soft murmurs and the pale arabesques of incense smoke. Dizzy from the scents of myrrh and olibanum I stepped outside into the sun, where tolling bells and cooing doves blended into a single bittersweet accord of spring. A little girl sat in the grass, weaving sticky dandelion stems into a wreath. 'The mass is about to start. Why aren't you inside?' I asked the girl. She gave me a coy look. 'My father is a priest. I've heard it all before.'

I shared the little girl's weariness about church rituals, and whenever the priest said 'place yourself in God's hands',

I thought about Sergiy and his belief that the church bred submission, taught passivity and clouded the rational mind. Nevertheless, I kept returning to Saint Nicolas, drawn as much by the mystical force of an unfamiliar religion as by my growing friendship with Pani Olga. On sunny days we aired out linens on the grass, shooing away the mangy dog that sat near the church entrance like a Chinese guardian lion.

'This is a tree of life.' Pani Olga's fingers traced the embroidery on a rushnyk depicting a fantastical plant. From its branches sprouted opulent blossoms. 'It means that the embroiderer dreamed of a long life and a big family.'

'And this is one of the oldest rushnyk patterns.' Pani Olga pointed to the broken zigzag, saying that similar motifs appeared on Trypillian pottery. The Trypillian civilisation flourished on the territory of Ukraine more than seven thousand years ago, and its distinctive clay pots with geometric motifs filled many archaeological museums in the country.

'This is Beregynya, a safe keeper.' Pani Olga drew my attention to a figure, ample of hip and bosom, holding branches laden with grapes and flowers. 'It was embroidered by someone to protect a loved one from harm.' The image had none of the Orthodox sobriety and harkened back to the old animistic religion of the Slavs, who worshipped the spirits of plants, animals, birds and rocks.

'This is a real marvel!' Pani Olga exclaimed excitedly, startling the dog that sniffed around us. 'This rushnyk was embroidered in the sixties, but do you see these yellow and blue hues? Take a look at the bend of the leaf here. Doesn't it look like a trident? The embroiderer must have been aware that such a shape could lead to an accusation of Ukrainian nationalism.' A trident was the coat of arms of independent Ukraine, a symbol powerful enough in Soviet days to secure passage to Siberia.

Pani Olga then unrolled a small towel embroidered in black. 'If people went through a difficult period or had a question they couldn't resolve, they embroidered their feelings onto a fabric and tied such a rushnyk on a tree.' Each cloth in my friend's hands became a record of aspirations, dreams and anxieties. She read the moth-eaten fabric like books, decoding messages and sentiments in the designs and colours.

'How do I embroider "family ties, raptures and returns" onto a towel?' I asked.

Pani Olga looked at me and squinted. 'I thought that you were on a pilgrimage and I was right.'

'Am I? I'm trying to make sense of what's going on and only becoming more confused. I think that my grandmother finds my presence awkward.'

'I'm sure that's not true. Nothing is more important than family. Even when we fight, we remain a family.'

I thought about Vladimir and said nothing. Pani Olga didn't press me further. She shared her struggles as a widow with two children and complained about her private tutoring job.

'The students don't want to learn. They ask me to write their term papers for them. And I do it, because I have no other way to make money. I contribute to the corrupt system I despise.' Pani Olga was originally from Russia, 'a true-blooded Siberian', as she called herself, and she moved to Poltava after she married her Ukrainian husband, a fellow Esperanto professor.

'My husband and I believed that one day Esperanto would be the universal language,' she said. 'Instead, it became the language for two. We used it when we didn't want others to understand us. Then my husband passed away, and now Esperanto is dying inside of me.' Pani Olga lowered her face and turned away.

I wanted to comfort her, but when I leaned in closer, she was already her smiling, bubbly self. Whenever Pani Olga revealed anything painful or sorrowful about herself, she neither dwelled on it nor sought my sympathy. She accepted humiliations and heartbreaks, because she also knew that every moment held the potential for a miracle. She treated her rushnyky as the manifestations of such miracles.

Pani Olga picked up a rushnyk embroidered in blood red. Firebirds with long, peacock-like tails sat on a tree festooned with stars and flowers and looked up to heaven.

'After my husband died, I became obsessed with embroidery, gathering patterns, cataloguing different techniques and meeting other embroiderers,' she said. 'It reminded me that life was still beautiful.'

The afternoon light cast oblique shadows on the grass and rouged our faces, but the air felt cold. Pani Olga handed me the rushnyk. The stitches were so tiny that they were hard to tell apart, and yet they formed a lovely pattern.

'Such pretty firebirds,' I said, shivering.

'These are roosters. A rooster symbolises a call to repentance. Remember the gospel story of Peter's denial of Christ and his eventual redemption?' Pani Olga said. She looked at her wristwatch and saw that it was time to prepare for the afternoon service. She folded the rushnyky and sprang to her feet.

'Why didn't you try the Rooster House if you're looking for your uncle?' Pani Olga asked.

My legs tingled and I struggled getting up. 'People at the regional archives told me that criminal cases are still closed to the public.'

'Then that's how it is,' Pani Olga said, offering me her hand. 'As for embroidering, the only way to do it is stitch by stitch. At first, it looks like runes, but then it forms a pattern.' Her grip was so firm that she pulled me straight up to my feet.

Six

Pani Olga's rushnyk metaphor sounded sensible, but applying it to my search for Nikodim turned out to be complicated. I couldn't even use it to figure out my grandmother. Small misunderstandings continued to build tension between us. When she mentioned that I was too slow weeding the strawberry beds, I took it as a personal slight. When I asked her if she would be home for dinner, she assumed that I was chiding her for not spending enough time with me. And indeed Valentina found my help lacking and I begrudged her long visits to Sasha. To add to my frustration, Sasha shared news of my friction with Valentina with the other neighbours, and I felt as if they looked at me askance, convinced that I was as much of a failure as a granddaughter as a gardener. The war made every plan less certain and every disagreement more strident. In the end, the best we could do was to lose ourselves in our projects – Valentina planted the orchard and I catalogued Pani Olga's rushnyky.

'Stitching it all together is much more difficult than I

imagined,' I said bitterly one day, reminding Pani Olga of her rushnyk analogy. 'Stitch by stitch, you said, but it seems that the more I try, the more everything unravels.'

'You are too impatient,' my friend said, adjusting her crown-like braids. 'Give your grandmother time. Meanwhile, why not visit villages where your grandparents lived and see what you can find? Talk to people. Breathe the air. Didn't you say that you haven't travelled around Ukraine enough? Who knows, maybe your grandmother might want to come with you.'

Pani Olga had a point. Several days later she and I made plans to travel by marshrutka, a type of shared taxi, to the neighbouring town of Reshetylivka. Pani Olga wanted to visit the Reshetylivka Rushnyk Museum and date a number of embroidery patterns that baffled her. I, on the other hand, was on a quest of my own. Before the Second World War, Asya had worked briefly as a teacher at the school attached to the Clara Zetkin carpet factory. Even if the trip would bring me no closer to Nikodim, it could help me find more information about my great-grandmother.

'Babushka, would you like to come to Reshetylivka with Pani Olga and me?' I asked Valentina when I returned home. 'We want to visit the Clara Zetkin factory and maybe the school where Asya once worked.'

At that moment Valentina was gesticulating at the TV and muttering something about 'boundless stupidity'. I didn't know if she was referring to the Russian government or the administration in Kyiv whom she detested for their incompetence despite her fierce patriotism. My grandmother threw me a glance that reprised her comment about the politicians. 'How can you talk of Reshetylivka when there is so much garden work to do?' she said. I shifted from foot to foot and remained standing in front of her.

'But you should go,' she conceded, turning off the TV. 'Ask them what a German Marxist has to do with Ukrainian carpets.' She treated my interest in rushnyky and villages as a strange fancy.

The Poltava countryside unfolded in a scroll of green orchards and black earth. Images flashed past the window: two white cats sitting on a haystack, still as Japanese dolls; a scarecrow wearing a chequered suit jacket and red tracksuit bottoms; a woman in a blue scarf herding a gaggle of ducklings so yellow they glowed in the grey morning light.

Pani Olga, on the other hand, didn't waste her time on the scenery. She had already learned her fellow travellers' biographies and shared a story about our embroidery quest in Reshetylivka. Several women joined the conversation, mentioning their grandmothers' rushnyky.

'Who has time for embroideries nowadays?' a middle-aged woman with orange highlights and a gold molar said.

'In Europe they protect their heritage,' a young woman next to her offered.

'In Europe they are rich and they can afford it,' Gold Molar retorted, looking around the bus for support. She had no trouble finding it. A man in a brand-new Adidas tracksuit rolled his eyes. 'In Europe they have money and culture, but they also have the rule of law. Here, on the other hand, we have to pay for the law to be applied as it should be. My son's teacher hints that unless I slip her extra money, like all the other parents do, she will give him a low grade. My son studies hard, and yet I must pay his teacher to grade him fairly. Will this country ever change?'

Bribery was such a common occurrence that soon everyone was clamouring to share their woes. 'Well, we're Europe. But *that* Europe doesn't want to admit it,' Pani Olga said, chagrined by the turn the conversation had taken.

'Like it needs us and our problems,' Gold Molar replied.

'The West will help us. Don't give up,' the Adidas man said, and the whole bus laughed, recognising the famous line from Ilf and Petrov's picaresque novel *The Twelve Chairs*. Since the European Union could only 'express concern' or 'express grave concern' over the war on its borders, the ironic quip stung. The situation was hopeless, it meant. Silence fell and the mood on the bus became sombre.

When we arrived at Reshetylivka, a town like other small Ukrainian towns with its mix of neat, brick houses, apartment blocks with ugly tiled facades, Soviet-era war memorials and patches of kitchen gardens, I tried and failed to find the traces of its old artistic heritage. Pani Olga explained that the Reshetylivka masters created many original techniques in embroidery, weaving, carpet making, wood carving and painting. Legend had it that in the sixteenth century the town's cobblers were renowned in Europe for their unusual red-tinted leather. Moreover, Reshetylivka originated bile po bilomu, white-on-white, the most complicated of all embroidery techniques.

A woman at the bakery in the town centre laughed when I asked for directions to the Clara Zetkin factory. 'You're twenty years too late, sweetheart. Zetkin was finished off in the 1990s.' Only in Ukraine could the Grandmother of German Communism die twice.

'Everything is gone,' the woman added. 'I was once a weaver too, and now I sell pastries. Take these ones,' she pointed to some crumbly rounds studded with peanut halves. 'These are actually fresh.'

Pani Olga didn't seem to consider the demise of the factory to be bad news for our quest, and after thanking the woman, she bought a packet of peanut cookies. Stepping out of the sweet fumes of the bakery, she steered me towards the low barracks in the distance. 'Nothing disappears completely,' she said.

The barracks turned out to be the Reshetylivka Arts College, and as soon as we entered the dark hallway smelling of dust and paint thinner, I knew we were inside a Soviet-era institution. The college had bi-coloured walls, dirty brown at the bottom and dirty white on top, in the manner that must have been prescribed by government standards circa 1980. The plaster on the walls sported deep cracks and mildew spots. Peering into one of the classrooms, we saw a group of five girls and one boy bent over embroidery hoops, their fingers flying over the fabric. The linoleum floor was littered with yarn and bits of fabric. Another girl was watering the scrawny spiderwort plants on the windowsill, oblivious to the streams of water gushing out of their perforated pots. 'The profs? They must be in the staffroom,' she said, throwing us a quick, uninterested glance, and we retraced our steps through the hallway and wandered in the darkness until we found the staffroom. There, one half of the tiny space was occupied by fabric samples and the other by two people drinking tea. A plump woman with a handsome, dimpled face and dark brown hair introduced herself as Nadia Vakulenko, the embroidery teacher. A melancholy-looking man twisting a cigarette in his fingers turned out to be the painting teacher, Petro. Neither asked us why we were barging into the staffroom and Nadia invited us to have tea with them. We squeezed into the cramped space and offered the teachers our peanut cookies.

When Pani Olga explained that we had come all the way from Poltava to take a look at the local embroideries, Petro nodded absent-mindedly, but Nadia grew excited. She offered to take us to the Rushnyk Museum herself, and we set off, leaving Petro to his contemplations and his cigarette.

Walking down the main street named after the leader of the

Bolshevik revolution, I observed that Lenin was ever-present in Ukraine. The further east one travelled, the more likely one was to live on Lenin Street, shop on Lenin Boulevard, go to Lenin High School and work at a factory bearing his name. After 1991, streets in Lviv and Kyiv had been renamed, but Poltava and its environs retained their Communist trappings.

'We've been petitioning the local government to change the street name for years, but they tell us that we have to wait, that it isn't the right time. When is the right time, then? Why do I have to walk down a street named after that bloody tyrant?' Nadia said.

'But the truth is that many people don't care. Or until now they didn't. I think that the time for change has arrived at last. It's not about the name of this or that street, but about losing our sense of our own history.'

In the rush to rebrand, authorities chose not to revert to old names, but to create new heroes. It struck me as ironically Soviet in spirit.

Nadia and Pani Olga exchanged a glance and laughed. 'You've been away from Ukraine too long, my dear. Did you expect that the Soviet way of life vanished along with the state? We have a long way to go before we learn how to do things in a way that's not Soviet,' Nadia said.

Despite being a small-budget affair, the Rushnyk Museum displayed an investment of much love and care. The rushnyky on display were decorated in a variety of styles, from white, lacy motifs to sumptuous red and blue ornaments, and Nadia opened one glass case after another for me to marvel at the rich textures and colours.

A collection of photographs from the Clara Zetkin factory caught my attention. I looked for Asya in the hazy sepia prints even though it was unlikely that as a schoolteacher she would have been photographed with the weavers. In one image a group of women dressed in ornate embroidered dresses worked on a rushnyk with a tree of life motif. Lenin monitored their work from a red corner, a niche in Ukrainian homes traditionally reserved for icons. It was clear from the unnatural position of their hands and the overly elaborate clothing that the photograph was staged, a promotional picture about the advances of Communism in the embroidery department. Underneath it hung another image with the serene, solitary mood of a Vermeer painting. It showed a woman standing in front of an open window. She wore a headscarf pushed back to reveal her dark hair and she leaned over a pile of rushnyky with determined concentration as if nothing but these bundles of cloth existed. The light flooding the room through the embroidered curtains bleached the linens and her face to mere outlines. It could have depicted Asya. Enraptured, I stared at the photograph until Pani Olga tapped me on the shoulder and told me that she and Nadia were leaving.

'Different regions have their own styles as distinctive as their personalities,' said Nadia, when we returned to the college.

'People in Poltava are calm and laid-back, like their flat landscape, so their embroidery is soft, pastel and low-key,' interjected Petro, who still sat in the staffroom, sighing and rolling his cigarette. 'In the western regions, especially in the Carpathians, people are energetic and dramatic, and their embroidery is bolder and brighter. That's the difference between the people of the plains and the people of the mountains. People embroider what they see around them.'

Petro himself was a man of the mountains, but these days he had to content himself with living on the plains of Poltava. 'I got married,' he said simply, and I wasn't sure whether the loss of the mountains or the acquisition of a wife was the source of his melancholy.

If people transferred their environment onto the canvas, then the Reshetylivans must have lived in a world of blooms, stars and snowflakes. Embroideries with the local patterns of cherry blossoms and intertwining vines embellished with grapes and cornflowers rendered Pani Olga speechless. Then it was my turn to be at a loss for words. Nadia unfolded a white linen shirt. 'I just finished this vyshyvanka,' she said. In Ukrainian, vyshyvanka means 'an embroidered shirt'. The tailoring of Nadia's shirt was plain – a straight, loose bodice with a rounded collar and full three-quarter sleeves – but its simplicity served to highlight the embroidery decorating it. The main motif was kalyna, viburnum, a plant that symbolised the innocence of youth with its white flowers and the passion of love with its red berries. Nadia wove both patterns into her embroidery, letting the full branches of berries embrace the small bunches of blossoms. Tiny stars around the main elements enhanced the airiness of the design. Nadia explained that she achieved the filigree effect by removing threads and embroidering over the remaining fabric. The embroidery appeared like the finest of laces, and I couldn't believe that it was the result of needlework. It was the famous white-on-white Reshetylivka style.

Nadia said that the white-on-white embroidery didn't allow for any mistakes, and that an error in counting even a single thread left the whole pattern crooked. To make it even more complicated, knots aren't allowed in the finished work, since the reverse has to look identical to the front side. To give a design luminosity and form, a master uses threads of different finishes and angles each stitch in such a way as to catch the light. I couldn't imagine what level of skill it took to create something so exquisite, but as I stood in the glow of the embroidery's beauty, the shabby surroundings that had so depressed me when I first walked into the college receded. I was only aware of the garment that felt as light as butterfly wings in my hands.

Neither Nadia nor Petro had any idea as to why the embroidery factory was named after Clara Zetkin, but they had many opinions about its demise. The factory employed thousands of people in Reshetylivka and its environs, and the college was part of the factory training programme, bestowing degrees in art, embroidery, carpet weaving and other crafts. Once the Soviet Union collapsed, the factory fractured, and the power struggles among its directors led to its final collapse and bankruptcy. Only the college remained.

'They've killed the Clara Zetkin factory, and now the college is on the brink of collapse,' said Petro. 'Can't you tell that we are on a government budget?' He pointed to the cracking plaster and wires sticking out of the walls. Like many technical colleges across Ukraine, the Reshetylivka College struggled to stay afloat because of a lack of financing and a demographic crisis. College-aged students were too few to fill the registration quotas, and arts as a vocation had little prestige. The students who enrolled did so because the government college offered them free tuition and a stipend, and they were unprepared for the meticulous work that awaited them as embroidery artisans.

'My dream is to have the Reshetylivka white embroidery recognised as a UNESCO cultural treasure,' said Nadia. 'I know that with this strange war going on there are other important things right now, but I can still dream, can't I?'

We missed our bus back to Poltava and had to hitch-hike. We stood on the road, trying to look like respectable passengers, but cars whizzed by and splashed us with mud. The bells of the freshly painted mint-green church standing near a large pond sounded the evening prayers. The wind tossed up the long, supple branches of the weeping willows growing at the edges of the pond. They arched gracefully and fell onto the water, scrambling the reflection of the church into gold and green shards. Rain came down with brute force. Through the grey haze we saw several armoured vehicles and a truck carrying soldiers on the eastbound road. Pani Olga and I huddled under my umbrella, our eyes on the convoy. It rolled slowly past us, its dull roar drowning out the bells and the rain. The soldiers' faces were ashen and dusty, and they sat in silence, staring into the distance. Why at that moment was I thinking of the white-on-white embroideries? Perhaps I was searching for evidence that beauty and art can survive the worst turmoil of history. I held onto this idea as a lifebuoy as the convoy rolled on and on, interminable.

Back in Bereh, I recalled too late that I had forgotten to inquire about the Reshetylivka archives and my family's links to the town, but before I could decide what to do next, I fell asleep. That night I dreamed of tangled threads and white embroideries.

Seven

Two months had passed since I arrived in Ukraine. Spring faded into summer. My short trip to harvest roses in the south of France came and went, and I returned to Bereh bearing Provençal souvenirs for Valentina and Dmytro. The memory of the trip lingered in the honeyed scent of roses planted by Asya years ago. The vine trailed along the fence and festooned it with small fragrant blossoms that my great-grandmother used to distil into rosewater. These interwoven recollections filled me with melancholy longings that I couldn't place. In Bereh, my life outside of Ukraine with its research assignments, gallery visits and outings with friends seemed far away and not quite real. I missed Brussels and my husband, but I still couldn't bear to leave Bereh.

The days had grown longer and the sun bleached the last of the cherry blossoms, reducing pink petals to grey dust. When I recalled that only a few weeks ago finding Nikodim seemed like a matter of a few conversations with Valentina and a couple of visits to the local archives, my naiveté exasperated me. Occasionally I leafed through Sergiy's journal to verify that I hadn't dreamed up Nikodim, and I rubbed my finger over the place where Sergiy's pen etched his brother's name into the paper.

One morning, as I stepped out of the shower, I spotted a strangely shaped piece of Styrofoam in the far corner. The house had no space for a bathroom, so Valentina had outfitted a large storage shed next door with a bathtub and a toilet and we had grown accustomed to taking showers amid farm supplies, canning jars and rust-covered sickles. The object that caught my attention looked more peculiar than the rest. Intrigued, I flipped it around and came face to face with Vladimir Ilyich Lenin. The leader of the 1917 Revolution was depicted in profile, his goatee jutting out towards the bright Communist future and our bathtub. Lenin's head was lopped off from the rest of the body just under his ears, but it was still as tall as I was. As I stood propping it up with one hand and holding my bathrobe with another, I came to the unsettling conclusion that for two months I had been taking showers with Lenin as my Peeping Tom.

I soon confirmed that the Soviet song 'Lenin is Always With You' didn't lie. Lenin was omnipresent in our house. In another shed I found a poster depicting the architect of the Soviet state as a cherubic little boy smiling out of a large red star. Under the tarp in the former henhouse, I unearthed two portraits of the older, tougher Vladimir with a halo around his bald head. In the summer of 2014, statues of Lenin around Ukraine were being torn down, and the government debated anti-communism laws, but here I had enough artifacts for a Lenin-themed museum. I recognised the portraits from my childhood, when they kept vigil over Sergiy's desk, but I was surprised to see that we still had them.

'They are Sergiy's,' said Valentina when I showed her my discoveries. She was reading the morning's newspaper and sighing; the headlines were mostly dire. 'He refused to throw them out, even after the Soviet Union collapsed. Only after his death did I remove them from the house.'

'Why did you keep them?' I asked.

'Why should I throw them out?'

Valentina handed me her newspaper and pointed to an article about another deposed Lenin statue. 'In Roman times, they reused the representations of the emperors, so why not learn from the ancients?' she said. 'Shave off the goatee, fix his potato nose, remove the tie, and there you go – Taras Shevchenko.' Transforming the creator of the gulags into the Ukrainian national bard would appear obscene to many people, Sergiy included. I said so to Valentina, but she only laughed.

'Your great-grandfather was a man of iron-clad principles,' Valentina said, and I had to agree that it described Sergiy well.

Everything about Sergiy was proper and correct: his biography, his support of the Bolshevik Revolution, his participation in the Second World War, his work in education. His permanent frown lines and the steely stubble on his cheeks lent him a severe appearance that was softened by his mane of unruly white hair. We were proud of our brave great-grandfather dressed in a suit decorated with prestigious Red Army honours. The only person who didn't hide her occasional irritation with his burnished hero aura was Asya. Whenever Sergiy brought up the war, she would roll her eyes. 'Talking about that again? Like a broken record,' she groaned.

On the mornings when Asya went to the market, Sergiy and I ran the household. After he drank his first cup of tea, scalding hot and with a large slice of lemon, Sergiy made breakfast. He cut up salo, a beloved Ukrainian delicacy of cured pork fat, with the flourish of a Michelin-starred chef. The moment a drop of water hissed on the shiny black surface of a frying pan, Sergiy tossed in the ivory dominoes of salo. To the golden pool of sizzling fat, he added tomatoes, onions and eggs that I had fetched from the henhouse, shooing the clucking chickens from the pungent warmth of their nests. Sergiy moved slowly around the kitchen, his heavy prosthetic leg clopping on the wooden floor. We ate straight out of the skillet, dipping moist chunks of brown bread into the barely set yolk.

On the wall of the dining room, among family photos and Lenin portraits, hung a reproduction of an old map. It was covered with a thick network of sinuous lines – rivers and borders – and the goosebumps of forests and mountains. Sergiy woke up at dawn to weed the garden and by the time we had had our breakfast, he was mellow and in the mood to talk. He gently released the map from its hook and spread it out on the table.

'This is the first map of Ukraine,' Sergiy said. He reached for a pencil and pointed out Poltava. He traced the pencil over the dark line representing the Vorskla River. 'Bereh is right here.'

I listened with rapt attention as Sergiy explained that the map was drawn by someone named Boplan, who came to Ukraine in the seventeenth century, when its lands were part of the Polish-Lithuanian Commonwealth. With approval, Sergiy added that though Boplan worked for the Polish king, he liked the Ukrainian Cossacks and admired their courage. 'He even wrote in his book, "They greatly value their liberty, and would not want to live without it. That is why the Cossacks, when they consider themselves to be kept under too tight a rein, are so inclined to revolt and rebel,"' Sergiy said. 'The Cossacks went into battle with these words on their lips: "Abo slavu zdobudem, abo doma ne budem".' Either we find glory, or we won't return home.

104

'What about you, dedushka? Did you say this when you fought the Germans?' I asked him.

'Losing wasn't an option for a Cossack,' Sergiy said.

The name Boplan sounded like Bohdan to me, and since the only Bohdan I knew was our next-door neighbour, I imagined the cartographer as a good-natured drunk in a sailor's shirt who drew maps in his spare time. Indeed, Bereh's Bohdan chafed under his wife's tight rein, and when they fought, he screamed that she treated him like a slave.

Later, I learned that Boplan was Guillaume Levasseur de Beauplan, a French military engineer in the army of the Crown of the Kingdom of Poland. When he journeyed east in 1630, he joined many adventure seekers for whom the eastern frontier was a fresh opportunity. Beauplan relied on his skills as an architect and cartographer to draw up maps and build fortresses, and after retiring to France in 1651, he published *Description d'Ukranie*, an unlikely bestseller which remained in print more than three centuries later. Equally famous was his map of Ukraine with its astonishing level of detail about towns, borders and landscapes. Sergiy's having this old map wasn't unusual. Many a village hall across Ukraine displayed it proudly, with their specific location marked by a pin. 'Look, we existed then and we exist now,' they meant to say. After Ukraine gained independence, Beauplan's name appeared on street signs and memorial plaques edging out those of the Communist heroes. If one were to believe local historians, Beauplan left no village in Ukraine unpassed.

If Beauplan was an unknown figure to me in those days, the Cossacks were certainly not. At school, we had to memorise passages from Nikolai Gogol's *Taras Bulba* by heart, a story about the Cossacks of the Zaporozhian Sich and their fight against Polish overlords. Images of Cossacks, complete with wide pants and embroidered shirts, appeared not only in editions of Gogol's stories and school textbooks, but also on official posters. A Cossack stood next to a maiden in a be-ribboned flower wreath and chequered skirt – the same outfit Valentina wore as a young woman in many photographs. Next to the Ukrainian pair stood a Russian one – always in the centre and at least a head taller. They were flanked by thirteen other couples representing the Soviet republics.

Sergiy's comments about the bravery of the Cossacks matched what I had learned about them at school. The first Cossacks were a ragtag bunch of outcasts and adventurers, who escaped serfdom and religious persecution in the fifteenth century by settling behind the rapids of the Dnieper River. They earned their living by cultivating the land and pillaging border towns, but by the time Beauplan had arrived in Ukraine, the motley crew had grown into a well-organised military power that took raids as far as Istanbul and recognised only the authority of their elected leader, the Hetman. Led by Bohdan Khmelnytsky, the Cossacks inflicted severe defeats on the armies of the Polish–Lithuanian Commonwealth – and in the process massacred so many innocents that in Jewish accounts the uprising was remembered as a time of darkness. This part was omitted from our school lessons, however. In 1648, a watershed moment in Ukrainian history, the Cossacks carved their own state out of the Commonwealth, with Poltava as its centre.

It all ended quickly. In search of friends, the Cossack state allied with its eastern neighbour, the state of Muscovy, and signed the infamous Pereyaslav Treaty in 1654. But where the Cossacks saw collaboration, the Muscovy tsars saw new colonies, and they appeased the Cossack nation's budding ambitions while they needed their services to police the frontier. Once that goal was accomplished, Ukraine became a colony itself.

The original Cossack polity was all but a flash in the pan.

The Cossacks themselves were hardly perfect heroes, but more durable was the romantic idea of them. In the Soviet period, they were either lauded as the vanguard of the people's struggle or harangued as the expression of Ukrainian 'bourgeois nationalism'. Sergiy adhered to the former viewpoint, and it was no accident that in his diary he wrote, 'Our native village of Maiachka in the Poltava Governorate was a Cossack settlement, and that's why we supported the Bolshevik Revolution'. Maiachka was the village where Sergiy grew up, and in my childhood imagination it was as mysterious as other places on Beauplan's map. In reality, it was a short drive from Bereh.

'Babushka, I would like to go to Maiachka,' I told Valentina later that day. I had found a tattered copy of Beauplan's map, along with Sergiy's portraits of Lenin.

'Maiachka? Why do you want to go there?' she asked, pushing aside the dusty map I was showing her.

'I'm curious to see where Sergiy grew up. He often mentioned the Cossack heritage of Maiachka and talked about Beauplan's map—'

Valentina didn't let me finish my sentence. 'But we have potatoes to plant!' she exclaimed.

We had already planted potatoes, but Valentina was either worried that we hadn't planted enough or that the variety we had planted wasn't appropriate. My first experience planting potatoes had been so gruelling that I wasn't eager to repeat it. I was also getting frustrated at Valentina using the orchard as an excuse.

'Fine, I already understood that you aren't interested to go. Then I will go alone,' I said.

'But the potatoes,' started Valentina, and I interrupted her. 'I will help you when I'm back. I will only be gone for half a day at most,' I said.

'Do you know anyone in Maiachka, by the way?' I asked her after a pause. Valentina was flipping through her notebook filled with various planting schedules.

'I see that you already made up your mind,' Valentina said, closing her notebook. 'No, I don't know anybody in Maiachka. We rarely went there.' She got up abruptly from the table and went to the corridor to check on seed potatoes sprouting white roots.

I didn't understand why my grandmother was upset over my short trip and I even considered postponing it. But her glum silence during dinner and curt replies to my questions exasperated me so much that I resolved to go despite her objections.

The following day I consulted the directions for Maiachka on my iPhone and took a bus from Poltava. I tucked Beauplan's map into my bag as a talisman, but without Sergiy's help, I couldn't read it – its orientation stretched Ukraine and turned it upside down. When I saw a sign for Maiachka appear on the road, I jumped out of my seat and asked the bus driver to pull over. 'The village is straight ahead,' he said, pressing on the accelerator and speeding off in a cloud of dust.

The grey ribbon of the highway and the wheat fields were the only landmarks around me. I imagined that I saw the red-tiled roofs of the village, but the midday sun was beating so mercilessly that my eyes teared and no matter how much I strained, I couldn't see anything apart from the endless fields and bottomless skies. I shielded my eyes and walked slightly off the main road until I came across a row of gravestones. I walked further and saw that I was in an old graveyard fringed by a grove of birch trees. Their slender, silvery trunks looked transparent in the white sunlight and their leaves fluttered in the wind. I shivered despite the heat, and backed out onto the main road.

Standing on the edge of the highway, I recalled that in

Ukraine, cemeteries marked the approaches of the village, and so I once again turned around and walked into the graveyard. Shutting out the creepy whistling of the old birches, I pushed my way through tall grass that left thick smudges of pollen on my clothes. The ancient tombs stood adorned with careening crosses, while the newer ones had stone tablets with pictures of the deceased. I walked past a matriarch in a white headscarf whose granite tomb towered over a smaller one of her husband. At the grave of a girl with a shy smile and be-ribboned braids, I disturbed a woodland snake that slithered slowly into the undergrowth. It was the only living being I had encountered among the tombstones and sun-bleached plastic flowers.

And then I came face to face with Sergiy. He stared at me from a black-and-white porcelain photograph set into a block of granite – the piercing gaze of the deep-set eyes, the frown line between the eyebrows, wide forehead and mane of white hair. 'Ivan Pavlovych Berezko,' I read on the tombstone and recognised Sergiy's older brother, the one who survived the wars and spent his life in Maiachka. I could see from the dates below his name that he lived for eighty-six years, from 1898 to 1984. I scribbled the dates down in my notebook, adding them to the bits of information about the Berezko family that I had gathered so far.

I crossed the cemetery looking for graves of Sergiy's parents or other siblings, but Ivan's tomb was the only one bearing the name of Berezko. Droplets of sweat rolled down my back. The grasses crushed underfoot released a dry camphorous scent that made the warm air seem hotter. After two hours of fruitless searching, I gave up and headed towards the houses on the edge of the village.

A group of grandmothers in triangular headscarves sat on a bench under a mulberry tree. Upon seeing a sweat-drenched tourist with a backpack, an exotic species in a Ukrainian village, they turned towards me and before I even had a chance to address them, they asked in unison where I was going. Replying to this question required time, and so I dropped my backpack to the ground and sat down next to them.

I explained that my great-grandfather was born in Maiachka and that it was the first time I was visiting his native village. The idea made the women curious and they whipped out mobile phones from the pockets of their black aprons. After a volley of calls around the village, they told me that I should find one Konstantin Teliatnik, who was friends with the Berezko family. 'Follow this road and when you see a dark blue house, enter and tell them that Tonia sent you,' one of the grandmothers told me. Their readiness to help me reminded me why I enjoyed being in Ukraine, despite the war and turmoil, and I clung onto these reminders of humanity to convince myself that everything would be well for all of us.

A thirty-something woman didn't appear surprised by either my visit or my explanation. 'Grandpa is starting to forget things,' she said, showing me into Konstantin Teliatnik's room. A bald old man was reclining under the bed covers. He had powerful arms covered with tattoos and his fingers fidgeted over the quilted blanket, as if he were searching for something. The room smelled of a prolonged illness.

'This young lady wants to ask you a question about the Berezko family,' the granddaughter said loudly, leaning over Konstantin. He fixed his watery eyes on me. I asked him if he knew whether any Berezkos still lived in Maiachka. 'Maiachka was such a beautiful place,' he began, moving his eyes from me to a spot in the corner of the room. 'The Oril River, forests, fishing. Of course, I remember the Berezko boys. Ivan and Sergiy, you say? They were older than me.'

I held my breath, waiting for him to continue, but Konstantin's eyes dimmed and he grew quiet. 'I remember fishing with Sergiy,' he said. 'Or maybe with Ivan.' He looked up at the wall in front of him and rested his gaze on two photographs, one of Konstantin as a young man radiating health and good spirits and another of a woman in an embroidered shirt and a jacket.

'That's him and my late grandmother,' his granddaughter observed. 'She passed away recently and Grandpa has been on the decline ever since.' Konstantin started coughing and shaking so violently that I could do nothing but apologise for my intrusion and leave.

On the map, Maiachka had a peculiar layout, stretching in all directions like an octopus. It was established as a frontier post in the eighteenth century and populated with Cossacks to protect the empire's borders. My great-grandfather recalled the family's large whitewashed house, which sat on the side of Maiachka closest to the Oril, the river mentioned in Cossack chronicles as a source of unearthly bounty. When Sergiy was born at the turn of the twentieth century, Maiachka was anything but bountiful. After the Bolshevik Revolution it descended into mayhem and once again became an unprotected borderland. The Civil War of 1917–1921 may be called Russian, but it was fought mostly on the territory of Ukraine, a region that was reluctant to join the Soviet state. Sergiy was thirteen when the Bolsheviks occupied Poltava in the winter of 1918. By the time he turned fourteen in the spring, the Reds had retreated and Ukrainian forces – supported by the Germans – had retaken the territory. At seventeen Sergiy became an orphan and the head of the family. His parents died in the typhoid pandemic, while his older brothers joined different partisan groups and left him to take care of the land and his sisters. As I walked past single-storey houses surrounded by cherry orchards, I wondered which one belonged to Sergiy's family and how he survived the war. When my great-grandfather worried senseless about us, we rejected his smothering care and told him that he exaggerated unnecessarily. His eyes clouded over with a mixture of sadness and reproach and he grumbled that we were lucky to live without knowledge of 'how terrible the world can be'.

Whenever I saw passers-by, I stopped them to ask if they had heard of the Berezko family, but it seemed that I followed a trail of vanishing stories. 'Grandmother would have known this, but she passed away last week.' 'Before Olka lost her memory she could tell you many stories about Maiachka.' 'If only you came earlier when the older folks were still alive,' people said, sighing. 'I never even thought of asking my grandparents about their past. What difference would it make to me?' one woman said, shrugging. The memory was fragile, and unrecorded stories disappeared like ripples on water.

When I came face to face with Lenin, I wasn't at all surprised. It seemed fitting that Sergiy's village still had a statue of him in its main square. Painted metallic yellow, he stood glittering in bright sunlight and eyeing a large brick building. I followed the direction of his glance and discovered the village council office.

At that point in my search, I had told my story so many times that explaining it to the woman sitting behind a desk full of paper files was effortless. I said that I was looking for my relatives and that I would be grateful for any information from the village archives. The head of the village council, Taisia, was a heavy-set woman in her sixties, with brusque manners and delicately manicured hands. As she listened to me, she screwed up her eyes and nodded. Then she picked up the rotary-dial phone and in a loud voice asked for the collective farm records to be brought into her office.

'Yes, I mean all of the collective farm records that we have,' she said. The woman on the other end of the line sounded dismayed enough for me to hear her high-pitched indignation. 'All means all,' Taisia repeated and put down the receiver. A moment later a young woman appeared bearing a tower of folders. She shot me a withering glance, but Taisia motioned for her to leave and closed the door.

'I know Ivan Berezko's daughter-in-law. She still lives in Maiachka and perhaps she might be able to tell you something about the family,' Taisia said, pausing to glance at me. I sat on the edge of my chair, grasping the table in front of me.

Taisia continued, 'But if you're undertaking proper research, first you should examine the collective farm records. They mention things like the names of the head of the household and family members, their dates of birth, their occupations, their level of education and sometimes even a new address if they moved out of the village. Of course, I'm not forcing you.'

'I'd like to do it,' I said, inhaling deeply to control my agitation. I was willing to stay overnight in this office with the stacks of newspapers and drooping geraniums on the windowsills only to be able to comb through the archives.

'I will help you,' Taisia said and put on her glasses. 'This stack is mine, and that one is yours.'

It took us more than two hours to find the first mention of Sergiy's brothers Fedir, Nestir and Ivan. The collective farm records confirmed that Fedir didn't survive the Second World War and had neither wife nor children. Nestir and Ivan lived side by side, but while Nestir's children left Maiachka, Ivan and his family stayed. The plot on which they grew wheat, rye and barley – the records were precise about the crops – lay on the edge of Maiachka, not far from where the Oril River curved around the village. This too matched Sergiy's descriptions of his childhood home.

'I found a record on someone called Fekla Berezko,' Taisia said. 'Not sure if it's relevant.' I looked over her shoulder at the spot she was marking with her painted pink nail. 'Fekla Zakharovna Berezko. Vera Nikodimovna Berezko. Nikolai Nikodimovych Berezko. There is a note next to Fekla Berezko, "Nikodim Berezko, husband, born in 1900".' I could hear my heartbeat reverberating in my ears. 'Nikodim,' I whispered. Taisia glanced at me quizzically.

The collective farm records showed that Fekla came to Maiachka in 1938, with only her son and daughter; the records mentioned a household of three souls. It meant that Nikodim must have already vanished by then. She worked on a small plot of land and was listed as a housewife. During the Second World War, Fekla and her son Nikolai continued living in Maiachka, but her daughter Vera was taken as an *ostarbeiter*, a slave worker, to Germany and was listed as missing. The records were silent on the fate of Fekla and Nikolai after 1945, but I already had more information than I had hoped to find coming to Maiachka.

Taisia wrote down the address of Lyuba Porfirivna, Ivan Berezko's daughter-in-law, on a piece of paper, walked with me into the main square and pointed to the big road behind the village. 'Follow this road straight ahead,' she said.

I asked her about the golden Lenin, bemused that he was still standing. 'Of course he's standing,' she said, drawing up defensively and daring me to contradict her. I didn't. I thanked Taisia for her time and generosity, but she cut me off and said that she was only doing her job. I adjusted my backpack and took the road she indicated. When I turned around to glance once more at Maiachka, I saw the head of the village council standing under the glittering statue of Lenin and waving at me. I waved back.

I left behind the village, with its collective farm barracks and Lenin, to enter the world of Sergiy and Asya's childhood. Apricot orchards and old-fashioned wells punctuated the landscape, and green wheat fields lined the road. Before long I spotted a small whitewashed house. 'Look for a crooked apple tree and a thatched henhouse,' were Taisia's instructions. I knocked on the door, but nobody answered. I sat down on a bench under the apple tree, stretched out my tired legs and fell asleep.

I opened my eyes with a start to find a short old woman with a round face, blue eyes and wispy white hair shaking me by the shoulder. Her mouth fell open in surprise to reveal one golden tooth. We stared at each other.

'Why are you sleeping under my apple tree?' she asked me. I said that I was her relative, and she looked panicked. When I explained how I thought we were related, the woman shook her head. 'We aren't real relatives then. I was married to Arkady Saenko, Ivan's stepson.' She sounded relieved.

Relative or not, she introduced herself as Lyuba Porfirivna and invited me to have a cup of tea. Her house was a traditional Ukrainian hut, large and spacious. I saw a wood-burning stove and a svolok, a massive beam that supported the house. Asya once told me that in the olden days, the svolok was venerated, and incense and small offerings would be left in a special spot above it, for the spirits. Our Bereh house was a simple brick construction, and the idea of a sacred pillar mesmerised me. In Lyuba Porfirivna's house, bouquets of immortelle and dried roses were tied to the svolok. The walls of the house were draped with colourful carpets and a large embroidery of a swan-filled pond. Above a bed piled high with lace pillows hung several sepia portraits. 'My late husband, Arkady,' Lyuba Porfirivna said, pointing to a serious young man in a military uniform.

'His mother didn't want me,' she said, taking out a family album and showing me their wedding photographs. A blonde girl in a white blouse, black skirt and socks rolled over her pumps looked shyly into the camera, clutching her fiancé's hand. The mildew stains on Arkady's face made it difficult to read his expression, but his body tilted protectively towards the girl. Lyuba Porfirivna rubbed the image, but the stain was indelible. 'Arkady's mother wanted him to marry a city girl, while I was a milkmaid on a collective farm near Maiachka. He said, "And who am I? A peasant like the rest of you." So we got married. I milked cows and he drove the milk truck.

'Ivan Berezko was so good to me that I called him father. His first wife died during the war and he married Arkady's mother a few years later.' Lyuba Porfirivna showed me a photograph of her mother-in-law, a thin woman with a pointed nose and morosely pursed lips. 'Ivan kept telling his wife, "Children are all we have. Let them live their lives but hold onto their love."'

'But Ivan had one problem.' Lyuba Porfirivna tapped her neck in a typical Ukrainian gesture to indicate that Ivan's nemesis was vodka. 'He could never resist a drink. There used to be a Sunday market around here, and he would go there to meet his friends. He would come home late, limping and stumbling. One of his legs was shorter than the other, and when he was drunk, he could barely walk. "You can hear the old man singing," Arkady would say. It meant that he needed to go and fetch his stepfather before he fell into the ditch along the road.'

I recalled that Sergiy rarely touched liquor.

'There were bad times and there were good times,' Lyuba Porfirivna said, looking at Arkady's portrait on the wall.

The sun was setting and a burnt orange glow spread over the wheat field in front of her house. The rustle of leaves in the evening breeze sounded like an urgent whisper.

'Where will you go at this late hour?' Lyuba Porfirivna asked me. The thought of returning to Poltava hadn't crossed my mind earlier, but now I realised that I had no idea where to find a bus at this time of night. I grabbed my backpack and rushed to say goodbye, but Lyuba Porfirivna barred my way.

'Stay here. I can't let you roam the country roads this late,' she said. 'Heaven forbid something happens to you and then I won't be able to forgive myself.' She pointed to a narrow cot near the tile-inlay stove. 'You don't mind sleeping there, do you?'

I accepted Lyuba Porfirivna's offer and called Valentina to tell her that I would stay overnight at the village. 'Fine,' she said. 'But you should have called me earlier, because I was worried.'

I hung up and tried to stifle my guilty feelings as I helped Lyuba Porfirivna make dinner. I peeled potatoes and then descended into the cellar to look for a jar of pickled tomatoes. She put the potatoes to boil in a battered tin pot and sliced rye bread and salted pork. We ate at a small table under a grape arbour, skewering potatoes from the pot with our forks and mashing them into pork fat. After a day of roaming the cemeteries, accosting strangers and poring over archives, I was famished. Lyuba Porfirivna glanced at me from time to time with maternal concern. 'How did you end up here in Maiachka?' she asked me.

I said that I was looking for Sergiy and Ivan's brother Nikodim. Lyuba Porfirivna was silent for a moment and chewed slowly.

'He put the whole family in danger,' she said.

A shiver ran down my spine and my hand holding a fork trembled. 'What did he do?' I asked.

'He was arrested. It was something political.'

'But what did he do?' I tried not to raise my voice, but I couldn't help speaking louder.

Lyuba Porfirivna looked at me helplessly. 'It was so long ago, and my memory is fading. Ivan said that he was bound to ruin the whole family. But I don't know why. I hardly remember my own life.' She got up and went into the house to fetch tea. I sat, unable to swallow another bite.

When we were washing the dishes later, Lyuba Porfirivna mumbled something under her breath and then said, 'They came and took him away.'

'Who were they?'

'They, them,' she repeated. She put her face into her hands and started crying.

She cried silently, but her body shook in violent spasms and occasionally a stifled sob escaped from her open mouth. Startled, I chided myself for bringing back painful memories to this lonely woman. I hugged her, feeling the sharp bones of her body under her housedress, and wiped away her tears. Lyuba Porfirivna and I were strangers passing briefly through each other's lives, but at that point her sorrow was mine. 'Sorrow will pay no debt,' I remembered , was one of Asya's favourite sayings, but sometimes one needed to cry and I held Lyuba Porfirivna tightly in my embrace until she quietened.

We bolted the door and turned off the light. Lyuba Porfirivna murmured and sighed in her sleep. I lay on the cot and stared at the ceiling. The silvery moonlight fell onto the tiles of the stove. On some tiles there were pictures of shepherdesses, on others, roosters with elaborate tails. I listened to a cricket chirping behind the stove and an owl hooting in the garden. Who was taken away? Nikodim? Arkady? Someone else? Then I too fell asleep.

I woke up the next morning as dawn was breaking. Cool air smelling of crushed grass, fresh cream and cow dung entered the room through a small window. Lyuba Porfirivna's bed was already made, and on the dining table stood a jar of milk and a basket of eggs. I found my hostess outside feeding chickens. She was throwing handfuls of grain to a feisty bunch of hens. The rooster dug the earth with his talons and looked at me suspiciously with a single red eye.

'Last night I told you that Ivan said that *he* was going to ruin the whole family. I made a mistake. Ivan wasn't talking about Nikodim. He was talking about his younger brother, Sergiy.'

I looked at her, stupefied. What was Sergiy, the serious and responsible brother, planning to do that could have harmed the whole family? But Lyuba Porfirivna hummed a song and swept the yard. She didn't know anything else or perhaps she didn't want to talk about it.

Riding a bus back to Bereh, I thought that with each piece of puzzle solved, another greater mystery revealed itself. The countryside appeared past the window as a patchwork of wheat and rye fields in green and yellow. Occasionally the quilt was broken by homesteads surrounded by cherry groves, and I wondered who lived in the small whitewashed houses and who tended the orchards.

∼

Our gate stood wide open, a sign of trouble in Bereh. I dropped off my backpack in the yard and ran into the house. At the dining table, Sasha was holding Valentina's hand and measuring her blood pressure. They both looked at me as I walked in.

'How could you leave your grandmother alone in her condition!' Sasha said, glancing at the tonometer.

'Sasha, everything is fine,' Valentina said weakly. 'It's just a little strain. Why are you treating me like a decrepit old woman?'

'What happened?' I asked out of breath, unbuttoning my jacket.

'150 over 90!' Sasha said as if announcing a football score.

'Where is your blood pressure medicine?' I asked, dropping my jacket on the chair and rummaging for the medicine box under the cupboard. 'How are you feeling?'

'I'm fine. Stop fussing over me,' Valentina said. 'I called Dmytro, so he is on his way here.'

'You shouldn't let your grandmother do such hard work like planting potatoes,' Sasha said.

'Why did you plant potatoes? I promised that we would do it together. Couldn't it have waited for one day?' I said.

'No, it couldn't wait. It's already June.'

Sasha nodded, agreeing with Valentina. 'In the city, potatoes are available all year around, but to plant them, you need to follow the calendar.'

'Thank you for explaining. I had no idea,' I said and immediately became annoyed with myself for adopting Sasha's passive-aggressive tone. Sasha sighed, folded the blood pressure cuff and put it back into its box.

'Call me if you need anything. You know that I will do anything for you,' she said to Valentina, who patted her hand and thanked her.

'Why were you so rude to Sasha? She came over the moment I called her,' Valentina said.

I found Valentina's blood pressure medication and gave her a glass of water to chase down the pill. I watched her drinking it slowly.

'You allow Sasha to say the most ridiculous things to me and you never defend me,' I said. I couldn't disentangle my exasperation from my guilt and worry.

Valentina didn't say anything. She sipped her water and rotated the mug in her hands.

'Why go to this godforsaken Maiachka?' she said at last.

I sat down at the table. 'I wanted to see where Sergiy grew up.'

'And what did you see? What would you even find there?'

'I found Ivan's grave. I met our distant relative, at whose house I stayed. I told you last night.'

'She's not our relative.'

'Well, not a blood relation, but she was very kind.'

We sat in silence.

'And then I found something about Nikodim.'

'What Nikodim?'

'Sergiy's older brother. The one who disappeared. Remember I asked you about him?'

'Ah, that again.' Valentina put down her mug and picked up her medicine box. She snapped it shut and her lips formed a hard line.

'I want to find out what happened to Nikodim. It's tragic how he disappeared.' I was stammering.

'And what about the family? What about those who had to live with the consequences? Is it not tragic?' Valentina was now staring straight at me, her whole face as hard as stone.

'It's tragic, of course . . .' My words came out garbled and frayed.

'I don't want . . . No, I forbid you to disturb the past.'

I got up from the chair to move closer to her. 'But it's important to know the past,' I began. I felt the ground underneath me become soft and unstable.

'Are you now lecturing me?' Valentina's cheek twitched and her face turned crimson. 'You are never at home these days. Either you're touring villages or photographing pieces of decaying cloth.'

The lime burns on my fingers started to sting. I stood frozen, unable to speak. Unable to point to the whitewashed orchard or the neat strawberry beds. Unable to find words to defend myself or to apologise. I opened and closed my mouth like a fish thrown ashore.

'And then you will go back to Brussels and things will be as before.' Valentina choked and stifled a sob. 'It's as if you care more about this Nikodim, who vanished decades ago and who has no relevance anymore, than about . . .' She cut herself off and opened a drawer to keep her hands busy.

My throat tightened so much that I couldn't find my voice. 'Fine,' I said at last. 'I will not do anything.'

I turned around, yanked Asya's coat off the rack, threw it on my shoulders and pushed open the door. It was a warm day, but I was shivering violently. I stormed across the yard, threw open the gate to the orchard and ran in, breaking through brambles to find the deepest, most secluded spot, where as a child I had buried 'secrets'. They were little bundles of cloth filled with flowers and colourful candy wrappers. An even better place for a 'secret' was a hollow in a tree trunk. I leaned against a cherry tree and ran my fingers over its craggy trunk. I found a hollow and took my notebook out of my pocket, tore out the sheet covered with notes about Nikodim and wrapped it into a handkerchief. I stuffed it deep into the hollow and pressed my face against the tree trunk. I will leave, I will leave tomorrow, I thought. Everything I do is wrong. My jelly-like legs gave way, and I dropped to the foot of the cherry tree, staring blankly ahead of me.

I didn't count whether two hours had passed or two days. I was in such a daze that I could have been asleep. I sat for such a long time that my body congealed into a crouched form. Something tickled my foot and I saw the tendril of a periwinkle plant. I unfolded my body like a crumpled sheet of paper and stood up, glancing around me. I noticed that the whole orchard was carpeted with periwinkles, but since it was summer they only sported green leaves, their blue flowers having long faded. 'Take these and scatter them everywhere,' Asya had told me one day, filling my small palm with tiny black seeds. The soil was soft and damp and the seeds disappeared into it. I couldn't believe that they would ever reappear. 'You will see the flowers next year when you come,' Asya said. 'Everything needs time.'

Here in the orchard, I felt Asya's presence more than anywhere else in Bereh. I imagined that she was still around, cutting gladioli or experimenting with a new method of grafting grape vines. The periwinkle plant that awakened me wrapped itself around the cherry trunk and its elongated leaves appeared glossy and bright against the rough bark. Nothing disappeared without a trace and everything needed time.

I caressed the periwinkle and knew that I couldn't leave. If I left Bereh now, it would be the final departure, without the possibility of return, and I wasn't ready for it.

I brushed the grass and soil off my hands. I no longer felt angry at Valentina. I saw that I couldn't just step into another person's life and find a place waiting for me. Both of us filled our absences with other presences. My presence reminded her of my absence, because sooner or later I would leave and she wouldn't know when I would come back, a year later or maybe ten. I thought that I was doing the right thing, but I was going down the wrong path. I wrapped Asya's coat tighter around me and returned to the house.

'Where did you go? I called out to you, but you didn't answer. I called your mobile, but you left it at home.' Valentina stood at the threshold holding her phone in one hand and an address book in another. She didn't know how to save new numbers into her Nokia. Her face was pale despite its deep tan. 'Do you want tea and raspberry jam?'

I put a kettle on the burner and reached into the cupboard for our teacups. 'I was thinking that we could clean up Asya's samovar and use it for tea,' Valentina said, following my movements with her gaze. 'Tea doesn't taste right without a samovar, don't you think?' Her eyes were red and damp.

I nodded and sniffed, trying to push my tears back in. Valentina came closer and hugged me, pressing me tight against her. 'I'm sorry. Let the past remain in the past, but I will not let you leave. Don't even think of it,' Valentina said. I nodded, the sobs swallowing my words.

PART 3

Embroidery Threads

Eight

I lent my camera to Pani Olga so that she could complete the embroidery catalogue on her own. Valentina and I pruned the orchard and planted tomatoes. We cooked traditional dishes that neither of us had made for years. We watched Turkish soap operas together. Sasha didn't visit us, though when we planted, we saw her working in her own garden.

My mother came to stay with us for the rest of the summer. Valentina and I outfitted our summer kitchen as a bedroom, ironed linens and wrote out menus. The memories of our summers in Bereh uplifted both of us, and we spent the days before my mother's visit in pleasant anticipation.

When she arrived, my mother transformed our household. We no longer rushed outside in the morning to tend to the orchard and instead spent hours over breakfast. 'I know that the orchard is all important in Bereh, but let's hope that it can grow on its own for a few days,' she remonstrated with Valentina, and my grandmother had no choice but to agree. I wished that I had been similarly forthright with Valentina from the start, but I had grown to enjoy our orchard routine. It allowed me to learn about my formidable grandmother on her own terms.

My mother and I have lived apart ever since I started college at seventeen, but she remains my confidante. As I shared with her my struggle to find Nikodim or my frustrations about my time in Bereh, she told me to be patient. 'Don't rush it,' she said. 'Life is so difficult right now. Let's take it all one day at a time.'

If I scandalised the village by wearing rubber boots and not looking like 'a real American', my mother would commit no such offence. Her luggage was full of elegant things like linen summer dresses, strappy sandals, matching belts and a collection of stylish jeans. In the mornings, she held fashion shows for the delighted Valentina and then she left to visit friends in Poltava, skipping down the main dirt road in pink kitten heels.

'Your daughter looks like an Italian movie star,' Antonina said to Valentina. She was one of the oldest Bereh denizens, and her brush with fame came in 1968 when she saw Sophia Loren during the filming of *The Sunflowers* near Poltava. My mother appreciated the compliment and gladly played her assigned role of Valentina's glamorous daughter. Only her slenderness caused consternation among Bereh's older residents for whom 'you've gained weight' was a compliment. 'Does your daughter have TB?' they inquired, genuinely concerned.

Though Valentina apologised to me for losing her temper, we never raised the topic of Nikodim again. I wasn't ready to give up on finding him, but having made a promise, I couldn't act against my grandmother's wishes. My mother also didn't think that I should pursue the search if Valentina was opposed, and we accepted that this man might remain a mystery.

At the same time, Valentina and I talked more, even when my

mother wasn't around. She opened up in ways I didn't anticipate, and it so delighted me that I no longer pondered why my grandmother was so adamant that I forget Nikodim. Yet her stories about the past captivated me, and on some days our tea after dinner extended past midnight as we talked.

'Babushka, how did Asya and Sergiy really meet?' I asked one evening. My mother was already asleep and Valentina and I sat in the dining room, the cold tea coating our cups with brown film.

'It was in 1933,' Valentina said. 'Your great-grandmother worked as a primary schoolteacher in Mala Nekhvoroscha. It's a village in the Poltava province, not much bigger than Mykhailivka, where she was born.'

'Did she want to teach in a village?'

'What choice did she have? You received an assignment and off you went. But I will tell you one thing. She had a love interest in Poltava, so she probably didn't want to go anywhere near Mala Nekhvoroscha. And then the famine started . . . ' Valentina swirled the remnants of tea in her cup.

The 1930s were hungry years in many parts of the world because of the Great Depression. The Soviet Union had little international trade, so it remained isolated from the aftershocks. The suffering of the capitalist world elicited gloating remarks about the death of the decadent system, and the Soviet press made a big fuss about receiving immigrants from 'the rotting West'. Asya didn't care about politics and followed the news just enough to appear informed. She accepted that Stalin was the wise father of the nation and that when he announced the new economic policy of industrialisation, it would be for the common good. She didn't grasp how Stalin's plan would affect people like her parents who lived in the countryside. The bright Communist future needed the collectivisation of land, whatever the cost. 'If only one man dies of hunger, that is a tragedy. If millions die, that's only statistics,' Stalin said.

In the early years the Bolsheviks emphasised land redistribution in their electoral campaigns, and even if the peasantry remained suspicious of their motives, such promises eventually had an effect. By 1929, however, the major collectivisation drive reversed the land redistribution reforms. If in Russia, with its ancient tradition of collective farming, it was a painful process, in Ukraine, where the national history was shaped through struggles for land, it was a harrowing tragedy. The loss of land was seen as tantamount to death. But what could the peasants do to protest? Burn their harvest? Slaughter their animals? Many villages tried resisting and fought the brigades sent to supervise the collectivisation, but such separate actions weren't enough to block an effort supported by the government and backed by the Soviet army and militias.

Soon a collective farm appeared in Asya's village. Her parents had a small vegetable garden and a cow. Asya's mother, Pasha, refused to sign over their land, but because they couldn't fend off the pressure from the authorities, the family reached a compromise. Oleksiy, Asya's father, worked on the collective farm, while Pasha tended their own plot.

Asya's family was fortunate in that they weren't executed or exiled along with 300,000 other recalcitrant farmers to the newly constructed system of penal colonies in Siberia and Central Asia. Reading about those years, I always found it hard to comprehend the intimacy of the violence. Most of the arrests and deportations were done by members of the community – a member of the state police, a state procurator and a village party leader. The chilling reality of the Great Famine in Ukraine, and the reason it remained an unprocessed tragedy several decades later, was that decisions on life and death were often pronounced by neighbours, friends and relatives. The same people who christened each other's children, worked the land together or raised toasts in each other's honour were signing each other's death warrants. Sometimes the party leaders were sympathetic. Sometimes the community was strong enough to stand together. Sometimes fate was a roll of the dice, a matter of chance. Pasha was allowed not only to keep her cow but also her ornate display of icons. Also, their land was on a steep hill, impossible to work by tractors. Sometimes geography was indeed destiny.

'When Asya arrived in Mala Nekhvoroscha to begin her teaching, it was 1931, and the harvests were already poor,' Valentina said. 'People who were forced to join the collective farms had few incentives to work hard, while that summer had been cold and wet. But Asya was more worried about her new work than the harvest. She was also anxious about meeting the school director, who was described as "a principled Bolshevik".'

'Sergiy!' I said, and Valentina nodded.

'Asya told me that she was a little disappointed, because she had imagined a tough guy in a leather jacket, while Sergiy looked like a student – a soft oval face, smooth cheeks, and a tendency to blush when he greeted her. The first time she saw him, he was wearing an embroidered shirt, and so Asya called him "a Bolshevik in a vyshyvanka". Never to his face, of course.'

In the meantime, the situation in the village deteriorated. Despite the bad harvest, the requisitions of grain were taking place as scheduled. In Mala Nekhvoroscha, requisition brigades were made up of young people from the poorest families, the local young Komsomol leaders. Sometimes their mothers came along. The brigade – a gang, as the locals called them – threw open the gate and searched the yard and the house, and even dug up the clay floors and unravelled the straw roofs. Though Asya was a teacher and exempt from the requisitions, when the brigade visited the house where she lived, her silk scarf and purse departed with them.

Asya also noticed watchtowers guarded by armed sentries in the fields. Any unauthorised collection of food was deemed theft, punishable by immediate execution. Villagers whispered about the 'five ears of wheat' law that stipulated that even a child taking crops from the collective-farm fields could be shot or imprisoned. Asya didn't believe it at first, but then the whole village was forced to watch as the requisitions brigade savagely beat up her neighbour Orisha for picking up fallen grains after the harvest. The brigade took Orisha away and nobody saw her ever again.

With the start of the school year, evidence of starvation was in plain view. Death by starvation was a horrifying end. Too slow. Too cruel. The body's psychological and metabolic defences didn't give up when one wished they did, and so the torture lasted for weeks, if not months. Funerals in the village became a daily affair. Soon the funerals ceased because the gravediggers were dead. Every day Asya rushed home from school, trying not to notice the corpses with bloated bellies at the side of the road.

'Sergiy saved Asya from hunger,' Valentina said. 'He slipped extra provisions into her bag, and one day when Sergiy brought a loaf of bread and proposed marriage, she accepted.'

'What about her young man in Poltava?'

'Nothing came of it, I suppose.'

Asya experienced famine in a small village, and she wasn't aware that mass starvation was spreading across all of Soviet Ukraine. Millions of people perished in Soviet Russia and Kazakhstan, but the black soil region of Ukraine, known to seventeenth-century travellers as Arcadia, bore the brunt of Stalin's policies. Every eighth person in the Ukrainian territories fell victim to the Holodomor, the Great Famine. One million children under the age of ten died. The toll of the famine was more than three million. My great-grandmother survived. Valentina was born in the autumn of 1934.

'That's why you wanted to plant potatoes that day and became upset about my trip to Maiachka,' I said. Valentina nodded.

'When you owe your existence to famine, you become branded with fear. I know that it's absurd, but I can't help it.'

'Back home in Brussels I always keep a 10 kg bag of rice, as if I'm haunted by the fears of events I haven't experienced.' I remembered the look on my future husband's face when he first saw my pantry. 'Are you one of those survivalists, by any chance?' he asked. I didn't know how to explain that I grew up in the Soviet Union.

'And I also keep a 10 kg bag of flour and several bags of sugar,' I added.

Valentina threw her head back and laughed.

'Why is my food hoarding so funny?' I asked, also laughing.

'We could cry over it, I suppose,' Valentina said, wiping her eyes. 'But we might as well laugh.'

The next day Valentina surprised us by announcing over breakfast that she wanted to visit Mykhailivka. 'I would like to see where my mother grew up,' she said and looked straight at me. I jumped out of my chair and embraced her. Making this trip had been one of my dreams, but I didn't imagine that it would be possible given Valentina's reluctance to leave her orchard untended.

'Don't get too excited,' Valentina said. 'You will be helping me plant tomatoes before we go.'

～

On the appointed day, after a heated discussion over the quantity of food to pack for our short trip, my mother and I piled into a taxi, with Valentina in the front seat as the navigator. The driver, Yaroslav, was a lanky man in his late thirties with a walnut-brown tan and day-old stubble. With the skill of a professional interrogator, Valentina had learned his life story before we had even left the environs of Bereh. He was twice divorced, had a daughter from the second marriage, and when not driving a taxi, he transported equipment for drilling rigs.

'Why is it that Poltava has so much gas and oil and we have to pay twice our pension for utilities? What do you think, Yarik?' my grandmother asked, switching to the familiar form of Yaroslav, because being much older she could skip formalities.

'The system doesn't benefit the small guy. But I'm not an economics expert. I only transport the equipment,' he said.

The road took us through small villages on the outskirts of Poltava, around meadows fringed with pine forests and over the plains of Central Ukraine. My grandmother forgot about the gas bills and gazed at the scenery, calling our attention to places she knew. Her garden work occupied her so completely that Valentina never left Bereh, apart from an occasional trip to the Poltava market. She grew animated as she pointed out familiar roads and homesteads.

Mykhailivka resembled Bereh, with the same arrangement of the faux-Grecian House of Culture, school, grocery store, main street named after Lenin, and an empty pedestal where the man himself once stood. The buildings in the village centre were brightly painted and draped in climbing roses. The house that Valentina called 'ours', even though it had been sold years ago, was renovated, but she recognised it as soon as we turned the corner.

'Do you expect that the new owners will just welcome you?' my mother asked as Valentina stepped out of the car.

My grandmother nodded confidently and said, 'Yes. After

all, they live in *our* old house.' She brushed wrinkles out of the smart beige suit that she wore for special occasions and added, 'One could say that we are almost relatives.' Valentina pushed open the gate, and my mother and I followed her.

The house was a one-storey dwelling under a heavy tin roof. One wing of the building was made of whitewashed clay, but the other, newer one was of brick. The large yard was filled with lumber, and an old man in a dusty suit was splitting logs. When he saw us, he dropped his axe and wiped his brow. Learning that we had come to see our ancestral home, he shouted in the direction of the house, 'Vlad, Liza, we have guests.' 'My son and daughter-in-law live here,' he explained, motioning for us to step inside.

Vlad was a tall youth with light blue eyes and a mane of tussled brown hair. He wore a torn sweater and smudged jeans. 'I was fixing the chimney,' he said shyly, offering us his elbow to shake instead of his soot-covered hand. The house smelled pungently of sour milk, damp clothing and wet clay. My mother excused herself and stepped outside. But Valentina and I lingered, taking in our surroundings. 'Here is where we slept,' my grandmother said about a small room near the entrance. 'And here we had the red corner where Asya's mother Pasha kept her icons.' Valentina pointed to a spot above a wood-burning stove. 'She prayed for her youngest son Vasyl to return safely from the war.'

'Did he return?' Liza, Vlad's wife, asked. Two toddlers were tugging at her skirts and she shushed them.

'Yes, he did,' Valentina said. The red corner in the house was bare, but on the refrigerator, I spotted a Post-it note: 'To pray for: paying off the debts, fixing the roof, for peace.'

We stepped outside. The contrast between the lived-in odour of the dwelling and the fresh breeze made me light-headed. Valentina's lips quivered. 'I still remember as if it were yesterday how my father announced that he had joined the army. He thought that we would be safer in Mykhailivka and brought us here. We stood waving goodbye as he climbed a lorry with other soldiers, and we waved until the dust settled on the road. Then I don't know what came over me, but I started running down the road, crying and calling my father's name. It was the autumn of 1941 and the leaves were already changing into different shades of red,' she said.

I took my grandmother's hand. She looked at me and said, 'He didn't have to go. He had draft protection, but he made up his mind to enlist long before Germany invaded. It was probably the only time in his life he did something contrary to Asya's wishes.'

Valentina said that Asya feared the war. Dark warnings had been in the air for years, with a brief lull in 1939 when Hitler and Stalin became friends and signed a pact that carved Eastern Europe into spheres of influence. Sergiy criticised the government for the so-called Molotov–Ribbentrop Pact, named after Soviet Foreign Minister Vyacheslav Molotov and German Foreign Minister Joachim von Ribbentrop. He believed that the agreement bought Hitler time to prepare the wider attack. 'Nazis can't be our friends,' he kept saying, and Asya begged him to be quiet, because as far as the Soviet government was concerned the Nazis *were* our friends and that was the end of the conversation.

The Soviet volte-face in June 1941, however, didn't shake Sergiy as much as the evaporating might of the Red Army at the start of the war. He cried in despair when he learned that Ukrainian cities were being abandoned to Hitler's armies. Lviv on 30 June, Berdichev 15 July, Bila Tserkva 18 July, Kirovohrad 30 July. On 19 September, the Germans occupied Kyiv. The Red Army surrendered to the Germans in the Battle of Kyiv on 26 September, one day before Valentina's seventh birthday. Though the official news put an optimistic spin on the events – 'the enemy sustained heavy losses of armies and morale' – Sergiy knew that it would be a matter of days before German forces entered Poltava. He knew what the occupation meant. He and Asya had already been teaching for a few years in Bereh when the war had started, and since the village was close to Poltava, he knew that it wouldn't be safe. Ignoring Asya's objections, he took the children to Mykhailivka.

Sergiy joined the Lenin Military Political Academy and left for Chelyabinsk, the city known as 'the Gateway to Siberia'. Almost a year later he was sent to the Voronezh Front. He and Asya had visited Voronezh, a pretty town on the Don River, during one of their rare joint trips, and its name evoked their 'belated honeymoon', as Asya called it. However, by 1942, the city was in ruins, abandoned to the Germans, who used the area to launch an attack on Stalingrad. Sergiy's diminutive height, the source of his mother-in-law's mockery, was the main reason he was assigned to the tank division – the cramped space inside the famous T-34 Soviet vehicle favoured shorter soldiers.

Back in her mother's house, Asya was at a loss. It wasn't clear how long the occupation would last and whether she would ever see Sergiy again. Some of her neighbours were quick to point out that the Germans were powerful and strong – one only had to recall how easily they beat the Red Army – and that one might as well adapt to the new circumstances. Asya didn't want to adapt. She knew that Sergiy would never forgive her. On the other hand, her parents and her two young children depended on her and she continued working as a schoolteacher in Mykhailivka, even when the command changed from Soviet to German. She didn't feel any responsibility to defend the Great Idea the way Sergiy did, and instead, she tried to protect her family. 'The human heart is a strange instrument,' Asya said about surviving those days. 'It grows used to pain and it hopes against hope.'

'Another hero during those days was Pasha,' Valentina said. 'Remember how I told you that she released the cows the Germans had confiscated?' Valentina motioned to the dilapidated hut further down the yard. 'The occupants used our summer kitchen as their canteen, but Pasha still went about her business right under their noses. One day she was finally caught. A German soldier hit her hard with the butt of his rifle and left her for dead. Not so! The next day Pasha was up and the cows were free. Thank God, the Germans didn't shoot all of us.'

Valentina and I walked around the small yard, careful not to stumble over the piles of lumber. 'Asya left for work in the morning, and I looked after my little brother Yura,' she said. 'He was still a baby, cute and fat, waddling behind me in his long dress like a duckling. Next to us lived Evgen Tychyna, the brother of Pavlo Tychyna, and he taught Yura to pray. He climbed on a table and recited in a voice too low for a little person, "God Have Mercy on Us".'

Pavlo Tychyna was a prominent Ukrainian Soviet poet, and I had to learn so many of his odes to Communism at school that I winced hearing his name. Valentina noticed my grimace and said, 'The brother of the poet who glorified Stalin taught my brother to pray. I keep remembering the strangest things.'

The house and its little orchard stood on a steep hill that ended in lowland filled with bird cherry and juniper shrubs. 'That's where your great-great-grandfather Oleksiy is buried,' Valentina said, holding on to me and looking down.

'These stories are heartbreaking,' said Liza, who accompanied us on our walk. She picked up her youngest daughter and held her tightly.

'Life is unpredictable,' Valentina said.

'Unpredictable and strange. If someone told me last year that I would be living in the Poltavan countryside, I would never have believed them. We're from Crimea. We had a house near the sea, and we rented out rooms in the summer to tourists. When the occupation started, Vlad decided that it wasn't safe for the children and we came here, to live with his father. Mykhailivka is a haven for us too, but I miss the sea. I feel claustrophobic here.' She choked up and bent down, pretending to pluck weeds from the garden path.

Valentina thanked Vlad and Liza for their hospitality and left our phone number in case they needed help settling in, then we drove out of Mykhailivka. 'The village looks charming,' I observed, trying to dispel the melancholy mood overtaking us. The neat houses covered in morning glory and wild grapes looked quaint and cosy.

Yaroslav shook his head, taking one hand off the wheel to gesture out of the open window. 'If you walk further, you can see many abandoned homes. The government cuts energy supplies to villages in these areas as it uses the land to drill for gas. Ironic, no?'

I thought that it was tragic, not ironic, but I didn't argue. My mother hoped that the new president-elect, Petro Poroshenko, would fix the system, but neither Yaroslav nor Valentina were hopeful. 'All politicians are the same. In Europe they might be better, but here they are all liars,' Yaroslav said. 'Or they become liars once they reach a position of power, and power—'

'And power corrupts,' Valentina finished his sentence.

As my grandmother read the road signs, she forgot current events. 'Rakivka, yes, I remember that town. My friend used to live near a creek there and we caught crawfish with homemade traps. And I remember Zhyrkovka too.'

'How does a seven-year-old child remember so much?' I

asked, though I too had many vivid memories from the same age. They all involved either Asya and Bereh or my paternal grandmother Daria, and Hlibivka, a village where Daria and Vladimir owned a summer cottage.

'Memory is like that. As I told you earlier, I keep remembering the strangest things,' Valentina said.

We passed a sign announcing the village of Shmaliukivka. 'My uncle, Platon Bylym, lived there,' Valentina said. 'We stayed with his family at the end of the war.'

Valentina pointed to a tree grove that grew larger as we approached it. 'That's where Asya taught during the war. The school was inside an old manor house that had rooms decorated with stucco angels holding cornucopias. It was bombed towards the end of the war, but if I remember correctly, it was over there, where you can see a patch of lilacs.'

I thought of Pani Olga's favourite phrase, 'Nothing disappears without a trace.' It had a peculiar ring in Ukraine, a place where too often the material manifestations of the past were destroyed and history rewritten. I could understand at last what Pani Olga meant as I listened to my grandmother conjuring up the places she knew out of landmarks that made sense only to her – thickets of lilacs, sun-bleached piles of bricks, dips in the land. The Soviet conception of history was that it could be made anew, bent to the will of those in power, but as Valentina, Pani Olga and other people I had encountered in Ukraine knew, history was fluid. The past was ready to reveal its legacy at the most unexpected moments, be it through embroidery patterns or old trees. To find what you wanted, you needed to know how to look at things. I was slowly learning to see. While sometimes I felt like a stranger in this land, I was also growing aware of its inexorable pull on me. Seeing Ukraine as if for the first time was as captivating as learning about my family history.

'Shall we stop by Shmaliukivka?' I asked, and Valentina told Yaroslav to take the exit.

Shmaliukivka was a large village, and Valentina remembered that Platon lived not far from the collective farm, kolkhoz. The kolkhoz, however, was nowhere to be found. We made several turns around the village and stopped near a junction where a large sunflower field merged into vegetable plots.

'Is this the collective farm?' Valentina called out to a man in a red baseball cap emblazoned with a hammer and sickle. He was selling milk and eggs on the side of the road. He came over to the car and leaned over to hear Valentina better. The tattoos on his hairy arms included a large-breasted mermaid wrapped around a dagger.

The man scowled, revealing rotting teeth. 'Welcome to our thriving kolkhoz,' he said and pointed to the carcasses of buildings in the distance. Then he extended his thumb towards the sunflower field, 'And this is owned by an oligarch.' After the fall of the Soviet Union, the collective farmland was divided among the workers, but the lots were too small to be profitable, and the prohibition on the sale of land made the development of medium-scale agriculture impossible. Into the void stepped the large agro-holdings, with the necessary financial and political levers to exploit the land to their advantage. Even more predatory was the regulatory system with its Soviet-era bureaucracy, Byzantine rules and rapacious appetite for bribes. The business elites, the so-called oligarchs, benefitted from the system. 'The flowers of capitalism,' the man said, spitting in the direction of the sunflowers, and ambled back to his stall.

'That man is a bandit,' Valentina said out of his earshot, and I nodded, thinking of his prison tattoos and provocative Communist Party cap. 'Did you see the price he wanted for milk?'

Having driven around the village once more, Yaroslav halted near a couple working on their vegetable plot. The woman eyed us suspiciously, but the man, wearing only a pair of boxer shorts and a hat made out of newspaper, was glad to take a break and came over to the car, lighting a cigarette.

'The house of Platon Bylym? I don't know if I heard of any Platon around here. Wait a minute! Let me ask Petrivna.' He waved to a grey-haired woman in a red dress taking a goat out to pasture and beckoned her to come over. She did, tugging the rope of the reluctant beast behind her.

'The house of Platon Bylym?' Petrivna asked. 'There are many Bylyms around here, but none of them are Platon. He lived here during the war, you say? Then we have to ask Aunt Maria. She's ninety and still remembers the old times.' The woman kicked her goat to stop him from bumping our car with his horns. 'Malchik, calm down, you stubborn creature.' Petrivna called her goat 'little boy'.

Valentina and I got out of the car near a small blue house that belonged to Aunt Maria. Tall hollyhocks swayed near the shuttered gate. 'And there she is,' Petrivna said, waving to a child running down the street. As the child approached us, I realised that it was an elderly woman withered by years to the proportions of a young girl. She was wearing a green headscarf tied tightly under her chin, a black dress that hung loosely on her thin body and a white apron. The goat herder laughed at our astonishment. 'God willing, all of us run like this when we are her age.'

Aunt Maria had the toothless smile of a baby, watery green eyes and a sharp mind. 'Yes, of course, I remember Uncle Platon. How could I forget him? Platon lived in a big white house not far from here with his wife Galia and his sister Odarka. I was an orphan, all alone in the world, and they took me in, cared for me, and made me feel a part of their family.' Aunt Maria spoke rapidly, holding my hand in a tight grip. Hers was small and callused.

Aunt Maria looked from me to Valentina. 'Was Platon your relative?' she asked, and Valentina explained that he was her uncle and that we had come to our native village after a long absence.

'Your uncle is long gone, may he rest in peace, but if you take this road past the sunflower field and turn right, his house is the third on the left. They are Bylyms too.' Aunt Maria walked us back to the car, still squeezing my hand and smiling her gentle smile. 'It's important to remember,' she said. 'When you're my age, you'll know that life leaves you nothing but memories. I'm grateful that mine are still vivid.' She kissed me goodbye and stood by the side of the road, watching us drive off.

Back in the car, I reflected on how in places where men are taken to fight in wars, women assume the role of memory keepers. Asya was my source of stories, while Sergiy's remained elusive. Valentina also held the key to our family archive. Ukrainians commended their women for their resilience and strength, but I now saw that they played another important role in preserving the Ukrainian story.

My mother refused to leave the car when we arrived at Platon's house. She wasn't enthusiastic about the trip in the first place, and now she was tired from the long drive and the talk of war. 'Take your time,' she said. 'I will just rest in the car.'

Valentina and I rang the bell and a tall, stout woman emerged from the stables and opened the gate. She asked us to wait till she finished milking the cow. She wore a dark blue running suit complemented with a sequined blue bandana and matching apron. 'I'm Raisa,' she shouted over the sound of the liquid hitting the bucket. 'Kolya, where are you? Entertain our guests, will you?' she hollered again.

Kolya emerged from the house yawning and rubbing his eyes. 'What's all this noise?' he grumbled, but when he saw us, he smiled broadly and invited us to take a seat under a grape pergola. He introduced himself by his last name, Bylym, which was also Asya's maiden name. This Bylym was short and stocky, and his black mesh T-shirt displayed his muscles and tattoos to their full advantage. 'Good thing your mum stayed behind. She would be shocked to discover such a relative,' Valentina whispered to me and chuckled. Tattoos in her mind always equalled a criminal past.

Kolya was affable and generous to a fault. 'Girls, what about a little drink to celebrate our meeting?' He held up a bottle filled with an amber-coloured liquid. 'From our own apples and 100 per cent organic.'

'Don't you be plying the ladies with your rocket fuel!' Raisa said, as she carried a bucket full of frothing milk into the house. She returned with a plate of cakes, a crystal carafe and dainty glasses. 'They can try my cherry ratafia,' she said, arranging the glasses on the table.

Kolya picked up the bottle of apple moonshine and brandished it in front of his wife. 'Rocket fuel! This potion can cure everything from high blood pressure to the common cold.'

'And give you an uncommon headache,' Raisa retorted. 'Anyway, you already look like you've tried your panacea.'

Kolya's flushed face turned a shade redder. 'A little drink does no harm,' he said and poured us the cherry liqueur, while topping off his glass with his own brew.

'Platon Bylym was a generous man whose house was open to everyone, rich or poor,' Kolya said after we had toasted. 'I bought this house after he passed away. I rebuilt everything, but I kept the orchard he planted and the sheds.' Valentina asked if they were related, both being Bylyms. 'There are many Bylyms around here,' Raisa said. 'We are just namesakes.'

'Where is your cellar?' Valentina asked. 'When my brother and I were children, we hid in the cellar here during the German retreat.' Kolya opened a shed near the stables and showed us the steps leading into the basement. I descended slowly, groping the damp walls to keep my feet from slipping. The further down I climbed, the colder and mustier the air grew, and when I finally reached the bottom, I was shivering in my thin summer dress. Using Kolya's flashlight, I could see the rectangular space lined with shelves holding jars of pickled tomatoes and cucumbers. The sounds from outside were muffled, giving the impression of being underwater. I was numbed by the cold and suffocated by the heavy smell of mildew. My grandmother and her brother stayed in this cellar for several weeks. 'Weren't you cold down there?' I asked Valentina as I climbed out and stepped into the sun to shake off the lingering chill in my limbs. 'I don't remember. I only remember being scared and yet curious. From time to time I'd even climb and push the trapdoor ajar. I could see men running with rifles, their heavy boots flashing past my eyes.'

'I'm sorry to talk of such sad things during our first meeting,' Valentina said, but Kolya shook his head.

'No need to apologise. Whose fault is it that we all suffered so much? Will the suffering of this land ever end?'

Raisa insisted on us having tea before we started our journey back to Poltava. 'For some reason I don't remember Uncle Platon during those days,' Valentina said, returning to the pergola. Kolya looked at my grandmother and bit the end of his moustache. 'Don't you know that he was taken prisoner by the Germans during the war? He even had a family back in Germany, but he reappeared in the 1950s and continued to live in this house. He had some trouble with the NKVD. Or did those bastards already call themselves the KGB? Being a prisoner was equivalent to being a traitor. They summoned him a couple of times to Poltava, but in the end, they let him go.'

An awkward pause fell over the table. 'We didn't keep in touch with that side of the family,' my grandmother mumbled, looking down.

'Families are complicated,' Kolya replied and refilled Valentina's thimble with ratafia. 'Let's drink to the memory of Platon Bylym,' he said and downed his glass in a single gulp.

'And to the memory of those who didn't return from the war,' Valentina said.

Sergiy returned from the war. He survived the carnage at the Voronezh Front. He survived the charnel house of Prokhorovka, the massive tank battle that was a watershed point in the Second World War, even if it was a defeat for both sides. He survived the Battle of Kursk, the one that changed the course of the war and left innumerable casualties, but during its last days a bomb exploded near his tank. Sergiy remembered blacking out and then waking up in a hospital in the town of Penza. He was told that he earned two medals for his brave conduct. But he had lost his left leg.

Sergiy could have remained in the army. He was offered a bureaucratic position in the military tribunal, but he couldn't bring himself to sign death sentences for young boys who had either mutilated themselves to escape from the front or deserted the army ranks. He had experienced enough of life in the barracks and he longed to be with his family. He also wanted to resume teaching, his true calling. War had turned him into a pacifist. He never talked about his decision, and I wish that I had asked him to explain.

Valentina finished her drink and concluded it was time for us to leave. 'I hope that you can stay longer next time. We will then have a proper meal, and if you like fishing or swimming, Kolya will take you to some first-rate spots,' Raisa said, as we took our leave and exchanged phone numbers.

She pressed a package of cakes into Valentina's hands. 'Blood relations or not, you are no longer strangers to us,' Raisa said. As custom demanded, Valentina refused three times before accepting the cakes.

Yaroslav pressed on the accelerator and off we drove past the roofed wells, whitewashed huts, potato fields and the yellow carpet of sunflowers.

'Look, it's snowing,' Valentina said, rolling down the car window and catching a handful of poplar fuzz. 'The snows of June . . .'

For the rest of the drive home each of us was lost in her own thoughts. I pressed my forehead to the window and in the blurred landscape I could distinguish neither green orchards nor yellow fields. I only saw two children hiding in the cellar, Asya walking down the winding country road to school and Sergiy climbing into the tank. 'I'm not afraid of hell,' Sergiy often said. 'After what I've seen, nothing can be worse.' As he lay dying, a man whose life spanned almost a century, his last words were 'Battalion, charge ahead!'

Plum-coloured clouds gathered quickly and menacingly, racing ahead of us. The horizon darkened and gusts of wind churned the poplar fuzz in the air. 'A storm is coming,' Yaroslav said.

'It will pass,' Valentina said. A few heavy drops fell on the windshield, the air smelled like overheated iron, and then as suddenly as it started the tempest vanished. 'You see, it passed,' Valentina observed with satisfaction. She started singing an old tune about the silvery poplars and the snows of June and hummed it for the whole ride back home.

The subsequent weeks left a luminous impression in my memory. Outwardly nothing had changed in the pattern of our

147

days, with their orchard tasks, meals and trips to Poltava, and the three of us, my grandmother, my mother and I, fell into a rhythm dictated by the languorous summer days. As the Ukrainian army was at last winning victories and retaking towns in the eastern breakaway regions, it seemed like this war could be over. We drank toasts to the future of Ukraine. The snows of June were melting, but in our euphoria we took no notice.

~

'Something terrible happened in Ukraine,' read the text message from my mother. With numb fingers, I typed 'Ukraine' into Google and pressed on the news tab. At first, I couldn't understand anything. A plane. Smoke. Crash. Amateur videos of charred bodies in sunflower fields. I had left Ukraine only a few weeks before, saying goodbye to Valentina and promising to return in September as soon as I sorted out my Ukrainian visa. The trees in our orchard were bent to the ground under the weight of fruit, and roses filled the air with the opulent fragrance of melted honey. I couldn't connect the Ukraine I had left behind with the grisly images on the news.

'Flight MH17, en route from Amsterdam to Kuala Lumpur, was travelling over conflict-hit Ukraine on 17 July 2014 when it disappeared from radar. A total of 283 passengers, including 80 children, and 15 crew members were on board.'

I dialled Valentina. She was watching the news. We only exchanged a few words when her voice turned faint and distant as if she were on another planet, a planet where planes fall out of the sky and people die in sunflower fields. I kept redialling but the lines were jammed. I was alone in my Brussels apartment. The silence was heavy, punctuated by the soft hum of the air conditioner. I sat on the floor in the middle of my bedroom. My attention was drawn to a black-and-white photograph of Asya on the mantelpiece of our fireplace. Asya held small Valentina in her arms and both wore chic hats and serious expressions. The photograph was taken shortly before the Second World War started. The Brussels communication tower visible from our bedroom window glowed red and blue, the way it usually did, but today it seemed ominous and grim. The European Union offices down the road must have been issuing another 'we're concerned and perturbed' statement in response to the tragedy.

The phone rang and shook me from my daze. My mother was on the line, speaking so fast that I had difficulty understanding her. 'Do you know what the representative of the Russian parliamentary committee said on TV? That it was engineered by the Americans!'

'Mum, stop watching the Russian news,' I managed to insert a sentence into her torrent of words.

'But I need to know what *he* is thinking,' she said, sounding like a political strategist. Nobody could figure out what Putin had on his mind, and the idea of my mother trying to decode it by watching Russian news made me laugh.

'That's better,' she said. 'When you picked up the phone, you had such a frightening, empty voice. We must stay brave.'

As July drifted into August and the fighting in Ukraine intensified, I failed to stay brave. As towns were taken and lost, hundreds of innocent people died and thousands were displaced. Then the names of people my family knew started appearing in the lists of the dead and missing. Some were civilians who were caught in the crossfire, others were in the army. 'I hate the phrase our leaders use constantly these days – "heroes don't perish",' Valentina said. 'Of course they perish. They die! And they become heroes only because they weren't afraid of death.'

Returning to Ukraine in September turned out to be impossible. With my American passport, I could only stay for three months at a time, and then I had to wait for six months before I could return. Obtaining a visa turned out to be more complicated than I anticipated, so I had no choice but to wait. Away from it, I felt Ukraine more intensely than ever. I experienced a similar emotional rollercoaster to when the war first started, except that now I felt nothing but gloom. I couldn't do a damned thing. I couldn't even be with Valentina. An emptiness grew within me like a black hole pulling in all joys and pleasures. I was either vacant and distracted or bitter and angry. I was angry that the Russian government was instigating this war, that the US could do little more than sanction a few Russian businessmen, that the European Union was proving ineffective and feckless, that the Ukrainian elites cared more about lining their pockets than about the country, that people were dying in this senseless, frightening war, that the war wasn't going to stop. I saw war and death in every headline – Syria, Gaza, Myanmar. It was a hot, sweltering August and it seemed as if the whole world was aflame.

I was afraid of losing my Ukraine, the Ukraine I had begun to know and love. Every recollection of Bereh became warmer and brighter. I talked to Valentina and relived the memories of my Ukrainian spring in all their vibrancy. I recalled our cherry orchard in full bloom, the quilt of wheat fields in the countryside and the splendid curves of the Vorskla, and lost myself in daydreams to escape the ever-darkening reality.

～

During those last weeks of August, I became a *flâneuse* in Brussels, observing life around me like a visitor in a museum. It reminded me of my early months in the city. My first impression of Brussels set the tone for my experience. My husband and I had emerged out into the chaotic area near Gare Centrale and found ourselves in a grey mash up of curvy nineteenth-century mansions and Brutalist cement boxes. Eventually we made our way to Quai aux Briques, an esplanade dotted by baroque and medieval buildings. We drank hot chocolate as rain darkened the facade of the Sainte-Catherine church and turned the square into an impressionist painting. 'I could live here,' I said to my husband.

Brussels, with its mosaic of neighbourhoods, held many hidden treasures and rewarded the curious. I wandered for hours in Schaerbeek admiring the Art Nouveau architecture, strolled through the Italianate arcades of the Galeries Royales Saint Hubert and explored the Congolese markets of Matongé. Or else I lingered at the Moroccan cafes overlooking the three-tiered Baroque church in the neighbourhood of Saint-Josse-ten-Noode. Vegetable sellers set up intricate displays of aubergines and tomatoes. Families strolled arm-in-arm, exchanging greetings in Turkish. Men in black suits drank tea out of pear-shaped cups and played backgammon, while making admonishing remarks to the boys carried away by their game of football. I liked that Brussels had its numerous layers, that it was unpredictable and even that it sometimes exasperated me. Even after the initial excitement of novelty wore off, I found the city beguiling.

However, in August 2014, Brussels provoked resentment. I begrudged the elegant indolence of the well-attired ladies walking their poodles in Parc Royal. I stared glumly at the black-suited EU civil servants on their lunch break as if they were responsible for the tragedy in Ukraine. I found everything irritating, above all my anger and dark thoughts.

Brussels was giving up its summer languor in exchange for autumnal melancholy. One day a downpour caught me in the middle of my walk, and I took shelter in a real museum, Musée

Royal des Beaux-Arts. If Holly Golightly felt that nothing bad could happen at Tiffany's, Valentina had a similar feeling about museums and she had passed it on to me. I loved their smell of aged wood and the way the soft light and silence filled the exposition halls. I lingered in front of *Landscape with the Fall of Icarus* by Pieter Bruegel. The Flemish artist chose the moment when Icarus, his wings destroyed by flying too close to the sun, fell into the sea. However, the tragedy occupies a small part of the painting – a flash of white legs above the water. In the centre of the tableau, a peasant works in the field, his attention riveted by the furrows made by his plough. On the seashore a shepherd stares at the skies. He doesn't notice the agony of the drowning man. Ships glide past at full sail. Another second – and Icarus would have disappeared under the opaque green waves, but the world would carry on as before.

I remembered vaguely that there was a poem by W. H. Auden about this painting and I looked it up at home.

About suffering they were never wrong, The Old Masters ...

I reflected on the poem for days afterwards, reciting it to myself before falling asleep. It struck me as poignant, considering that W. H. Auden wrote it in 1938, a few months after Neville Chamberlain famously referred to the German annexation of Czechoslovakia as 'a quarrel in a faraway country between people of whom we know nothing'. Less than a year later, Germany and the Soviet Union partitioned the territories of their European neighbours under the Molotov–Ribbentrop Pact. The Second World War had started.

The poem was also a reminder that regardless of how much I let my suffering bind me, the world moved past me without halting, without changing its course. In a strange way, I found it consoling, because instead of expecting help or compassion from the outside, I focused on the sources of resilience within. I flipped through old pictures of my ancestors, who had survived more tragedies than should be allotted by fate. One of my favourite snapshots of Pasha, the great-great-grandmother I never knew, showed her standing in the yard of the Bereh house. She stared defiantly into the camera, with her feet planted firmly on the ground. She wasn't one to succumb to anguish.

Valentina demonstrated that she was of the same rootstock. She was anxious about the future like everyone else, but she continued to work in the garden, meet the neighbours and cook elaborate meals. To all of my pleas to start an application for a foreign passport, in case the situation deteriorated, she replied that she would never leave her home. Valentina and I made the months apart more bearable by making plans. I told Valentina that I would whitewash the orchard again; she said that we would take more trips together. I swore that I would weed the strawberry beds religiously; she assured me that she would organise the old junk in the sheds and give away the Lenin portraits. As long as spring came, as long as we were able-bodied, we would do it all, we said.

Still, the idea of an unresolved conflict with Vladimir weighed on me, and I wrote him a short email. My message bounced back. Vladimir's Skype account still looked inactive. He lived with his daughter and had a social worker who looked after him, and I supposed that if something happened to him, I would learn of it through the family grapevine. Perhaps Vladimir didn't care to resume our chats. Perhaps he was still angry. I could only wait for him to reappear.

I discovered over the course of those months that Asya was right. The human heart was a strange instrument. I accepted pain and I never ceased to hope.

Nine

In April 2015, as I stepped off the train in Poltava, the familiar scents of pungent greenery, scorched rubber and poppy-seed rolls made me light-headed. I understood the exalted sentiment of people falling on their knees to kiss the ground of their homeland. I remembered the first time I returned to Ukraine and my inexplicable feeling of being an outsider, but now I was at home and the sense of returning to my land stirred a complex emotion in me. I followed my own version of the homecoming ritual. Upon reaching Bereh and hugging Valentina, I went into the garden and touched the rough bark of the cherry trees.

'I used to do the same thing whenever I returned to Bereh,' Valentina said, leaning on the garden gate and observing me. 'Only then did it feel that I was truly back.' The young cherry trees Valentina and I planted had survived the winter and their maroon-streaked buds were turning into blossoms.

Valentina once again drew up ambitious plans for the garden, but this time she delegated the main duties to Uncle Tolya, a short, wizened man on the other side of his eighties. Uncle Tolya wasn't my uncle. In a Ukrainian village, anyone significantly older than you was called either Aunt or Uncle, blood relations notwithstanding. Uncle Tolya had a swarthy face and spiky hair thickly coated with brilliantine. His bushy eyebrows hanging over his beady eyes made him look like a hedgehog. I had seen him around Bereh on my previous visit, but that spring he became a permanent fixture in our lives.

Uncle Tolya always wore a grey suit, complete with a double-breasted jacket and peach-coloured shirt. The suit, like Uncle Tolya himself, belonged to another era, and its threadbare chic contributed to the aura of mystery surrounding its wearer. Out of an inner pocket Uncle Tolya would produce a screwdriver, a packet of roasted sunflower seeds, an embroidered handkerchief or a mottled apple, like a magician performing a trick.

'When I was a schoolboy, they said that the Earth is held by four elephants and even showed us pictures. Later they said that it rotates around the Sun. Now they say that it's moved off its axis. The end is coming,' Uncle Tolya would announce in place of a greeting, as if continuing an interrupted conversation. 'We might as well plant those cherry trees today.'

Uncle Tolya's main occupation was digging graves in the cemetery, and his work around death gave him a philosophical attitude to life. He also served as a village oracle, offering people advice on all matters of life and love – how to hatch chickens, propose marriage or plan a new business venture. Since in Bereh people could be hired to cast spells on cucumbers to make them grow faster, it no longer surprised me that a grave digger worked as a fortune teller.

We could never predict when Uncle Tolya might appear, ringing the bell of his old bike and braking with a flourish in front of our house. Some days he could be seen in our garden from dawn to dusk, and on others there was no sign of him and his bike. Though Uncle Tolya accepted money from Valentina for his help, he came when he needed human companionship. Digging graves was lonely work.

When Uncle Tolya at last arrived, he went straight to business. 'Tell me what I need to do,' he announced in the stentorian voice that contrasted with his small, lean frame. Uncle Tolya worked with lightning speed, and once he was done, the garden looked neater, the yard cleaner and Valentina happier.

After work, Uncle Tolya washed his face and hands at the water pump, shook out his jacket, and with obvious enjoyment, partook of Valentina's cooking. She filled the table with food, apologising for the meagre quantity and the poor taste of the delicacies she prepared, while he refused three times, before agreeing with a feigned reluctance to taste 'only a couple of morsels'. He and Valentina then went through another complex ritual of her giving him money for the work and him refusing it. In the end, he took what she'd offered, ate enough for three people, bid a formal goodbye and then stayed chatting with Valentina for the rest of the afternoon. It was the most enjoyable part of the day for both of them.

'All sea captains are alcoholics,' Uncle Tolya proffered. Or he assured Valentina that the Eiffel Tower was the tallest building in the world. Uncle Tolya had never been at sea, and his information about the Parisian landmark was a century out of date, but he delivered his statements with deadpan seriousness and accepted no arguments. 'Sergiyvna!' he would say in response to Valentina correcting him, using only my grandmother's patronymic in an old-fashioned manner. 'Don't listen to that witch box.' He pointed to the TV in the corner of our living room. 'It tells you lots of nonsense. Mark my words, even if a captain is not an alcoholic in the beginning, he will become one later.'

Valentina hid a smile and asked Uncle Tolya if he wanted a cup of coffee. He refused, saying it was worse than vodka. It was a meaningful comparison for Uncle Tolya, because in his younger days, by which he meant his sixties, he had had an alcohol addiction. He now claimed not to drink anything stronger than tea.

I left Valentina and Uncle Tolya to their chat and sat with a book in Asya and Sergiy's former bedroom. 'It's as sure as anything – the Earth moved off its axis,' I could hear Uncle Tolya expounding on his favourite theory. I wondered if he wasn't right about the present time being out of joint. We all felt it despite the limpid beauty of spring. The war in the east still rumbled on, but the acute fear gave way to anxiety about rising prices and a collapsing economy. Valentina stopped watching Turkish soap operas and spent hours glued to the television following debates about gas subsidies. Her pension had lost three quarters of its value since the previous year, and whatever remained was not even enough to cover the heating bill. When I suggested paying myself, she protested, her pride wounded. She accepted help from my mother and my aunt, but she felt it beneath her dignity to take money from her grandchildren. I learned to take quick showers in the freezing bathroom and did the grocery shopping at the Poltava market twice a week. I quoted lower figures to protect my grandmother's peace of mind, but even these white lies didn't reassure Valentina. My grandmother clasped her hands in distress as I told her the prices of milk, eggs and meat.

'Why are you worried about such things?' Uncle Tolya would say. 'Today you are alive, and tomorrow they'll put you over there.' He pointed his earth-stained thumb in the direction of the cemetery. He didn't watch television, and his attitude to things made me think of the prince from Lampedusa's *The Leopard*, 'All this shouldn't last; but it will, always; the human "always" of course – a century, two centuries … and after that it will be different, but worse.' It wasn't much of a consolation to Valentina, who watched her pension melt away day by day, but it was a reminder of Slavic fatalism to me.

Another person who adopted a philosophical approach to life was Pani Olga. '"See the birds of the sky, that they don't sow, neither do they reap, nor gather into barns. Your heavenly Father feeds them. Aren't you of much more value than they?"' she repeated, quoting the Bible. Over the winter Pani Olga lost her rental apartment and moved into the church's attic. When I first saw her, I gave a start, because her luxuriant braid was gone, and instead she sported a short bob. 'Someone less fortunate than me in the hair department will have a nice wig,' she said. 'Besides, short hair is more youthful.' Her permanent tutoring job was terminated without any advance notice, and she had to run the household and pay her daughter's tuition with income from sporadic writing assignments.

'I needed money more than my hair over the winter,' Pani Olga admitted at last, but she also refused my offers of help. I suggested that she stay with us in Bereh, where we could easily make room for another person, but the idea made her laugh.

'Thank you, but I live in the closest place to paradise,' she said, leading me up to the church attic filled with books, bundles of candles and baptismal vessels. Pani Olga put the kettle on and fetched mismatched cups. We drank tea brewed to the colour of coffee and talked about the embroideries she had unearthed during my absence and other new additions to her rushnyk archive. The greenish light of the desk lamp cast an eerie glow onto the icons, and the scent of incense and dried roses hovered in the shadow-filled corners of the room like a ghostly presence. Surrounded by crucifixes and censers, we forgot that there was another world out there until the church bell tolled and made the walls of the attic room vibrate. Then I remembered that the meat I had bought at the market for Valentina was thawing in my bags and that I needed to return home.

Valentina knew that I often visited Pani Olga while running errands in Poltava, and sometimes my grandmother asked me to show her the latest photographs of her archive.

'This embroidery looks familiar,' Valentina observed one day, watching me process the images. She pointed to a photograph of a red and black rushnyk with a band of intertwined roses and peacocks.

'Pani Olga said that it's called "Brocard roses", after the French toiletries maker who opened a factory near Poltava at the turn of the twentieth century. Each bar of soap came with a free embroidery pattern.'

'Where would Pasha get French soap?' Valentina muttered.

'Pasha?' I was sitting at the dining table with my laptop, while Valentina stood behind me to better see my screen. I instinctively looked up and glanced at the portrait of Asya's mother. Her eyes were such a pale blue that they appeared colourless in the black-and-white print, and her expression was hard and severe.

'Pasha embroidered rushnyky with roses and birds like these,' Valentina said, pointing to the photograph.

'What was Pasha like?' I asked, still staring at her portrait.

'Tough,' Valentina said, pushing her reading glasses to the top of her head and frowning. 'Too tough.'

Pasha emerged from Stalin's hunger terror with a cow and plot of land intact and she protected her family during Hitler's war. I could believe that she was tough.

'But Vasyl's death broke her and she made our life hell,' Valentina said. 'She tormented us. She was so mean, so unfair. She beat me.' Her words came out hoarse and dry. I looked down. I couldn't bear to look at Pasha, but I still felt her pale eyes on me.

Vasyl was Asya's younger brother, who died long before I was born, and I imagined him as he appeared in the portrait hanging in Asya's bedroom – a young man dressed in an elegant black suit, a lock of blond hair swept romantically over his high forehead. Vasyl played flute and saxophone in the Poltava symphony orchestra, composed music for the accordion and toured the USSR with his wife Lara, performing romances and ballads. He earned a good salary as a musician, and Lara, who looked like a brunette version of Veronica Lake, received small film parts. One day as he was riding home from a rehearsal, his motorbike slipped on a rain-drenched road and he died from a brain haemorrhage.

'At first Pasha lived with Lara and helped her take care of the children, but then Lara remarried and moved to Hungary with her new husband,' Valentina said. 'Pasha said that for her Lara had died and she returned to live with Asya.'

Valentina sat down and put her elbows on the table, resting her face in her hands. 'She didn't feel grateful for Asya's care. She spent her entire time embroidering rushnyky and draping Vasyl's portraits with them. She cried, asking why God took her beloved child. She wove cloth and embroidered it. Day after day. It was her only pastime, along with praying. It was hard for me to feel sorry for her back then.'

Valentina glanced at Pasha's portrait and looked away. 'But as they say, one shouldn't speak ill of the dead,' she said.

I hesitated and then asked, 'Why do you keep her portrait here then?'

'Guilt, perhaps. When someone leaves, we always feel guilty, especially if we feel relieved.'

A dull pain in the region of my heart made me breathless for a moment and then vanished. I sat staring out of the window.

'Pani Olga says that rushnyky were made not only for festive occasions, but also to pour out one's grief,' I said, after a while.

'I suppose,' Valentina said. 'Anything that distracts you is good enough.'

'Do we still have Pasha's rushnyky?' I asked, ignoring my grandmother's scepticism.

Valentina pointed in the direction of the sheds. 'I never throw away anything, but the devil will break his leg in that place,' she said, acknowledging that our storage was an utter mess. 'Perhaps Pasha's rushnyky are still there. Perhaps they have turned to dust.'

~

I didn't think that Valentina would search for old mementos in the sheds, so I launched a different type of investigation on my own. Away from Ukraine, I had become possessed by the idea that I hadn't explored the place where I was born. I accepted that Nikodim would remain a mystery, but I became determined to discover as much as I could around Poltava. I could barely control my excitement when I sat on a bus, a map in my lap and an as yet unknown destination in my mind.

Valentina complained to Uncle Tolya that she was worried about me taking trips in such uncertain times. 'Let the child go. We're old and our place is at home, but she still has energy in her legs, and she needs to go places,' Uncle Tolya said. 'Mark my words, the more you try to keep someone, the more they will want to escape. I made such a mistake with my dog.'

Thus unleashed, I left for the bus station to catch the next marshrutka heading to places like Hadiatch, Petrykivka or Dnipro, towns whose names had a familiar ring even though I had never visited them.

Sometimes I wandered through small towns with magnificent

churches and old palaces sitting next to picturesque ponds. Petrykivka, the birthplace of traditional Ukrainian folk painting, was one of my favourite discoveries. Arriving there, I was delighted to find that every wall and fence was covered with swirling clusters of rowan berries, dahlias and grape leaves, as if the drawings had escaped from the artists' easels and run riot around town.

At other times, the marshrutka dropped me off in towns that looked like they could be anywhere in the Soviet Union. I came to the historical town of Hadiatch only to find a dreary mishmash of prefab apartment blocks and concrete barracks. A bust of a bearded man stood in the middle of the town park, but no inscription identified it. A thirty-something man walking his dogs around the mysterious bronze persona saw me taking photographs and remarked that it was the bust of Mykhailo Drahomanov. 'He was born in Hadiatch,' he added with pride.

Drahomanov was an influential nineteenth-century Ukrainian political thinker, but the monument looked to be of the Soviet period, when Drahomanov was condemned as 'bourgeois-nationalist'.

'You youngsters are so ignorant,' an elderly street cleaner interjected, having overheard our conversation. 'That's Karl Marx. But if you like, he can be Drahomanov. That's probably what the town authorities intended when they removed the name plate a couple of years ago. It's easier than restoring Drahomanov's house.' He pointed with his broom towards a building down the street where the writer once lived – it was tragically dilapidated and boarded up.

Disappointed in Hadiatch, I took a bus to Reshetylivka. The town might have looked modern, but I recalled that it still retained its traditions and artistic heritage. Also, Valentina's talk of Pasha's rushnyky had reminded me of the embroiderers

I met during my first visit with Pani Olga, so I decided to drop in on them again.

Reshetylivka looked festive as the town prepared for Victory Day celebrations on 9 May. I lingered near a Second World War memorial being cleaned by a group of women and read the names of Reshetylivka's war heroes. Their names filled several enormous tablets from top to bottom and were too numerous for such a small town.

Students at the Reshetylivka Arts College were preparing for their final exams. The girls sat as if stitched into place and only their fingers were in motion. When I entered the classroom, Nadia Vakulenko was furiously shuffling through a pile of forms on her desk. As she looked up and recognised me, her eyes widened and she jumped up. 'I remember you. You came last year with another lady to see our rushnyk museum. I was hoping you'd return.'

'Bureaucracy is my nemesis,' she said, pointing to the papers on her desk. 'The Soviet Union is long dead, but our laws are of Soviet vintage. Would you like some tea?'

She stuffed the papers into a desk drawer and shut it with a loud bang. A student walked over to her to ask a question about her work. 'You have to work overtime to finish it in time for graduation,' Nadia said.

The girl glared at her half-finished shirt and pulled at the hanging threads. 'This is not my fault. My mum is sick and she makes me take our cow out to pasture,' she said.

Nadia sighed and put one of the sleeves into her handbag. 'Fine, do as much as you can today and we will see about the rest later.'

'Her mum has one illness only, and it is vodka,' she said as we left the classroom. 'But if the girl doesn't pass her exam, she will lose her stipend. I have to help her finish the embroidery.'

When I first met Nadia, I assumed that she was an ordinary teacher, and it was only months later when I read about the special rushnyk embroidered for Ukraine's president that I spotted her name and learned that she was an Honoured Embroidery Master and that her work was exhibited at galleries and festivals around the world.

'I probably mentioned it already, but we have a plan,' she said as we walked into the staffroom. 'The embroiderers of Reshetylivka have decided to submit our white-on-white embroidery as UNESCO Intangible Heritage. It's unique and intricate and it qualifies. Of course, it means dealing with the Ukrainian and UNESCO bureaucracy, but if we succeed, we will gain a new level of recognition. And I can finally open my own school.'

Nadia told me about the plans and showed me the stack of paperwork she had collected for the application.

'When I saw you walking into my classroom today, I couldn't believe my eyes,' she said, turning on the electric kettle. 'We need someone to translate some of the documents into English. It's only a couple of pages.' She looked at me pleadingly.

'Of course, I will translate it for you,' I said. I had no sense of what it took to convince UNESCO that a tradition had cultural value, but the idea struck me as exciting.

As the kettle hissed and sputtered, the other teachers joined us and soon the tiny room was filled with the clamour of voices. Petro, the painter whom I had met previously, still bore his look of resigned melancholy. A new face, Alla, a thin, blonde embroidery teacher, was energetic and upbeat, unable to sit still. The drawing instructor Vita joined us, bringing a jar of instant coffee and a bag of cookies to add to our potluck. Nadia presented me as 'a guest from Europe', an introduction that encouraged the usual and unanswerable question that

Ukrainians posed when they learned that I lived abroad. 'So, what's life like there?'

By now I should have come up with some standard answer, but people enquired with such earnestness that I wanted to reply honestly, capturing both the positive and the negative. 'What's life like over there? What kind of a question is that?' Nadia shrugged her shoulders, while I mulled over an appropriate reply. 'Every place has its problems. It's not like the streets in Europe are paved with gold.' She poured out the tea.

'You, dear Nadia, are a true Reshetylivka patriot,' Alla said, eyeing a plate of sweets and selecting an apple. 'You even refused to move to Kyiv when you were offered a promotion. Imagine, you could be living in the capital! Khreshchatyk, museums, everything the city has to offer at your fingertips.' Alla enumerated the beauties of Kyiv dreamily as she crunched through her apple.

'I would be wasting hours commuting to work in the crowded subway and spending my entire salary on rent,' Nadia replied. She drew open the curtains and pointed to an apartment building across the street where she lived with her two grown children. 'But Alla is right, Reshetylivka captured my heart. I first came here as a student to study weaving, but because the school had no openings in the carpet division, they transferred me to embroidery. I was disappointed at first, because I was convinced that I was already an embroidery expert. When I saw the different techniques used in Reshetylivka and the delicate needlework of the local masters, I realised how ignorant I was. I wanted to learn it all. I drew inspiration from the Reshetylivka air itself,' she said.

'I stand corrected,' Alla said, patting Nadia's arm. 'You aren't simply a patriot. You are a romantic.' Everyone, including Nadia, laughed.

'Here is someone who understands art and romance,' Nadia said, touching my shoulder. 'She first came here looking for the Reshetylivka embroideries and then volunteered to be our translator.' The teachers thanked me in turn, impressing on me the importance of this project for all local masters.

During a lull in the conversation, I said that my great-grandmother lived in Reshetylivka briefly before the Second World War and wondered if the town's archives might not have some information about my family.

Alla turned to the drawing instructor to her right. 'Vita, don't you know the woman who works at the archives? Take the girl there and ask them to do some digging in the system.' Vita agreed and as soon as we finished our tea, we went across the street to the archives centre.

The centre comprised a small room hidden on the ground floor of the town hall. It was lunch hour, and Vita's friend Roza was eating a sandwich at her desk while reading a detective novel. Vita piqued her curiosity by explaining that I was 'a foreigner looking for her relatives in Ukraine'. Roza closed her book and switched on the computer.

She said that the online database included the birth, marriage and death records for the whole of Poltava, and that the records often included additional details like registrations, residence permits, and perhaps some other relevant information. I gave her Asya's full name, and Roza typed it into the search window and pressed a button. The request came up in red block letters, 'Record Not Found'. My heart falling, I gave Sergiy's name, but once again the computer beeped and displayed 'Record Not Found'. We tried several different spellings, but it was as if nothing existed about my family, no sign of either life or death.

Then I remembered finding Asya's old letters, which she

signed as Vasylyna. 'Would you please try another name?' I asked, worried that Roza was tired of wasting her lunch hour on a fruitless search. 'My great-grandmother was baptised as Vasylyna, so perhaps the old records exist under that name.'

'Young women in the 1930s liked to pick short, modern-sounding names,' Roza said. 'My great-grandmother was called Agrippina, but she liked to call herself Ina.' I'd long been wondering why Asya decided to change her name, but it didn't occur to me that it might have such a simple explanation. She was a young woman about to leave her village and start a new life as a schoolteacher. She wanted a new name to match and so Vasylyna became Asya.

The page went grey and a small hourglass icon swirled as the machine hummed. 'I've got it,' Roza exclaimed. She could see Asya/Vasylyna's record with its strings of dates and numbers, leading to other members of the family. Roza dictated and I wrote down the information as fast as I could. I learned that Asya's mother's recorded name was not Pasha but Praskovia and that the exact date on which Asya and Sergiy registered their marriage in 1933 fell on 8 March, International Women's Day – and the worst period of the Great Famine.

Sensing that I was on a lucky streak, I asked Roza to search for Nikodim Berezko. My excitement must have been contagious, because even though her lunch hour was over and other visitors were waiting in the hallway, Roza obliged.

'Why don't you check with the Security Service of Ukraine, the organisation that inherited the KGB archive after the fall of the USSR?' Roza asked when I explained what had happened to Nikodim in the 1930s. Her computer searched for records. 'Mind you, it always gives me the creeps to walk past that horrid Rooster House.'

The computer flashed the red 'Record Not Found' message. Roza returned to the page with Asya's original name to access further recesses of the records.

'My great-grandmother had such an intense fear of the Rooster House that we always took a detour to avoid it. She called it the Rooster Trap,' I said, watching Roza's screen.

'My great-grandmother Ina's friend was arrested, but she was released after a couple of days. Her hair turned grey overnight. Whatever she saw there changed her for life. You can bet that she never went near the Rooster House. Maybe Vasylyna was arrested too?'

Roza continued chatting, but I didn't hear what else she said. I was dumbstruck. It didn't seem probable that Asya could have been arrested. Roza's remark was a conjecture based on no evidence whatsoever. People who were arrested by the KGB rarely returned home. And yet the idea planted itself in my mind. What else, if not a glimpse inside the Rooster House, could explain Asya's paranoid fear of the place, down to the mere mention of its name?

I left the archives. I realised that I should have stopped by the embroidery college to say goodbye to Nadia, but my thoughts were in a jumble. Asya arrested? How could my law-abiding, flower-loving great-grandmother, the wife of a war hero and upstanding Communist, be arrested? And yet, why did it seem impossible? Thousands of others like her had met the same fate. Still, I couldn't accept it. I had spent years studying political science, but I still struggled to connect the facts I had learned from books to my family's personal experiences. Examining their actions against the historical backdrop was much more difficult – and more painful – than I had anticipated. It wasn't surprising then that my great-grandparents spoke in riddles and that for many the Soviet legacy remained a traumatic topic.

Only those who either lauded or condemned it had no qualms stating their opinion.

I couldn't make out anything in front of me. Everything was a blur. When I reached the bus station in Poltava, I hailed a taxi and said, 'To the Rooster House'.

PART 4

The
Rooster
House

Ten

The grim sirens flanking the Rooster House seemed about to take flight. I walked up to the building and stood in front of it. The door of the Poltava headquarters of the Security Service of Ukraine (SBU) looked so heavy that I doubted my light push would make it budge, but it swung open with such ease that I nearly lost my balance and tumbled inside. The place that I had imagined as a house of horrors had an air of *fin de siècle* elegance. The polished marble of the ornate staircase glittered in the afternoon sunlight and the dark burgundy carpet hugging each step had not a speck of dust on it. The entrance hall was cool and smelled of expensive cologne. A tall guard in military uniform scanned ID cards at the checkpoint. Two men in grey suits and several soldiers stood in the hall and the moment I entered they turned around and looked at me.

I hadn't prepared an explanation. Until the last moment I hadn't imagined walking into the Rooster House, but now that I was there, I had to collect my thoughts.

'I went to the archives and there was something strange, maybe she was arrested.' I could hear my breaking voice echoing against the high ceiling. The guard seemed baffled. 'Actually, it's about my great-grandfather. Or rather, his brother.' The guard continued listening, a faint smile lifting the corner of his mouth. He must have assumed that I was deranged.

'His name was Nikodim, and he vanished,' I blurted out at last. The men in suits stared at me in a way that must have been taught at the KGB school – trying to peel away the protective layers and read my innermost thoughts. But perhaps my feverish imagination was playing tricks on me.

I tried again. 'What should I do if I'm looking for someone who disappeared in the 1930s? I think he was arrested. I called different archives and searched everywhere, but I keep bumping against a wall. Where else should I look?' My voice, still unnaturally high and strained, rang out in the hallway. Sweat beaded on my forehead and ran down the sides of my face.

The officer took out a pad and wrote down an address. 'We have an archival division. You can ask there,' he said, handing me a piece of paper. 'It's a five-minute walk from here, and it's called the Sectoral State Archive of the Security Service of Ukraine. They have a counter open to the public, and I'm sure they will be helpful.' He checked his wristwatch and confirmed that the archives should be open. I took the address, thanked the officer and fled.

However, the address he had given me didn't seem to exist. I spent two hours circling the neighbourhood, but yet again I came up against a wall. This time it was a literal wall, because the whole street was a construction site, and where the archival division should have been was only a steel fence. Whenever I asked for directions, people were dumbfounded. 'The SBU archives? Open to the public? Go to the Rooster House. Not that the KGBists over there will help you,' a woman watering a flower bed said. However many times the security organisation changed its name, it remained the KGB.

'We've lived here for more than fifty years, and this is the first time we've heard of any archival division,' was the collective reply of three grandmothers eating sunflower seeds and watching over their grandchildren.

'Young lady, why are you looking for the devil?' an elderly gentleman in a three-piece suit and a hat asked me and walked away before I could reply.

I took wrong turns and lost myself in the maze of narrow alleys, construction signs and abandoned houses. The Soviet-era building complex had numerous inner courtyards, and its numbering system included letters and fractions that didn't follow any logical order. Asya's calling the Rooster House 'a trap' was appropriate. I was in the post-Soviet version of the film *Labyrinth* and I despaired of getting out of it, to say nothing of finding my destination. Nevertheless, I went from building to building, from house to house, trying my luck. I discovered that while the archival centre was elusive, the former KGB offices were omnipresent, a reminder of the tentacles of the totalitarian state. Some were inconspicuous buildings in grey slate with metal detectors at the entrance. 'How the hell did you get in here?' an armed soldier shouted at me the moment I pushed open one door. I beat a hasty retreat, the rush of adrenaline making me dizzy. Other sites were silent offices in residential towers. The streets around them had no names.

At last, I came upon the archival division, hidden under the stone arches of a dark passage. The sign said that it was closed. My anxiety and long search left me too drained to feel disappointed. Now that I had found the building, I could pay a visit another day. But I still had the feeling of being in a twilight zone, where nothing was as it seemed.

Walking past the Rooster House on my way back to the bus

station, I noticed the officer who had directed me to the archives. He was smoking outside the door, catching the afternoon sun on his face and the admiring glances of women. When he saw me, he waved and asked if I had found the archives. I explained that the office had already closed and that I would have to return another time.

'We can call Elena Ivanovna, the officer in charge of our archives, on the internal line,' he said. He threw the cigarette stub into the urn by the entrance and gallantly held the door for me. I hesitated and then stepped into the hallway more bewildered than grateful. I expected an ambush of sorts, a ploy to detain me. The officer dialled the number and handed me the phone. The female voice on the other end of the line sounded like it belonged to someone who had no patience for small talk. I explained that I was searching for a missing person in my family and that I had exhausted all possibilities. I gave Nikodim's name. 'It would be difficult to find information based only on the name,' the woman said. I stared at the white marble wall in front of me and gripped the phone tighter. 'I also still need to understand what you're looking for and why. Most of the former KGB archives are still classified, so first I need to interview you. Would Wednesday, nine a.m., at our office suit you?'

I said yes. Then I remembered my promise to Valentina and said that I needed to speak with my grandmother first.

'Call me when you make up your mind,' said Elena Ivanovna and hung up.

My phone rang the moment I walked out of the Rooster House. I didn't understand at first that it was our neighbour Sasha.

'Come home at once!' she screamed.

Had Valentina learned about my visit to the Rooster House and become angry? I thought irrationally.

'Your grandmother fell and broke her back,' Sasha said, and everything around me came to a halt. 'I tried calling Dmytro, but he is in Kyiv.'

I ran down the street to the bus stop. It was empty, indicating that the bus had just left. I hailed a taxi, but it raced past me. I called a car service, but exasperated at being kept on indefinite hold to the soundtrack of tinny Mozart, I hung up. I scrolled through my phone to find another taxi company and Yaroslav's name darted past. I called him.

'Yaroslav, you probably don't remember me, but last year you took me and my grandmother to the villages . . .' I started.

'Vika. I remember. You were looking for your family roots. How is your grandmother?'

'Something awful has happened to her, but I can't find a car to take me to Bereh. I'm in the centre of Poltava.'

'I'm coming to get you. Where are you?'

I glared at the voluptuous red sirens. 'At the Rooster House.'

'What the hell are you doing at the Rooster House? Anyway, better not to ask questions about that place. I'm coming.'

Ten minutes later, Yaroslav's car pulled up and I got in. 'We'll be in Bereh before you know it,' he said and pressed on the accelerator, making his motor roar.

Once again the gate stood open and the yard was full of neighbours whom Sasha had called for help. Breathless, I pushed them aside and saw that Valentina was sitting on the bench rubbing her side. She looked flushed and embarrassed. 'I slipped on the grass and fell hard on my back,' she said. 'Nothing major happened. I only have a small bruise.' She showed us a blue mark on her arm. Her mobile phone rang and she picked it up. 'Dmytro, I'm fine. Nothing happened. Sasha is making a mountain out of a molehill as always,' she said.

'Even minor falls can be dangerous,' said Yaroslav, who

followed me into the yard. 'Let me take you to the hospital for a check-up, just to make sure that everything is fine.'

Valentina's face turned crimson and her mouth hardened. 'I said I am fine. I don't need any doctor to tell me something I already know.' She got up and limped into the house, leaving Sasha and the rest of the neighbours to shake their heads and file out of our yard.

'She is afraid of doctors,' I told Yaroslav, apologising for Valentina's brusque reply.

'My mother is like this too,' he said, getting into his car. 'But if she changes her mind, call me.'

The next day, Valentina woke up unable to walk. The fall aggravated injuries that she had accumulated over years of lifting heavy watering jugs and bending down to pull weeds. She made the strain worse by ignoring it, and worked through the kind of pain that would leave a younger person gasping for breath. She tended the vegetable beds in the sweltering heat and suffered heat strokes. She treated her wounds in the cavalier manner of Monty Python's Black Knight. Nobody in the family could convince her that taking care of herself was more important than taking care of the garden.

Now the pain radiating from Valentina's lower back paralysed her. She lay in bed, applying hot compresses. When I suggested going to the hospital, she became angry and shouted that doctors knew nothing. Valentina always feared hospitals, and her neighbours' stories about dilapidated government clinics and their poor service only reinforced her paranoia. Dmytro and I tried cajoling, threatening, even bribing her into accepting a trip to the best private hospital in Poltava, but we couldn't change her mind. The best we could do was to take care of the house until she recovered.

Uncle Tolya came to cheer up Valentina. 'My mother used to

say that to cure these aches you have to rub your back against a pine tree struck by lightning. But let me tell you, it's all nonsense. The only thing that fixes all pains is a coffin.' Digging graves for the dead, Uncle Tolya had little experience in comforting the living.

In time the pain subsided, but Valentina emerged from her illness with deflated spirits. She talked about her strength sapping away and whenever she brought up an event in the future, she qualified it by saying that she might not live to see it happen. The change wrought on her by the fall was so dramatic that I could barely recognise my energetic grandmother in the sullen woman before me. 'There is nothing to look forward to,' she often repeated. 'It's all downhill from here. Old age is such loneliness and darkness.'

'But we are here with you,' I countered feebly. 'What about your projects? You wanted to redesign the orchard . . . '

Valentina waved her hand, cutting me off. 'As if any of that makes any difference. I gave my best years to this land, and now I'm an old wreck.'

Such comments didn't seem strange to our neighbours who dropped in on Valentina. Like a Greek choir they took up the lament and shared their own woes. Some of their complaints were of the global variety, like the war and climate change. Others were of a distinctly local flavour, like the yellow mould on Sasha's apple trees or a new kind of potato blight Uncle Tolya had noticed. 'There is nothing good any more,' they said, as they took their leave to tend to their vegetable plots. The potato-planting schedule remained sacrosanct, world crises notwithstanding.

Valentina, on the other hand, lost interest in the garden. The seed packets and planting charts gathered dust. She could sit for hours in the dining room, staring at the floor and sighing.

179

Seeing her reduced to such apathy pained me. She frowned when I proposed planting carrots myself. 'What's the point?' she replied. I wanted to put my head on the table and weep. I expected Valentina to continue with her usual refrain about not living long enough to see the carrots ripen, but instead, she added dryly, 'You don't know a thing about planting carrots.' On this, my grandmother was correct.

One afternoon after tea, I sat at the dining table editing the photos I had taken during our trip to Mykhailivka, while my grandmother applied a hot compress to her back.

'Isn't it a nice photo?' I said, showing her the image of the two of us standing in front of the house where Valentina grew up.

My grandmother smiled. 'I bought this jacket in Kharkiv,' she said, pointing to the beige serge jacket she was wearing in the photo. 'It must have been six or seven years ago. Your mother wanted us to go to Kharkiv to see the place where we lived, and we had such a wonderful time. That was the last time I bought anything nice for myself.' She smoothed the creases on her jogging suit and looked at it with a critical squint.

'Babushka, let's go to Kharkiv then. You will show me where you studied, where you went on dates with Grandfather, where Mum was born. We will go to your favourite cafes. We will go to the museum. We will go shopping for new clothes.' My thoughts raced and my fingers typed 'tickets Poltava to Kharkiv' into the search bar of my browser before Valentina could reply. I expected her to bring up the orchard or her health as an excuse to crush my plans, but she smiled and said, 'Kharkiv is the place I truly loved.'

She didn't notice that her compress had slipped onto the floor. 'It was the place that I made my own. The other places, including Bereh, were selected for me, by my parents or my husband, but Kharkiv was mine.'

For Valentina, Kharkiv meant the happiest days of her youth and the thrill of her university years. She studied hard to obtain a coveted spot at the National University of Kharkiv, one of the oldest and most respected in the Soviet Union. When, despite her good scores, Valentina's name landed on the waiting list, Asya grew furious. She told Sergiy to remonstrate with the university administration. He protested that it was below his dignity, but Asya persisted. Contrary to Sergiy, she was cynical about the system and didn't believe in its fairness. 'Unlike those party apparatchiks whose children get priority placement, you fought in the war. Why should you be ashamed to remind them who made the real sacrifices?' Asya said. The sight of Sergiy on a crutch weighed down by his military honours was enough for the university administration to make room for one more student in the geography department.

The country was still recovering from the Second World War when my grandmother started her university studies, but it was the beginning of the upbeat 1950s and – after the death of Stalin – the Khrushchev Thaw. Valentina was filled with optimism. She listened to Khrushchev denounce Stalin, and she believed that the horrible deeds of the past were due to a single wicked man. She wanted to hope that the future would be bright. She was yearning to discover the city, meet new people and enjoy life. She wanted to forget about the dark days of war that still haunted her.

In Kharkiv, Valentina shared a tiny room with two other students, and when she wasn't studying at the library, she took to wandering around the Fine Arts Museum next door to her apartment. When my grandmother discovered it, the building still smelled of plaster and paint and the rooms were half-empty, a testament to wartime plunder. Nonetheless, even the bits of the collection that remained were impressive and included the works of masters like Volodymyr Borovikovsky, Dmytro Levytsky, Ivan Aivazovsky, Ilya Repin and Taras Shevchenko – the renowned Ukrainian poet was also an accomplished painter. Valentina had learned their names from books, but standing in front of the canvases she was struck by their beauty and power. Valentina could see how an artist used a brush to apply colour – she could even spot the grooves left by the hard bristles – making the paint fall in precise layers to evoke the texture of hair or fabric. She observed the way flecks of white created the glint of lace, the opalescence of pearls or the shimmer of sunshine on water. Then she saw how images came together to tell a story about love, beauty, betrayal or death. Words were superfluous. She could read the canvas and understand it. It was as if she had lifted a veil and caught a glimpse of another world.

Valentina's awakening was bittersweet. In contrast to the pleasure of her museum visits, her chosen field of study was dull. Making her father wear his awards to secure her a spot in the geography department was a mistake, but changing course was out of the question. She enjoyed participating in student seminars, but she now saw in front of her a career with endless five-year plans and hours spent calculating the number of tractors needed to equip a collective farm. Valentina began filling her spare time with as much art as she could find, subscribing to magazines, joining archaeological expeditions, saving her meal allowance to attend plays and film screenings, and on a whim, dancing in the amateur folk ensemble.

Dance was the medium in which the shy young woman could best express herself. Valentina enjoyed falling under the spell of music, following its rhythm and making the melody flow through her body. She loved how a dance could be as tender as a waltz or as exuberant as a polka. Valentina's reputation as a fine dancer spread throughout the university and she was invited to perform a Hungarian czardas at the graduation ball. She made a beautiful costume complete with a tight black jacket and a full red skirt, and her dance was such a success that she did an encore. 'Someone loved your dancing so much that he asked for an introduction,' her friend Lina said with a conspiratorial smile after she saw Valentina backstage. 'His name is Boris.'

A few days later Valentina went to a student gathering at Lina's insistence. As soon as she entered, she saw two young men in bright green shirts in the centre of the room performing popular songs. They looked like mirror images of each other – the same tight curls brushed back to reveal high foreheads, the same olive tint to their skin, the same laughing blue eyes. One man was playing an accordion, while the other was singing. 'That's your Boris,' Lina whispered, pointing at the singer.

Boris and his brother Evgen were studying engineering at the Kharkiv Aviation Institute. By coincidence, the brothers were also from the Poltava region. Though they were impossible to tell apart – and the brothers exploited the smashing effect of their double good looks by dressing alike – the two men were polar opposites. Boris was studious and responsible, devoting his time to coursework and community projects, while Evgen could never pass up the opportunity to be the life of the party with his accordion and a collection of songs. He was flirtatious, funny and generous to a fault, but it was with the level-headed Boris that Valentina fell in love. Kharkiv in May provided the romantic *mise en scène*, and Boris and Valentina were soon married. A year later my mother was born and so Kharkiv marked a new page in my family history.

Every day I asked Valentina to tell me new stories about her time in Kharkiv and every day she delved into her memories with so much enthusiasm that our afternoon tea transitioned into dinner. Our evenings ended past midnight, when the sluggish wall clock measured out twelve grudging beats and reminded us that it was time to rest. But it was as if my grandmother had a store of stories she had longed to tell me and she didn't want to stop talking. Every night before we went to bed, I reminded her that once her back healed, we would visit Kharkiv. Every night Valentina agreed. I knew that she wasn't merely humouring me when she asked what we would do about the house and garden during our absence.

'I spoke about it with Dmytro, and he promised to stay here,' I said. 'And Uncle Tolya will look after the garden. Hasn't he been asking you to give him more work?'

'I've neglected everything, haven't I?'

'Resting is important.'

'No, enough with resting. We need to work.'

'First, we need to go to Kharkiv,' I said firmly.

'We will go, I promise you.'

Bereh denizens could accept the most eccentric and immoral behaviour from their neighbours, but not the neglect of the garden. The next day Uncle Tolya came and announced that whether we wanted or not, he was weeding the vegetable beds. 'By the time you two decide on anything, this place will turn into a jungle.' He picked up a watering can and a hoe and asked me to fetch a folding chair for Valentina. 'I will work and Grandma will command,' he said.

Valentina protested, but since Uncle Tolya wasn't listening, she followed him into the garden. As I was hanging laundry in the yard, I could see Uncle Tolya arranging a chair for my grandmother under the shade of a pear tree and setting out to weed the garlic beds. 'Today is a warm and sunny day.' Uncle Tolya's voice echoed through the orchard. 'It means that God has plans for everything.'

At first, Valentina sat quietly, twisting the tassels of her shawl, but as Uncle Tolya hacked away at the weeds, she sprang up from her chair and pointed at something in the vegetable beds. 'You're leaving all of these small dandelion shoots behind. One day of rain and they will be large enough to choke my garlic,' her voice rang out, impatient and bossy. She sounded more like the Valentina I knew.

From that day onwards, Uncle Tolya returned regularly to help Valentina. Some mornings he came bearing bunches of daffodils or bouquets of bird cherries that filled our house with the heady aroma of toasted almonds. 'Who suspected that a rustic character like Uncle Tolya could be such a romantic?' my grandmother said, burying her face in the foam of white petals. She went up to her vanity table and applied a few drops of her favourite iris perfume with a glass stopper. I wondered if there could be something more than warm friendship between Valentina and Uncle Tolya, but I didn't want to pry. They were polar opposites in many respects, but they clearly enjoyed each other's company. On the tea tray in the dining room a large mug with the fading design of a rooster always awaited Uncle Tolya's visit.

By the time the cherry blossoms faded, Valentina had recovered enough to make the trip. I bought the train tickets to Kharkiv and showed them to Valentina as a fait accompli. We were going to travel together again.

~

Kharkiv was waking up to the rustle of the street cleaners' brooms, the melodic whine of trams speeding down narrow alleys and the glare of the morning sun. Valentina and I took a bus from the train station, crossed a bridge over a muddy river and drove past old buildings draped in advertisements for manicures, beer on tap and legal help. The imposing blocks of the

Soviet novostroiki, literally 'new buildings' that were no longer new, sidled up next to modern churches that aimed to look old.

Despite the changes the city had undergone since Valentina was a student, I could easily imagine what she must have felt on her first visit. Kharkiv had neither the splendour of Kyiv nor the bucolic charm of Poltava, but it had grandeur. The buildings were massive; the streets were wide; the monuments outsized.

Kharkiv was also a town of memorial plaques. On every corner, a hero had died and a poet had penned a verse. I also noticed many blank spots where plaques had been removed. Some heroes were heroes no longer.

'Do you want to have breakfast first?' I asked Valentina when we reached the city centre. Our train to Kharkiv was too early in the morning for breakfast and my grandmother was so preoccupied with the trip that she had eaten very little the day before.

We selected a cafe on Sumska Street in Kharkiv's centre and sat down near a window overlooking the wide avenue. Valentina glanced around, pointing out the new buildings and lamenting the state of the old ones.

'But at least the food is much better than in the days of my youth,' she said, tasting the apple pancakes we ordered for breakfast. They were layered with fluffy mounds of soured cream and dusted with confectioner's sugar. 'When I was a student, this place used to be a diner, and you could get a sugar bun and a glass of kefir for a few kopeks.'

The pancakes were fragrant with cinnamon and vanilla, and ravenous after our train journey, we ate them greedily.

'I met Nikolai, Nikodim's son, here,' Valentina said. 'That's how I learned of his father's existence.'

My fork fell on the floor, splattering the tablecloth with soured cream.

'I was still a high school student when I went to Moscow to

visit my friend Aniuta. There I met her brother Vania. He was my first love.' Valentina either didn't notice my agitation or pretended to ignore it. I had not mentioned Nikodim's name since our explosive conversation a year ago, and Valentina's unexpected revelation blindsided me. I also didn't understand what Valentina's paramour had to do with Nikodim, and since I grew up hearing so much about my grandparents' love for each other, the idea of Valentina being infatuated with someone else made me forget the original topic. 'You had a first love! What about Grandpa Boris?'

Valentina laughed and waved to the waitress to bring me another fork.

'It was different. Vania and I exchanged letters, and when I was already a university student, he came to visit me in Kharkiv. Because he couldn't afford a hotel and I couldn't invite him to my room, he slept on a bench in the zoo. What's more, I went to visit Vania in Leningrad, where he was studying at the Nakhimov Naval School. I sold a few cuts of silk that Asya had given me and bought a train ticket.' Valentina giggled and savoured her own mischievousness. 'And Asya never learned about it!'

Then the letters from Vania stopped. Valentina assumed that the young man became bored with their long-distance relationship and had found someone else, but she was too proud to write to him and ask for an explanation.

'But something could have happened to him, or the letters could have been lost,' I suggested.

'A lady can't stoop to chasing men,' Valentina replied, puffing out her chest. She laughed again. 'Well, I was young and too proud.'

'Years passed. I was newly married, and while expecting your mother, I stayed at the university working on my thesis.

One day I received a letter from Asya about a strange visit from her nephew Nikolai Berezko, the son of Sergiy's older brother Nikodim. Until then I hadn't heard of either Nikodim or Nikolai. Asya said that Nikolai lived in Belgorod, but that he sent a telegram to them in Bereh about an urgent matter he needed to discuss with me. Asya told me to expect his visit in Kharkiv. Two weeks later, he showed up, saying that he had a letter for me – except that he didn't have it.'

'How odd,' I said.

Valentina nodded. 'I thought that he was a nutcase. So I suggested that we talk at a cafe because I was concerned about being alone with him.'

After a long, awkward pause, Nikolai explained that his wife, Valentina Berezko, had received a letter from someone named Vania, who said that she was still in his thoughts and that he was hoping to hear from her. Nikolai was convinced that the letter was written by Valentina's former lover and the couple had a row that almost ended in divorce. Nikolai wrote to Vania demanding an explanation. Then it became clear that Vania had written to the wrong Valentina. He saw a newspaper story about Valentina Berezko receiving an award for outperforming her factory norms and presumed that he had found the young lady with whom he had lost touch. He impetuously wrote a letter and mailed it to the factory mentioned in the article. Nikolai's angry missive made him realise that he had made a mistake, and he begged forgiveness for causing the couple undue anxieties.

'I no longer thought about Vania, and I was in love with my husband and anticipating our new adventures together. But I admit that remembering that young man who wrote me passionate love letters stirred many nice memories.' Valentina glanced out of the window and smiled at something. Then she shook her head and turned to me, 'But Nikolai brought no letter.

He said that he had destroyed it, because he was worried that if my husband read it, he would be angry.'

I suddenly felt melancholy. All of these stories were nothing but constellations of strange coincidences, all leading to a loss.

Valentina noticed my downcast expression and reached out to pat my hand, 'But what kind of a life would I have with a sea captain? As Uncle Tolya likes to say, "All sea captains are alcoholics."' We started laughing and we laughed until tears streamed down our faces and the other customers at the cafe looked at us quizzically.

'After that, Nikolai visited Bereh from time to time, bringing Asya supplies from the chemical factory where he worked. He didn't mention his family. He was a quiet and intense man and he made us, especially Asya, uncomfortable. At first, I didn't know why—'

'Did Nikolai mention what happened to his father?' I interrupted her, now impatient to learn about the connection to Nikodim.

'He never did. Asya herself brought him up. I overheard her having a row with Sergiy about going to the Rooster House to search for Nikodim and she blamed Nikolai for "digging it all up". Sergiy was reasoning with her, saying that all dangers were in the past, and that he needed to know. And Asya said that if everything was in the past, Nikodim could rest in peace there too.'

Valentina took out an embroidered handkerchief from her pocket and wiped her lips. I noticed that she had worn a smidgen of pink lipstick for our trip. I felt a pang in my heart. We were in the city that held my grandmother's brightest memories, and even here we were haunted by Nikodim's story. I also thought about losing my father and the sudden reminder of his departure stung me. I was haunted too.

189

'Sergiy promised not to do anything,' Valentina continued. 'I found him in the orchard later that day. He was pruning the cherry branches with fierce determination. His hands were trembling. I wanted to comfort him somehow, but he started talking. He said that Nikodim was the brother he admired the most growing up. When he was arrested, Sergiy was torn. He believed in Communism and the Soviet Union as an idea. He believed in his brother. Either it was a terrible mistake or Nikodim was truly guilty of a serious crime.

'Sergiy was ready to search for his brother, but Asya protested. The mere suggestion of filing a formal request about someone who might have vanished in the Rooster House terrified her. She forbade Sergiy to do anything. Sergiy's older brother Ivan was also worried that such an inquiry might bring harm to the whole family. In the end, Asya and Ivan and their fear of the Rooster House silenced him,' Valentina said. 'We never talked about Nikodim any more. We preferred to forget.'

But as I learned from Sergiy's journal, he never did.

'I was wrong to forbid you to search for Nikodim,' Valentina said, clasping my hand. 'It was a selfish thing to do, and I'm sorry. I didn't realise that I myself was living in fear of the Rooster House, but I promise you that if you want to continue your investigation, I will help you.'

Valentina reached out and stroked my cheek. 'Sergiy would have wanted you to find Nikodim.' I took her hand and pressed it to my face, feeling its roughness and warmth.

The day after we returned from Kharkiv, I ran into the cherry orchard to find the old tree with a hollow. I reached inside and felt a bundle of cloth – my notes about Nikodim that I had buried one year ago after a fight with Valentina. The paper was soggy and the writing illegible, but it didn't matter. I knew which thread to follow.

Eleven

The gate slammed with a violent bang behind me, shutting out the city with its crowds of early morning commuters, its tall lindens scattering their fragrant confetti of petals, its bus stops named after forgotten Communist heroes and its old mansions hiding their faded elegance under layers of Pepsi ads. I surrendered my documents to a uniformed guard wearing the Ukrainian yellow and blue insignia. He peered at my American passport, frowning and pulling on the tape that the consular official had used to add extra visa pages. 'Stay here,' he said, disappearing with my documents into the cavernous space to the right of the entrance. 'Never forswear a prison cell or a begging bowl,' was a proverb my great-grandmother Asya often quoted as a warning that life was unpredictable and you never knew what fate had in store. And here I was at the Poltava city penitentiary. I looked at the grey concrete blocks, barbed wire, and the metal bars on the windows.

The guard returned and escorted me to a small building near

the front entrance, held the heavy steel door and motioned for me to enter. 'Follow this way,' he said, still eyeing me with unconcealed suspicion. I stepped into the long, dark corridor and walked a few uncertain steps until I saw a puddle of light on the floor and a door left ajar. I knocked and walked in without waiting for a response.

In contrast to the grim surroundings, the archive division housed inside the municipal jail had the atmosphere of a typical administrative office, prosaic and dull. The room was lined with several rows of desks. Their yellowing Formica tops had a fine spiderweb of veins. The ziggurats of files and folders on top of the desks so riveted my attention that I didn't initially notice that there were other people in the room. A tall, dark-haired woman in a grey trouser suit shook my hand and offered me a chair. 'We spoke on the phone,' she said. 'My name is Elena Ivanovna, and this is my colleague from the archives.' She pointed to a thin, balding man in civil dress writing at one of the desks, but she didn't introduce him. His indifferent glance ran over me and returned to his notes.

After Valentina and I had returned from Kharkiv, I had called Elena Ivanovna at the Rooster House and said that I was ready to make an appointment. She invited me to the archives at the Poltava municipal jail and was now staring at me. 'What do you want to find?' she asked.

Asya's fairy tales featured a character called Ivan the Fool who was always going off on impossible missions to 'who knows where' and seeking 'who knows what'. I felt like a fool as I tried to explain to the officer that I was looking for a man who disappeared in the 1930s, that I was looking for someone of whom I knew so little that my search didn't make sense even to my family. I only had his name. Nikodim. This Nikodim vanished.

'When did he disappear?' Elena Ivanovna asked, turning on

her computer. 'When—' I couldn't hear her question, because some shrill noise I didn't recognise entered the room through the open window, deafening us. These sounds no longer frightened me.

'For goodness' sake, what are they doing?' she asked her colleague, wincing. 'Must they train here at this hour?'

Her colleague shrugged and pointed at the ceiling. Someone up there had decided that the new army recruits would train in the football stadium next to the town jail. I wasn't sure if he meant their superiors or some other all-mighty power. He closed the window. The sounds grew muffled and distant.

'So, when did this person . . .' Elena Ivanovna was more irritated with me and my foolish request than with the noise.

'Nikodim Berezko,' I reminded her.

'Yes. When did this Nikodim disappear?'

It was in the 1930s, but I had no year.

'What's the year of his birth?'

I shuffled in my chair and admitted that I didn't know.

'We might as well read coffee grounds,' Elena Ivanovna said. She hit a button below her monitor and her computer stopped humming. 'I can't base my search on such scant information.'

The muffled noise sounded like fireworks and I almost expected to see explosions of colour. But the sky looked blue and undisturbed through the bars on the window. The three of us remained silent. I cleared my throat, unsure what to say next. The audience was clearly over.

'Why do you want to find Nikodim?' Elena Ivanovna asked, folding her arms across her chest and looking at me. That summer day in the middle of the Russia–Ukraine war, how could I convey to a former KGB archivist that I was looking for an uncle missing for over almost a century because I wanted to make sense of the present and to understand my roots?

'Did you have any other people in the family who were arrested?' she asked.

I froze. I remembered my suspicions that Asya might have had her brush with the Rooster House, which was why she feared it.

'Vasylyna Oleksiyvna Berezko,' I said, and added hastily, 'but it's only a guess.'

She nodded. 'I will check through our archives. But I need at least this Nikodim's date of birth or the date of his arrest. Berezko is a common name.'

I promised that I would ask my family and left, feeling more desperate the closer I came to solving the mystery and the more it eluded me.

~

'Was Asya ever arrested?' I asked Valentina and at once regretted starting so abruptly. Valentina's face flushed crimson and the knuckles of her hands whitened around the teacup she was holding. I wanted to prepare my grandmother and to explain what I had learned during my visit to the former KGB archives, but the words escaped before I could control them.

My grandmother placed the cup carefully onto the saucer. 'As you know, Asya worked at the school in Zhyrkovka during the Nazi occupation and as a result, she was called in for questioning by the NKVD. She and Pasha spent the whole night preparing her suitcase and making plans for us children in case she wouldn't return.'

My grandmother rose and walked over to the armoire where she kept old porcelain wrapped in newspapers and stacks of yellowing linens. From the bottom of one of the drawers, she pulled out a beige paper folder loosely wrapped in a towel. 'Asya was never charged, but from then on she had to be careful. She was certain that her dossier was under close surveillance by the

KGB, and that she could be arrested again without any warning,' Valentina said, handing me the folder. I read the heavy-set letters in bulky serif type: 'Lichnoe Delo'.

'Lichnoe Delo' meant Private Affair in Russian, but the folder and its contents belied this notion. There was nothing private about the dossier kept on my great-grandmother, Vasylyna Oleksiyvna Berezko née Bylym.

The file contained the forms Asya filled out and the forms filled out for her, requests to acquire medical leave or job transfers. It read like an extended biography. It included her date and place of birth, her social class and that of her parents, information on her siblings and husband and their work assignments. The file asked whether she spoke any foreign languages (none), had defended a doctorate thesis (blank) or travelled abroad (never).

In another section, I found the personal statements on Asya written by her work colleagues. They contained anodyne comments – 'a valuable colleague', 'a respected educator', 'an upstanding citizen', but for someone in Asya's position, such phrases would have been the best recommendations. On a slip of paper as transparent as an onion peel I found a long description of Asya as someone 'politically and morally reliable' who was 'studying the history of the peoples of USSR in her spare time'.

A framed vision of a summer evening floated up in my mind: the tops of tall lilac bushes glazed red by the setting sun, the distant rumble of a passing train and the atonal symphony of frogs, nightingales and village dogs. The yard is covered with low wooden troughs filled with tulip bulbs. Our task is to clean off the excess peel and sort the bulbs by size. I'm only ten, but I have already learned how to do this, just as I learned how to clip rose shoots or to plant dahlia tubers. The earth-caked lumps become shiny marbles in Asya's nimble fingers, and the pile of rust-coloured peels grows bigger. She is sitting on a low stool, stretching out her legs covered with the bluish lumps of varicose veins. Her lavender house dress is fastened by red flower-shaped buttons. A tortoiseshell comb glints in the yellow light of a hanging lamp as Asya bends down to pick up yet another tulip bulb. 'Mother, enough with the tulips, come and eat,' Valentina calls from the house. Asya shakes her head. The sun is rapidly falling behind the lime trees on the horizon. Asya and I continue until we can no longer make out the bulbs in the dusk. Valentina drops her hands in exasperation and orders me to wash up and eat my supper. 'It's nothing but the garden during her every waking moment. Even on her deathbed she will be worrying about her garden,' Valentina says, looking at her mother.

My Asya wouldn't have read about the history of the peoples of USSR in her spare time, but the dossier in front of me wasn't about my great-grandmother. It wasn't a criminal file, because it contained no mention of infringement or misdeed. It was simply a dossier with work information and personal details, but it could have been used to make a case. The information collected seemed bland, but the thorough manner in which it was compiled and the repeated questions about her social class and educational achievements left the impression that her crime was to be inferred from the most irrelevant of details. Such minutiae uncovered and twisted by a prosecutor could lead to any conclusion. Asya could emerge as either innocent or condemned and she wouldn't be able to do anything about it. No wonder she lived in fear of the Rooster Trap.

Did the person describing Asya as 'politically and morally reliable' help her? Did the authorities find that a primary school-teacher wasn't worth the trouble of arrest and sentence? Asya was never summoned again to the Rooster House. However, the personal file remained. I flipped through the last few pages left

unfilled and was about to close the file when I saw a narrow strip
of paper with calligraphic handwriting in dark purple ink. It was
no bigger than a matchbox and it was sewn into the binding. I
had to pry the edges of the folder to read the sentence. 'Arrested
family members: Nikodim Pavlovych Berezko, brother-in-law.
Year of arrest: 1937.'

Valentina walked back into the room as I was reading the
file. I showed her the strip. 'So you've found Nikodim,' she said.

～

Once again, the prison gate closed behind me with a heavy bang.
It was to be my second meeting with Elena Ivanovna, the officer
in charge of the secret police archives. Once again I went with
the blessing of Valentina.

Elena Ivanovna asked me again what I was hoping to find. She
turned to her cabinet and sorted through stacks of documents.

I was at a loss for an answer. She meant either the type of
document or the sort of information, but for me her question
had an existential ring. I thought of journeys to places unknown
revealed by a labyrinth of family stories. I wasn't after an accusation or an acquittal. I was after the truth, but what this truth
was I didn't know. I repeated that I was looking for information
about my great-uncle Nikodim and that I had little to go on, other
than the bits I had gleaned: Nikodim Berezko as mentioned in
Sergiy's diary and the fact that he was arrested in 1937, as I had
learned from Asya's dossier. I also recalled that the collective
farm records in Maiachka noted Nikodim's date of birth as 1900.

Elena Ivanovna closed the cabinet and turned to face me. She
was holding a file. Its green cover was marked with smudged ink
stamps and lines of scribbled writing. 'Declassified.' The pages
held between thick cardboard covers had crumbling edges and
left a yellowish dust on the Formica surface of the desk.

'It was easier to find than I expected. Nikodim's full name alone sufficed. But I would like to warn you before you read it,' Elena Ivanovna said, still holding the file firmly. 'It was 1937. They had quotas to fulfil.' She pointed towards her desk and the floor-to-ceiling shelves stuffed with similar folders. One file – one life. There were hundreds of them in the small office. 'Read between the lines.'

She put the file in front of me and stepped out of the office, closing the door behind her.

The name on the folder read 'Nikodim Pavlovych Berezko'. I touched its stained cover and hesitated. Here was the document that I was hoping to find all this time and yet I couldn't open it.

When Asya had a rare afternoon off from her garden duties, she took me to the river. She sat on the shore while I tiptoed towards the water's edge. The beach had a thick fringe of rustling reeds on one side and where the water met the sand, a slimy ribbon of silt. The surface of the river was calm and black, reflecting the clouds and silvery poplars on the other shore. It looked bottomless and frightening. I stood, shivering and indecisive, testing the water with my toes. 'Close your eyes and jump in,' Asya called out. 'One, two, three – go!' I dived into the water, aiming for the deep part, but I kept my eyes open. As my feet lost contact with the ground, as the cold current pulled me under, as the sky turned murky green when seen through the heavy curtain of water, I felt heart-searing panic. But then some other force pushed me up, broke the dark surface and delivered me back to the blue sky and the sun and Asya on the shore.

I counted to three and opened Nikodim's file.

The first page included Nikodim's biography and the transcripts of interrogations, written in the same hand, presumably that of the police superintendent, and initialled by Nikodim. The portion mentioning his middle-class peasant background was underlined. The rest of the transcripts were machine-typed and included copies of statements made by others involved in the case. Every page was stamped and notarised.

The mechanical language of the transcript and the familiar phrases that I had often heard at school – 'counter-revolutionary conspiracy', 'agitator of the population', 'anti-Soviet views', 'bourgeois-nationalism', 'fascist Germany' – made the file seem like a canned plot, rather than a narrative from which to glean truth. Yet it was the only thread I had through the labyrinth if I hoped to find Nikodim. The only thread, not counting Sergiy's mention.

I started reading. I read between the lines.

Twelve

On 24 August 1937, three men in plain clothes knocked on the door of a straw-covered hut in the village of Lozuvatka and asked the head of the household, Nikodim Berezko, to come with them to the Poltava police station. It seemed like a misunderstanding, because Nikodim wasn't a man to fall on the wrong side of the law. He was a primary schoolteacher. His life before the revolution of 1917 was likewise beyond reproach. He helped his parents on their farm in Maiachka and took care of his siblings. Some said that as a young man he was responsible for a fire at the church, but others reasoned that it was only empty talk because he was open about his Bolshevik views. He was equally frank about his distaste for religion even though his devout parents baptised him with a classical Orthodox name. At any rate, the local court in Maiachka acquitted him of any crime in the arson matter. When the Bolsheviks seized power on 7 November 1917, plunging the country into civil war, Nikodim, two weeks short of his seventeenth birthday, joined the Red Guards. One year later, his volunteer partisan group joined the Red Army and Nikodim fought in its ranks for four years until he was severely wounded in 1922. He then settled in Maiachka, got married and found work at a watermill. The old injuries, however, made his life miserable, and instead of breaking his body further by lugging heavy flour sacks, he decided to continue his studies.

The year 1923 coincided with Soviet policies of Ukrainisation, the initiative that made the use of the Ukrainian language in government offices mandatory and also created opportunities for peasants to study. Lenin's vision included exporting the revolution to other countries, and Communist Ukraine was to be the model. The Bolsheviks reasoned that to urbanise Ukraine, they had to create a more hospitable environment for the new arrivals from the countryside, and that meant forcing the cities to speak Ukrainian rather than Russian.

Ukrainian language teachers were suddenly in high demand. As a Ukrainian speaker from the peasant class and a former Red partisan, Nikodim was guaranteed a position. He joined the Workers' College attached to the Pedagogical University of Poltava and completed his studies with distinction. With his diploma, Nikodim could teach adult evening classes that paid well enough for him to support his family. At one point, his wife Fekla, who stayed behind in Maiachka, came to live with him in Poltava and their daughter Vera was born there in 1926.

Towards the end of the decade, however, the honeymoon between the Communist Party and Ukraine was over, and 'Ukrainian bourgeois-nationalism' was pronounced as a threat to the integrity of the Soviet Union. Ukrainisation policies were replaced with aggressive Russification. Ukrainian-language printing houses and theatres, which had flourished in the previous years, were closed and their leaders purged. Nikodim emerged unscathed, but his services as a Ukrainian language teacher became obsolete. He lost his only source of income and had to return to Maiachka. He could barely make ends meet. His situation was so desperate that he stopped paying his Party membership fees and was expelled from its ranks. He contacted some of his Red Army comrades to ask for help, and one of the people who responded to Nikodim's letters was Iakov Vashlenko. Nikodim had met Vashlenko in 1917 when he had been part of Vashlenko's partisan group. The two men had fought side by side for five years. Vashlenko had left the army the same year as Nikodim because of wounds, and he had moved to Lozuvatka, a small village between Poltava and Dnipropetrovsk, where he worked as the chairman of the local council. He wrote that their new school needed a head teacher and suggested the post to Nikodim. As the last vestiges of the Ukrainisation policies were eliminated in 1934, Nikodim arrived with his family in Lozuvatka to start his new duties.

That same year Fekla gave birth to their second child, a son they named Nikolai, but the happy occasion was clouded by the family's ever-worsening financial circumstances. The primary teacher's salary was small, and with each year Nikodim's health worsened. Obtaining a pension or benefits proved more difficult than he had expected. The bureaucrats demanded proof of his participation in the Red Guard movement, and he collected reams of papers and testaments only to be sent back for more documents and more testimonies. He grew vexed that a loyal supporter who helped build the young Soviet state was reduced to begging and pleading for a measly pension.

Since many people in Lozuvatka experienced hardship, remarks critical of Soviet policies were common. The collective farms were managed badly, and the equipment was either not right for the soil or not properly maintained. Some people, for instance, grumbled that instead of buying tractors the collective farm should buy bulls, the traditional beast of labour in the Ukrainian countryside. Many people were bitter about the traumatic changes of the recent decade, especially the forced collectivisation that controlled all aspects of their lives. The survivors of the devastating famine of 1932–33 were disoriented and confused. The consequences of collectivisation were as disastrous as many had predicted, including people in the Communist Party like Nikolai Bukharin, who even dared to call the Stalinist approach 'irresponsible' in a *Pravda* article. If Nikodim could help it, he would avoid signing up his family for the Lozuvatka collective farm.

His hopes for a pension crushed, Nikodim could only commiserate with his former army commander Vashlenko, who ended up as his next-door neighbour in Lozuvatka. The war experience brought the two men together and Nikodim often dropped in on his friend after work. Their other neighbours came over, and since they were illiterate, Nikodim read newspapers out loud to them.

Newspapers were the main source of information about the world in Lozuvatka and the men listened eagerly. The reports from *Pravda* and *Izvestia*, the main newspapers in the Soviet Union of the 1930s, kept readers in a permanent state of exhilaration with their reports of record-breaking harvests of wheat, cotton production or steel output across the Union. In 1937, however, the threat of a new war was in the air. As Japan began an active policy of expansion and Germany rearmed, the Soviet media built up the image of an infallible state. 'Strong and mighty is the Red Army of the land of the Soviets! Firmly it stands on guard, protecting the borders of the great country, ever ready to crush an enemy should he even dare to attack the Soviet Union. More than once have those who have tried to test our Army's sharpness and vigilance received a severe blow,' the *Pravda* article pronounced.

However, such triumphalism alternated with paranoia, and so *Pravda* warned citizens to be vigilant about the malicious wreckers who were devising plans to undermine the Soviet Union. They illustrated their predictions with the Case of the Trotskyist Anti-Soviet Military Organization.

In Soviet newspapers of the 1930s, the appellation 'Trotskyist' embodied all evil. A prominent figure in the Bolshevik Revolution, Leon Trotsky later became critical of Stalin and his policies. He was exiled from the Soviet Union in 1929, but the case bearing his name, the Anti-Soviet Trotskyist Process, became a crucial part of the Stalinist purges. It was to be neither the first nor the last purge in the USSR, but in comparison to earlier repressions within the Communist Party, the purges of the 1930s were deadlier. As the net was cast wider in the search for internal enemies, more people were caught in it.

The newspapers published sensationalist reports identifying one celebrated figure after another as an enemy of the people. General Mikhail Tukhachevsky, the reformer of the Red Army, was accused of military conspiracy and espionage. Another famous case involved Nikolai Bukharin. Only a few years earlier Bukharin had been the General Secretary of Comintern's executive committee, and though he was ousted from power in 1929 over disagreements with Stalin over questions of collectivisation, he retained influence as the editor of *Izvestia*. This didn't prevent *Izvestia* from publishing reports questioning Bukharin's loyalty. One such letter to the editor from factory workers sent 'a warm salute to the brave workers of the NKVD and its leader, the loyal Stalinist Comrade Yezhov,' and asked the government to investigate the criminal activity of Bukharin and his supporters and 'to cleanse the Soviet soil' of such dangerous elements.

Nikodim didn't share his views as he read newspapers out loud to his neighbours, but when he was alone with Vashlenko, he was more candid, since he trusted his former commander and respected his opinions.

While Vashlenko didn't comment on the arrests of the top Red Army brass, he believed that the former Red Guards were persecuted by the Soviet government and that their rights were ignored. Vashlenko had had his own share of frustrations fighting to obtain a monthly pension, and he felt stepped over by the new career Communists who, in his eyes, were not true Bolsheviks. However, he could do little but talk, since he was a man with few means and even less influence.

In the summer of 1937, the purges gathered momentum. According to the logic of the Stalinist system, if wreckers had been discovered in the highest echelons of the government, then they must be present in all layers of Soviet society. In July 1937 the 'ex-kulaks' and other 'anti-Soviet elements' campaign was launched. The Bolsheviks defined an affluent peasantry as the kulak, someone who hoarded their wealth, and during the collectivisation drive anyone who resisted giving up their land was labelled as such. Sergiy's family, with its six hectares of land, would have run such a risk had the brothers not made the decision to surrender the land to the collective farm in Maiachka. Many so-called kulaks had already been executed or sent to Siberia in the early 1930s, but the new 'kulak eradication initiative' was of a different and a much more unpredictable nature. New groups were earmarked for elimination: priests, former opposition members, military officers, ethnic minorities and saboteurs in agriculture and industry.

Then, in July 1937, Stalin signed an order that turned the top-echelon purge into a society-wide witch hunt. He created the special NKVD triads to investigate crimes and mete out punishment with no right of appeal. As one of the People's Commissars commented, working with the triads was simple, because 'they taught people to destroy enemies in a quick and efficient manner'. The same efficiency was applied when drawing up the arrest quotas. The original Moscow quota for Poltava was set at five thousand five hundred. But the local Ukrainian authorities sent a letter to Stalin to increase it. Like their counterparts in the cotton mills and steel factories, the NKVD workers wanted to beat the official targets and display their zeal. Their request was granted.

~

When Nikodim was taken to the Poltava police station on 24 August 1937, the plain-clothes men didn't say that he was under arrest. They only asked him to come with them to Poltava. He said goodbye to his wife and the children and left.

At the Poltava prison, the secretary of the municipal NKVD branch, Nikolai Zdykhovsky, asked Nikodim to fill out a questionnaire, focusing Nikodim's attention on his background and pre-revolutionary activities. Nikodim didn't hide the fact that his family had owned several hectares of land before the revolution. 'He himself is a pauper and has nothing apart from a hut and a shed,' Zdykhovsky noted in the report. Nikodim then gave brief biographies of his siblings, and the secretary wrote down that his brother Mykyta served the old regime. He underlined it.

The next question appeared out of nowhere. Zdykhovsky asked whether Nikodim Berezko admitted to being a member of a counter-revolutionary organisation, the aim of which was to create an independent Ukraine. Wasn't he recruited into this organisation in 1936 by Iakov Vashlenko, a former Red Guard and Nikodim Berezko's former commander? Didn't Vashlenko, as the director of said organisation, gather people at his house for anti-Soviet conversations? Nikodim denied everything. He said that if they spoke negatively of Soviet power at times, it was because of financial difficulties and problems with food supply in the village. They thought that some local Communist leaders didn't respect the Red Guards despite their sacrifices, and how could they think otherwise when they were denied benefits and removed from positions of authority.

He said that neither he nor Vashlenko agitated people against the Soviet government. If they vented, it was only to each other. He said that he didn't know of Vashlenko's involvement in any anti-Soviet organisations. He signed his statement.

The interrogations continued.

The questions continued.

The probing continued.

Then Nikodim broke down.

He mentioned that one day as he read a newspaper, Vashlenko had interrupted him and said that in 1933 the famine was created on purpose by the Soviet government to force people onto the collective farms and crush the resistance of those who didn't want to join. Nikodim said that he disagreed with Vashlenko and said so, but that Vashlenko countered that the Soviet government took grain away from Ukraine when people needed it the most and sold it for hard currency abroad.

At first, Nikodim confessed to participation in the counter-revolutionary movement created by his former Red Guard commander, Vashlenko. Then he admitted his role as one of the masterminds of the anti-Soviet uprising – though he continued to deny that any of his neighbours were involved.

Did Nikodim believe that by giving some information to the interrogator, the tortures would stop and he would be left alone? It was a mistake that many accused made, not realising – or not willing to believe – that their accusation was dictated by the needs of the state to unmask the so-called enemies. Nikodim's actual misdeed was irrelevant. The only goal was a confession and more names.

In subsequent interrogations Nikodim gave names. He listed his neighbours Kovtun, Bondar and Burlaka as members he recruited into his anti-Soviet organisation. The interrogator noted that they all sang 'The Glory and the Freedom of Ukraine Has Not Yet Perished', 'the bourgeois-nationalist anthem'.

Having the confession and the names, the interrogator pushed Nikodim to admit that their group was receiving orders from higher-ups in Dnipropetrovsk and the instructions were allegedly delivered by the brother of his neighbour Trofim Chervony, who passed them to Nikodim under the guise of selling fishnets. Nikodim was presented with Vashlenko's confession that mentioned the fishnets and secret messages from Dnipropetrovsk.

Nikodim read Vashlenko's statement. Then he admitted to being one of the recruiters for the Trotskyist conspiracy to undermine the Soviet government and establish an independent Ukraine. He signed his confession.

NKVD records captured only a small portion of what had transpired in the room between the accused and the interrogator. Missing was the psychological pressure to cajole the accused into making a confession. Also missing was the torture. The Poltava NKVD in the 1930s had a reputation for its elaborate arsenal of 'enhanced interrogation' methods.

The fly buzzing around the room hit the window sharply. I started and looked up. In the distance I could see the grey blocks of the penitentiary buildings topped with barbed wire. In front of me were dark yellow pages filled with neat round handwriting and a signature, 'Nikodim Berezko'.

The NKVD files were a mixture of lies and bits of truth, and I followed the archivist's advice to read between the lines. Yet I knew that some parts of the files weren't invented. It dawned on me suddenly that Sergiy often talked about Nikodim. Bits of conversations returned to my memory with such clarity that it seemed as if someone had thrown open the window and let in the bright light. This realisation was so astonishing that I got up from the table and walked up and down the room.

Sergiy had five brothers, one of whom, Fedir, died as a soldier during the Second World War. Since my great-grandfather simply said 'my brother' when he talked about his sibling, I assumed that it was the fallen hero Fedir that Sergiy revisited in his recollections. I remembered him telling me a story about his older brother who was seventeen when he joined the Red Guards, the first one in the family, and how he forbade the twelve-year-old Sergiy from leaving his sisters behind, saying that he was the bright mind and that his role was to teach, not fight.

I opened my notebook and scrutinised the dates and events. Beyond a shadow of a doubt, the brother Sergiy mentioned couldn't have been anyone other than Nikodim. Sergiy talked with pride about *the brother* who had returned wounded from the Civil War and had applied himself so diligently to his unfinished studies that he not only obtained a school diploma but finished his Workers' College courses in the University of Poltava. The Maiachka records told me that the rest of the brothers remained on the collective farm in Maiachka, the same farm to which they eventually gave up their land. Nikodim and Sergiy were the ones who left for Poltava and pursued teaching.

Growing up around Sergiy, I heard his stories so many times that I either took them for granted or ignored them. But the older I grew, the more I argued with him. I was tired of his didactic stories painting the world as a cruel place that needed Communism as a solution. Even Sergiy's mentions of Cossack honour and bravery began to seem quaint and contrived. 'What did this revolution of yours achieve?' I said one day. 'Endless parades and endless lines?' I hated the mandatory marches to mark the Revolution of 1917 even more than standing in lines. The final years of the Soviet era were a time of endemic shortages, when even basic goods like toilet paper disappeared from store shelves. When that happened, we cut up old issues of *Pravda*. Sergiy was the only one who used it for its original intended purpose. In 1989, I couldn't understand why someone would give up everything for the wreck of the country in which we were living. Asya's cynicism was closer to my own. After I left Ukraine, Sergiy's stories faded from my memory.

Returning to Bereh, I had no difficulty hearing Asya's voice. The more I thought about her and the more I walked along the paths of the garden she had planted, the more I recalled our night-time talks and details about her life. But Sergiy's stories remained elusive.

I sat down at the table and picked up the file again. As I read more, I remembered some of them. The bitter irony of discovering his voice thanks to NKVD documents gave me pause, but I was too overwhelmed by the flood of recollections to dwell on it. The fragments were coming together to form patterns. I recalled how I once complained about Ukrainian language homework at school, mentioning that I didn't understand why I had to waste time on a language I didn't use at home. Sergiy was reclining on the seat of a decommissioned armoured vehicle that served as our yard chair. He shook his head and said that while language was not what made a person, it was the tongue my ancestors spoke. People were willing to die for the right to speak the Ukrainian language, he continued, as his older brother did, who perished fighting for a free Ukraine. The exact phrase Sergiy used was 'died fighting for "vilna Ukraina".' He said it firmly, enunciating every word and placing an emphasis on 'vilna'. Like Asya, Sergiy spoke Ukrainian to me. 'Vilna' meant free, liberated, but also independent and autonomous. Several years after we had had this conversation, Ukraine became an independent country, and the word 'vilna' acquired a different connotation for me. Back then, however, I had so little awareness of any national identity other than being Soviet that I couldn't have made the connection. I assumed that Sergiy was talking about Fedir, who died during the forcing of the Dnieper in 1943, and I grew embarrassed by my selfish whining. The story had a moralistic angle, but that day as Sergiy mentioned his brother, he grew quiet and sat for a long while lost in thought.

'Brother Nikodim, vanished in the 1930s fighting for a *free* Ukraine,' wrote Sergiy in his blue journal. For *vilna* Ukraina.

Sergiy wasn't one to use words casually. This trait of his was another recent discovery for me. Going over his teaching manuals or his letters, I was struck by the precision and clarity of his prose. He appreciated the power of words. During the war, Sergiy served as a zampolitruk, a political commissar in charge of the ideological education of the troops in his division. As the Red Army suffered a series of defeats in the early years of the Second World War, the political commissars became influential figures within their units. A political commissar was part chaplain, part propagandist, and one of Sergiy's responsibilities was to find the right words to boost the morale of the soldiers.

If Sergiy wanted to mention his brother who died during the Second World War, he would have used a cliché like 'died in battle with the Nazi occupiers'. But 'died fighting for a "free Ukraine"' had a completely different ring. Sergiy could only have been talking about Nikodim.

That was how I saw that not everything about the file was a lie. I also knew that Nikodim died halfway through his incarceration, because while the interrogation reports continued, they lost all semblance of truth.

I had read through the first part of the file so quickly that

I hadn't noticed that some parts were crossed out and rewritten. For instance, the counter-revolutionary organisation that Nikodim allegedly joined was at first defined as a Trotskyist conspiracy against the Communist Party and the Soviet state. 'Trotskyist conspiracy' was then crossed out and another hand wrote in: 'a Bourgeois-Nationalist organisation aiming to establish an independent Ukraine'. In another section, Vashlenko was described as commenting that the Trotskyist programme suited the Soviet peasants better than the current Communist Party ideology. The paragraph was crossed out and rewritten to say that Vashlenko had suggested that the Trotskyist programme was better for the Ukrainian peasantry than the Soviet regime. And so on. As Ukrainian nationalism became the main evil to be unmasked and destroyed, Nikodim's case had to fit the new storyline. After all, someone heard him sing the forbidden Ukrainian anthem and he didn't deny it.

From interrogation to interrogation, the case grew in magnitude and absurdity. The organisation became not simply a counter-revolutionary group, but a plot to undermine the entire Soviet state. Besides Nikodim, Vashlenko, Trofim, Kovtun, Bondar and Burlaka, new people were added to the list: anyone who had the misfortune of being close to the accused – their neighbours, the godparents of their children, their collective farm co-workers. Vashlenko was quoted as saying that the government was easy to destroy as long as everyone did something about it. So Trofim's uncle, who had broken the collective farm's mowing machine, was charged with being part of the Lozuvatka counter-revolutionary organisation and a saboteur. Another family member was arrested and accused of maliciously planting forest seedlings in such a way that they withered. Nikodim's supposed role evolved from a recruiter to an agitator, who as a schoolteacher had instilled anti-Soviet thoughts into the young, malleable minds of his pupils.

Later, as Stalin grew concerned about the USSR's borderlands and the international situation, the NKVD changed its rationale and Nikodim's case once again had to be revised. The documents framed Nikodim and Vashlenko's activities as a counter-revolutionary conspiracy to establish a bourgeois Ukrainian state supported by 'the fascist powers in Germany and Poland'. Their coup was to be timed to 'the start of the war between the USSR and the capitalist nations'. The organisation was discovered to have leaders and cells all over eastern Ukraine, reaching as far as the Black Sea shores of Odesa. According to the file, between 1931 and 1934 the Lozuvatka cell raised money for the foreign powers and through their Dnipropetrovsk contacts transferred money abroad to import weapons. A deposition mentioning the confiscation of a broken rifle from Trofim's home was duly included. Another document attached to the file was an interrogation of Nikodim's cellmate, a Pole, who said that during their incarceration Nikodim boasted of being part of a planned coup that received support and ideological directives from Germany and Poland.

However, Nikodim's case never went to trial, because he died by suicide after one of the interrogations. Or so the file said.

I read the warden's statement. Nikodim returned to his cell at 1.30 a.m. on 11 September 1937. At 6.30 a.m. he was awakened by the warden along with the rest of the prisoners. At 8.30 a.m. he received bread for breakfast. Nikodim asked the warden for matches. When the warden came with tea a few minutes later, he discovered Nikodim hanging from the 'grates of the door'. The warden found no sign of life in the body and determined that the arrested had hanged himself from a piece of lining he had torn out of his jacket. The statement concluded that during the interrogations the arrested behaved calmly and betrayed no suicidal intentions.

The details were many and they were too suspicious in their careful enumeration. Why did Nikodim ask for matches when he was planning suicide? Why did he decide to hang himself in the short interval between receiving his bread and the morning tea? Most of the NKVD interrogations happened in the late hours because sleep deprivation was a common technique. Presumably, Nikodim could have realised his plan at any time during the day – and not at the precise moment when he was most likely to be discovered. Moreover, since the grates of the door were located at eye level, hanging oneself from them would have been complicated. I read between the lines and the suicide story sounded as false as the idea that poor ploughmen and illiterate pig farmers sent money to Germany with plans to overthrow the Soviet government.

Eight people were charged with participation in the Lozuvatka conspiracy. The purported masterminds, Vashlenko and Trofim, were sentenced to hard labour, while the people they recruited, Kovtun, Bondar and Burlaka, were arrested and shot on 16 November 1937. No logic existed in the Soviet penal system. Perhaps the NKVD needed to fill their November execution quotas. By then, Nikodim was dead, whether by his own hand or someone else's. To the rest of the world, he simply vanished.

∼

I reached the end of the documents in the main file, but the folder contained more pages. One of them was a letter written on unlined paper that said, 'My husband, Nikodim Berezko, born in 1900 in the village of Maiachka, a participant in the Red Guard movement during the Civil War, most recently working as the head teacher of a Lozuvatka primary school,

Dnipropetrovsk region. On 24 August 1937, he was taken away by the constables of the Poltava region, for reasons unknown. When I went to Poltava to seek a meeting with him, I was told that he had been moved to Kharkiv. Since then, I haven't had any news about him. I plead with you to tell me why he was taken away and what happened to him. Fekla Berezko.'

The letter was dated 1955. Stalin was dead. Nikolai Yezhov, who had been appointed as the head of the NKVD in 1936 to lead the purges, was executed in 1940 for anti-Soviet activities. Lavrentiy Beria replaced Yezhov in 1938, and his own execution in 1953 bore a striking resemblance to the death of his predecessor.

For the first time since I had opened the file, I wanted to sob. The shameless, blatant lies that seeped through every line clung to me like leeches. The file reduced me to a spectator: mute, numb, helpless. I understood why Valentina was afraid of digging into the past. With each page of the file, I came not to the light, but deeper into the darkness, a darkness filled with disturbing, unanswerable questions.

I always thought that the most corrosive effect of the Soviet system was the hypocrisy. Everyone said one thing and thought something else. It was the most sensible way to behave if you wanted to survive. The hypocrisy was everywhere. It was in the cafeteria menu listing soup with meat that – as everyone knew – wasn't there. It was in the newspapers announcing that no accident had occurred at the Chernobyl nuclear power plant. It was in the slogans, signs and demonstrations. 'We pretended to work and they pretended to pay us,' ran a joke in the 1980s. Soviet life was permeated with such pretences, big and small.

Reading Nikodim's file, I saw that the absence of truth, rather than the presence of lies, was even more dangerous. The fog of lies and half-truths made it difficult to orient oneself, to use one's personal moral compass to analyse the situation. The universe defined by Soviet propaganda was one of crooked mirrors that warped reality. Words ossified into clichéd phrases and slogans lost all meaning. What meaning did the word 'democracy' possess when it was used to describe Stalin's Constitution – 'the most democratic in the world'. The Orwellian language of 'brotherly assistance' and 'liberation' hid occupations. 'Disarming dangerous elements' meant passing a sentence without evidence or trial. The labels 'saboteurs', 'wreckers', 'rootless cosmopolitans' and 'enemies of the people' transformed human beings into raw material to be removed, weeds to be cleared from a field.

Fekla's poignant letter reminded me why I had started my quest for Nikodim in the first place. I wanted to pay tribute to a relative who had been reduced to a crossed-out name in the archives. I wanted to commemorate his life, fragile and full of pain. I wanted his tragedy to be acknowledged – and as I saw it now, it was a tragedy that befell the whole family when he disappeared.

When Nikodim vanished in 1937, he left behind a wife and two children. According to Soviet law, the family of the accused was guilty by association, and after 1935 children from the age of twelve could be sentenced as adults and interned in the gulags. Fekla was spared such trials, but her life in a small village, in an atmosphere of fear and suspicion, with two young children and no means to survive, must have been a nightmare. She had to leave Lozuvatka soon after Nikodim's disappearance. She went to Maiachka, where her husband's brothers lived. Did they also fear being associated with her? Did they believe that Nikodim had done something wrong? She lived apart from the family in Maiachka. Whose punishment was more severe? His, dying that same year, or hers, continuing to live as the wife of 'the accused'? She and her children would be reminded of their status every time they crossed the threshold of a government institution or applied for work. Finally, the most sadistic torture was to conceal from someone what had happened to their loved one and why.

When Fekla sent her letter in 1955, the newspapers began writing about mass amnesties after the death of Stalin. In another cruel twist to the story, she would have to wait for seven years to learn her husband's fate. In 1962, Nikodim's case was at last pronounced as lacking 'a criminal matter', and the file included a standard certificate of rehabilitation, along with a statement revealing Nikodim's suicide and a bland line of condolences.

All people accused of the Lozuvatka conspiracy were rehabilitated 'due to the lack of a criminal matter' or 'due to the lack of a proof of guilt'. All but one received their rehabilitation posthumously. The only person to emerge alive from the ordeal was Trofim's brother, the unfortunate fishnet salesman, who survived ten years of hard labour.

Nikodim's file looked thin relative to the other folders I saw on Elena Ivanovna's desk, but it appeared to me like a well of misery. I didn't know if it had an end – there were more pages after Fekla's letter.

In 1993, Nikodim's son, Nikolai Berezko, by now a fifty-nine-year-old man living in the newly independent Russia and approaching retirement age, wrote to the Security Service of the newly independent Ukraine (USBU, as it was then known) explaining that he needed a certificate of Nikodim Berezko's rehabilitation. Their family had never received it, but he knew that his father was innocent. Nikolai was applying for pension benefits, but he was told that his papers couldn't be processed without proof of his father's rehabilitation. Even after the end of the Soviet Union, children were held responsible for the crimes of their fathers. Nikolai also wanted to know how his father had died and where he was buried.

Nikolai received a reply. He was notified that the certificate of rehabilitation was given to Fekla Berezko in 1962. The USBU had no knowledge of the burial places, the letter said, not mentioning that the corpses from the NKVD prisons were dumped into a sand canyon outside Poltava. 'Unfortunately, this is all we know about the tragic fate of your father, a victim of the Stalinist repression,' the letter concluded.

In 1995 Nikolai sent another letter begging the authorities to send him the certificate of rehabilitation, which he needed to receive his pension benefits. 'It's not possible to obtain anything without this certificate,' he wrote. 'I implore you to send it to me.'

The next reply to Nikolai explained that since his family should have received the certificate of rehabilitation, he needed not the certificate of rehabilitation but a duplicate of the certificate of rehabilitation, 'a completely different document, necessitating an inquiry at the public prosecutor's office of the Poltava region'. For his father's death certificate, he had to write a letter to the civil registration office of his father's last place of residence.

Nikolai followed this Kafkaesque trail and wrote letters to the public prosecutor and the assorted public prosecutor office divisions in Poltava. He wrote to the civil registration offices. He wrote again to the USBU, which by then had become the SBU. He included copies of all correspondence but was sent deeper into a morass of bureaucracy. 'I beg you, gentlemen, help me,' he wrote in his last letter. 'I can't receive my pension benefits without this form.' Nikodim had vanished more than half a century ago, but his tragic tale continued to haunt those near to him.

Nikolai's call for help was the last page of the file. I didn't learn if Nikolai ever received the document confirming that his father was innocent, but his ordeal eerily resembled Nikodim's travails in proving his Red Guard status half a century earlier.

On the reverse of the paper cover, someone included a careful tally of the pages included in the file. Ninety-one. Or 102 including Nikolai's letters. Elena Ivanovna mentioned that I needed to fill out a form identifying my access to the file. It would increase that count to 103. I had originally believed that each file contained a single fate, but I was wrong. Each file in that office contained many destinies and maintained its own secret life.

If I multiplied this story by the number of Great Terror victims, the magnitude of the pain and horror was incomprehensible. Between 1937 and 1938 more than 190,000 people were arrested in Ukraine alone. The purges claimed more than a million lives. 'When you cut down the forest, woodchips fly,' Yezhov said as he directed the juggernaut of the NKVD. That by 1938 he himself was among the dead timber brought me no consolation.

I signed my name on the line in the file, handed it to the officer in charge of the KGB archives and rushed out of the prison to find myself back in the bright summer day of Poltava. I could not read one more line of the file. I needed to breathe deeply and leave behind the darkness that clung to me.

I wanted to hear Valentina's voice. I reached into my bag and found my phone. 'Babushka, I'm coming home,' I said. I heard the rustle of leaves and realised that my grandmother was in the orchard and that I needed to be there with her.

$\sim$

I had photographed the file with permission of the officer, and several days later, Valentina and I read it together. We talked about Nikodim when I first returned home, but neither one of us wanted to look at the documents. Then as time went by,

Valentina asked me more questions, and so I downloaded the photographs and showed them to her.

She listened to my explanations and sometimes asked me to repeat the dates or people's names, but apart from that, she said nothing. We sat side by side at the dining table, and as the hours slid by, dusk and heavy silence enveloped us. The thick glass of the window made the world outside appear hazy. The tea roses trailing along the fence glowed crimson as the shadows thickened. Valentina was staring somewhere into the corner, playing with the arms of her reading glasses.

I was about to shut the computer when Valentina stopped my hand and said, 'Poor Nikolai! These letters of his asking for proof of his father's rehabilitation are heartbreaking. The organisation might change its name ten thousand times, but it's still the same cruel, inhuman machine. It was like that in the Soviet Union. It remains like that in independent Ukraine. I still can't believe that anyone was willing to help you find this archive. Are you sure you're not concealing something from me? Did you give them a bribe?' Valentina looked hard into my eyes. When I was a child, this gaze of hers made me break down and spill all my secrets, but now my conscience was clear and I held her stare.

'I didn't give anyone a penny,' I said. 'The people I encountered were genuinely helpful.'

'Sergiy would have been proud of you. Another thing I thought of when reading Nikolai's letters was Sergiy's own struggle to obtain his pension,' she said.

As a war veteran and an invalid, my great-grandfather was entitled to a supplement, but as Valentina explained, he was denied it on the grounds that he lacked certain documents. He wrote letters to officials and they responded asking for further documentation of his injury and his participation in the war effort. When one paper was obtained, another document was needed, and the rigmarole went on without an end in sight. Sergiy was partially successful in obtaining his pension, but he remained ineligible for the supplement. Valentina's eyes were red, and she turned towards the window, wiping her cheek with the back of her hand.

'But Sergiy retained his belief in Communism, despite the injustices he suffered. It made Asya so angry at times, this stubborn loyalty of his,' Valentina said through tears.

'You were right about this search being painful and even dangerous,' I said, hugging my grandmother. I had thought that knowing more would elucidate things, but it also threw into relief the ugly reality of life. The past into which I delved for stories was a repository of pain for her. The more I experienced this anguish and misery at various junctures of my search, the more I understood my grandmother's reluctance to open that Pandora's box.

My grandmother rubbed her face as if trying to shake herself out of a daze and said, 'All this time you were searching for Nikodim, I kept hoping that you would find nothing and give up. I underestimated how important it was to know the truth, whatever that truth might be. Once I came to this realisation, I only hoped that the truth wouldn't harm you.'

We watched the shadows fill the yard beyond the window. The lightbulb flickered. The old wall clock measured out seconds in tinny beats.

'Asya couldn't forget about the famine of the 1930s and Sergiy couldn't forget about his brother,' Valentina said softly, as if talking to herself.

I thought then that when they aren't told, the stories of painful events turn into black holes that devour everything around them. The traumas can't be seen, but the gravity surrounding them becomes so strong that it absorbs everything in their proximity.

'The deeper Asya and Sergiy buried their stories, the more their secrets troubled them,' I said, and Valentina nodded.

From the window we could see the yellow glow of streetlamps. Valentina got up from her chair and pulled the stiffly starched curtain closed. She was convinced that the neighbours spied on us through the windows once the lights were on. The dark paranoia, our inheritance from the Soviet era, was hard to discard.

'Did you notice that Nikodim never mentioned Sergiy?' Valentina asked, sitting down next to me again. I admitted that I hadn't. The realisation that Sergiy had talked about his brother was so staggering that I missed the lacuna in Nikodim's file. We scrolled through the photographs again, enlarging the pages with Nikodim's biography. 'See here, Nikodim mentioned having only six siblings – Mykyta, Fedir, Nestir, Ivan, Oksana and Odarka. He didn't mention his youngest brother, Sergiy.' My grandmother tapped the screen. Sergiy was mentioned nowhere in the file. Did Nikodim omit him because he was worried that the shadow of his arrest might fall onto his brother, who by then was making steady progress up the career ladder? The NKVD could have found him anyway had they wanted – and as Asya's personal dossier showed, they eventually did – but the absence of Sergiy's name in Nikodim's file seemed significant. As did Sergiy's mention of Nikodim in his diary. Some mysteries remained despite my efforts to uncover them.

Thirteen

Valentina went to bed early, leaving me alone with Nikodim's file. I read it again. I thought that the more I examined it, the more it would reveal to me. The archivist told me to read between the lines, to look for omissions and inconsistencies. Then I noticed it.

'He left no note.' A line in blue ink appeared under the prison warden's report detailing Nikodim's suicide. I enlarged my blurry photograph and read the sentence again to make sure that I hadn't misunderstood.

'He left no note.'

Neither did my father.

The thought triggered a fuse in my brain that detonated an explosion in my chest. The walls around me vanished and the ceiling collapsed. Eyes glued to the computer screen, I put my hands over my mouth to stifle a scream, though I wasn't sure if any sound would emerge. I did everything to suppress the recollection. I obliterated the memory as much as I could, but it remained deep inside me. Now it rushed to the surface and the pain overwhelmed me.

My husband and I were watching *The Leopard* one evening when I received a call from my stepmother, Karina. She and I spoke on the phone every other week, often during her afternoon coffee breaks. After she and my father moved to California, they found work at a medical supply factory in the Bay Area, bought a house and even arranged to ship their two dogs from Kyiv to San Francisco. 'You become responsible for ever for what you've tamed,' my father said, but I wondered whether he truly understood what the Little Prince meant, because in many ways my father didn't abide by this philosophy.

My parents married within a month of meeting each other. My mother was a university student, and my father was a handsome acquaintance of her best friend, Lana. He had black hair that fell in soft waves around his cheeks and the large brown eyes of an Indian movie star. He courted my mother by showering her with flowers, and the intensity of his infatuation won her heart. Valentina had misgivings about the marriage, because she couldn't understand how her future son-in-law, who didn't have steady employment, planned to support his family. My mother wouldn't listen to her objections. For their honeymoon, my father proposed a trip to Georgia, where the newlyweds rented a small house on the beach and drank red Kindzmarauli wine while watching the sunset over the Black Sea. My mother's letters back home waxed poetic about her husband's ability to brew Turkish coffee and play guitar.

These skills, however, weren't enough to make their family life harmonious when the couple returned to Kyiv. They had to share a two-room apartment with my father's mother, Daria, and his older brothers, Vladimir and Valery. Tight living arrangements complicated daily life, but the worst part was that my mother discovered that she had nothing in common with my father. He didn't even try to take her wishes or feelings into account. 'All men are selfish,' Daria used to say. At first my mother was too proud to reveal to her parents that her marriage was a failure from the start and she tried to make the relationship work, but after almost a decade she knew that it was time to leave.

My parents divorced when I was eight years old. After the Chernobyl accident in April 1986, my mother pulled me out of the local school and took me to Bereh. The Poltava region was considered safe and I stayed with Asya and Sergiy until the autumn. Then my mother enrolled me into a boarding school in Crimea, and when I returned to Kyiv at the end of the year, my parents were living with different people on opposite sides of the city. Even with the strained family composition, they gathered to celebrate my return, pretending that nothing dramatic had occurred.

I was confused and upset, though I instantly liked my Azeri stepmother, Karina. She included me in every trip she took with my father and invited me to stay with them. I decided that the parties responsible for the divorce were my mother and her tall blond mathematician, Alex. My father promised that when I turned fourteen, I could live with him and Karina, and while it meant waiting six long years, we would see each other every weekend. I couldn't wait to turn fourteen.

At first, my father would pick me up every weekend from Alex's house, where my mother and I moved after I returned from Crimea, and take me to our old apartment. He would then take a nap, while I read English books with Karina, painted with Daria or practised yoga with Vladimir.

Then the visits became rarer. My father promised to come but never did. At first, I waited. Then I stopped expecting him. When I turned fourteen, my father never mentioned me living with him and Karina, and by then I wouldn't have wanted to anyway. Alex was the one who watched my school dance performances, helped me with maths homework and inspired my wanderlust and fascination with languages.

After my father and Karina moved to the US two years after I did, I visited them in California during my university holidays. Karina and I could talk about books and movies for hours and we took long trips to explore San Francisco, but I had little in common with my father. Sometimes I felt that being alone with me made him uncomfortable. I waited for him to explain something or say something that would make everything fall into place. But he never did. He wasn't part of any meaningful event in my life. He didn't congratulate me on graduating *summa cum laude*; he didn't cheer me when I received a full scholarship from Yale; he didn't attend my wedding. Sometimes he didn't respond to my invitations; sometimes I didn't offer them. In those rare moments when my mother complained about my father, she called him 'indifferent'. It may not have sounded like a damning accusation, but for her it was, and with time I understood its full gravity. Indifference can inflict more damage than crude betrayal.

I distanced myself from him. My father was busy with his own interests and he seemed reasonably comfortable in his new American life. He didn't need me.

The first year I started working as a freelance journalist was exciting. I travelled, gathering materials about the fragrance industry, interviewed perfumers and tracked down farmers in far-off places. I kept in touch with Karina, but after my last trip to California, I rarely spoke to my father. Karina updated him on my adventures, so if he wanted to reach out, he knew where to find me. One day he emailed me out of the blue asking if I could look at photographs of a few houses and offer my opinion.

He sent me a zip file with the three-dimensional blueprints of identical-looking houses, sketches of solar panels and information about green energy. He even called me to talk about the California real estate market, boasting that he had figured out how to make the system work. He said that he was going to hit a gold mine and that he would buy a house for me and my husband in California. He said that we would travel together as we once did and that all of us would return to Ukraine and repair our cottage in Hlibivka. I hardly listened to him, irritated by yet another incomprehensible switch of my father's personality. He had made so many empty promises to me before that I had run out of faith. It hurt less if I kept my expectations low, so I said that I had to leave for work.

When Karina called a couple of weeks later, I motioned to my husband to mute the television. He paused the film, leaving the image of Burt Lancaster and Claudia Cardinale frozen in a blurred waltz.

'Hi, Karina,' I said. 'Aren't you supposed to be at work?' With our three-hour time difference, I knew that she should have been at the office.

'Your father shot himself,' she said. I didn't understand her and I wanted to say so, but my lips were fused shut. Cold paralysis took over my throat, my chest, my arms, my legs. I was sitting in front of a round Turkish table I used for writing and for making kutaby, paper-thin Azeri breads filled with herbs, the way Karina taught me. Bits of dried flour were stuck in the grain of wood and I suddenly thought that I needed to scour the table.

'Your father shot himself.' Karina repeated, with an edge of accusation.

'Your father shot himself,' she said, a third time.

'He didn't leave a note.' She was crying. I heard the dogs barking in the distance. There are moments between sleep and

227

awakening that are surreal. You wonder, will it end, and if it will, what will happen? I grew up reading fairy tales and I never lost the belief that after a nightmare, there must be a dreamy awakening. But sometimes a nightmare is endless. I didn't cry. I stared ahead of me at the table. Then I howled like a wounded animal. I wanted to scream, but the sound that came out was a howl. This is the only thing I remember.

I don't remember flying to California for the funeral. I don't remember how I made a speech about my father at the service, because everyone else was too shocked to say anything. I don't remember it but I was told that my speech was moving. I don't remember the cemetery. I don't remember the ceremony. I don't remember how I told my stepmother that I wanted nothing of my father's inheritance. I refused to accept it as I refused to accept my father's departure. He left without explaining anything. It was his biggest betrayal, and I couldn't forgive him. The pain I felt was so intense that I couldn't reminisce about my father. I decided to forget him. I decided to leave everything behind. A year later, my husband and I left the US and moved to Belgium to start a new life in a new country.

～

Nikodim's departure left a black hole, just as my father's had.

I stared at the laptop. Then I did something that only a year earlier I would have been afraid to do. I put my father's name into my email inbox and clicked 'search'. Strings of archived messages came up. I read them, remembering what happened before and what happened after. My father's emails were brief and few. Vladimir's messages also came up. They were longer. At first, he was asking why my father wasn't responding to his emails. Then when he learned about the tragedy, he began to console me. I remembered that we also spoke on the telephone during those early days and that he encouraged me to remain strong. Vladimir was my biggest source of resilience during those first terrible weeks because he was close to my father and me and understood us better than we did each other.

One of the last emails from Vladimir around that time concerned our pact. We agreed that until I was strong enough to process what happened to my father, he would not bring him up again. I didn't know when this moment would come, but my grief was so profound that it froze everything inside of me.

The night receded and lingered behind me only in the dark shadows near my unmade bed. Through the gaps in the shutters, I could see the lavender shimmer of sunrise. I could hear Valentina tossing in the bedroom next door, sighing in her sleep. The pile of notes I had written while reading Nikodim's file sat on the table. My writing was jagged and uncertain. I thought that the Rooster House trapped my grandparents and frightened them into submission, but as I sat in front of the messages from another time, I realised that I too was trapped. I couldn't confront my fears and my pain. I buried them. And they sprouted in the darkness of oblivion into something that was stifling me. I could change continents, countries and cities, but how could I escape when every bar in my cell was constructed by me? I was so afraid to be abandoned that I abandoned myself and my memories. You cannot escape what you pretend doesn't hold you. You cannot be free if you are afraid of confronting reality.

Every departure leaves a void. In Ukraine, on the Monday after Easter, people return to the cemetery to share a meal with their departed loved ones. They set up tables right in the graveyard and for one day a year they commune with the dead, remembering them, forgiving them and asking their forgiveness and help. I never once thought of offering my father a share of that meal. I never forgave him for leaving. So I forbade myself to grieve.

I needed to speak with Vladimir. Confronting what I feared was one way to escape the trap. Another was to seek forgiveness and make peace.

PART 5

The Caves
and Mysteries

Fourteen

'Trapped but not caught' was how Vladimir described himself. He and my grandmother Daria were spending the summer holidays in her native village in Russia when they learned that Hitler had declared war on the Soviet Union. The advance of the German troops was so rapid that Daria couldn't return to Kyiv. The village was occupied and they were cut off from the rest of the world.

One day Vladimir developed a fever and then felt a strange stiffness invade his body from his legs and all the way to his neck. A neighbour told Daria that a German doctor in another village was treating patients and she brought Vladimir to see him. The doctor was tall and wore small round glasses, and when he bent to take Vladimir's temperature, the boy saw his own reflection in the lenses. 'Polio,' the doctor said, waving for another patient to come in. 'Er ist so gut wie tot.' He is as good as dead.

But Vladimir didn't die. He didn't die as he burned in fever.

He didn't die as he lost all sensation in his limbs. He didn't die when the villagers scalded him with boiling water, trying to resuscitate his lifeless legs. He lay on the bench in his grandparents' dark hut and watched the termites burrow holes in the wooden pillars that supported the walls. Without opening his eyes, he knew from the sound of the cricket in the corner whether it was morning or evening. He could tell by the smell of the bread whether it included more sawdust than usual. When he learned to move his fingers, he could tell the weather by the texture of the clay wall that was his constant companion. When spring came, Daria carried him to the forest where he felt grass growing under him. To escape the trap of his ailing body, he turned to his own dream world and used his imagination to fill the void.

After the war ended, Daria and Vladimir returned to Kyiv. He had treatments and multiple operations, which the Soviet medical establishment – and Vladimir himself – considered a great success. He learned to stand and walk, but he could never fully straighten his crooked spine, nor could he use the right side of his body. His thin frame remained contorted by polio, with the top of his body leaning forwards and to the left as if he were in a boxer's stance. When Vladimir walked, he hobbled. When he needed to use his right hand, he picked it up with his left. But his fingers moved so deftly that he could take apart and put together the most complicated machinery.

Vladimir's fascination with mechanical devices was inspired by a neighbour, a military captain, who, taking pity on a sick boy, gave Vladimir a Fotokor-1, a folding-bed plate camera, and taught him the basics of photography. Taking a cue from its name – Fotokor was an abbreviation for 'photojournalist' in Russian – Vladimir recorded everything around him. He then asked his father for books about film and sound recording and copied the designs of different components in a notebook. He dreamed of studying engineering and at school he took extra-curricular lessons in physics and technical drawing.

However, when the admission committee of the engineering faculty saw Vladimir, they rejected his application. 'Can you even hold a pen?' someone mocked him. 'Try physics.' Vladimir suffered the same humiliation at the physics department. His extreme disability made people think that they need not even feign kindness. But Vladimir neither took offence nor accepted failure. He applied to the economics faculty of the University of Agriculture and was accepted. Like Valentina, he thought that playing with numbers was innocuous. He later became a senior accountant at a machine factory.

During my childhood, Vladimir no longer worked and lived off his disability pension. He had already sojourned in jail on charges of 'capitalist propaganda', an episode of his life he didn't conceal. I even suspected that he thought of this experience as a personal achievement, showing he could be just like others. He credited his ability to lead such a 'normal life' to yoga, and his room was outfitted with a wide platform bed on which he slept and practised asanas. As a child, I loved his abode for its fascinating collection of medical posters, books in languages I couldn't understand and jars with fermenting vegetables and sprouting seeds. He treated me to his sour fizzy drink concoctions, which he claimed to be elixirs of life, and he taught me yoga exercises. When Vladimir wasn't in medita-tion, he disassembled radios. His bookshelves were filled with samizdat publications on Ayurveda and manuals for semi-conductor devices.

My father shared the same interest in technology, and I also remembered him building transistor radios. However, he didn't have Vladimir's persistence and he flitted from project to project, never finishing anything. The half-finished plans and associated bundles of wires accumulated in our apartment before my mother either threw them away or gave them to Vladimir to use in his own experiments.

After Ukraine became independent, Vladimir moved to Israel with his former wife and his daughter. Though they had been divorced for more than two decades, his former wife insisted that he accompany them. In Tel Aviv, he still repaired electronic devices, experimented with Ayurvedic recipes, studied Hebrew and practised yoga.

When I read our exchanges after my father's death, I scrolled to the winter of 2013 and retraced our correspondence up to the day when our disagreements turned into a rift. I read each message carefully, his responses and my own.

What struck me this time was not the nature of his comments, but rather the memory of my vehement reaction to them two years ago. Since then, I had already spent long enough in Ukraine to know that even my grandmother, who considered herself a patriot, missed some aspects of life under the Soviet Union. I had met people who lost all stability and security after 1989 and for whom capitalism was a cruel farce. Placing Vladimir's opinions in that context made them less outrageous than they once appeared to me, even if his dismissal of the tragic famine of the 1930s still stung. The truth was that Vladimir was family, and I missed him.

However, reconnecting with him turned out to be as complicated as finding Nikodim. My paternal grandmother and Vladimir's middle brother had long passed away. My cousin in Tel Aviv was much older and we were never close. Vladimir was the only person from my father's family with whom I kept in touch, but our communication had always been virtual, and its dangerously fragile nature revealed itself in the bounced-back emails and undelivered messages. His phone number was out of service. He was nowhere to be found.

My mother combed her old notes for any contacts from her married days and she sent me the list of addresses in Kyiv. I told Valentina that I would be leaving for a few days to stay at Lola's apartment and booked a train ticket. My grandmother knew that Vladimir and I had a falling-out, and it troubled her. When my parents were still married and lived with Vladimir and Daria, Valentina visited often and grew to know Vladimir. She no longer kept in touch with my father's side of the family, but she chided me for losing patience with my uncle. 'Blood is thicker than water, and you two deserve each other,' she repeated whenever the subject of our fight came up. 'To argue about a country that no longer exists! It sounds like a joke.'

But not being able to get in touch with Vladimir was no light matter for me. I worried that I had made an irreparable mistake and that it was too late to fix it. I sat on the train and fought back an overwhelming panic.

~

Like London and Paris, Kyiv is a city defined by its river. The Dnieper cuts it in two: the Left Bank, with modern apartment blocks and residential complexes; and the ancient Right Bank, the place where Kyiv took its roots at the end of the fifth century CE. Even though I grew up in the modern section of the Right Bank, I recognised the Old City as soon as I saw its hills adorned with the golden domes of the Monastery of the Caves, the Kyivo-Pecherska Lavra. One of the addresses my mother had given me was in the neighbourhood near the monastery, and I headed there as soon as I got off the train.

Having found the street, the alley and the house number, I was elated to see the name of Vladimir's friend, Grigori Goldberg, on the mailbox. I rang the bell, but the silence on the other side of the door was unbroken. I waited and tried again. Perhaps he was out. Perhaps he too had vanished.

I wasn't sure about anything. I returned to the main street and walked into the lavra. The gateway was small and dark, and stepping inside the courtyard, I was dazzled by the sun glancing off the gilded domes. Christian monks settled the caves on these hillsides in 1051. The founder of the lavra, Saint Anthony, retired to an underground cell and when the monks discovered his corpse years later, they saw that it was miraculously preserved. Other monks followed suit and sequestered themselves in the labyrinth dug into the hills over the Dnieper River and soon the caves became a necropolis and a place of worship. Though I wasn't raised in a religious family, the lavra's antiquity and mystery beguiled me even as they left me apprehensive. As a child, I visited the lavra caves once with my father, and I still recall the fright instilled in me by the sight of mummified eleventh-century fingers resting on emerald velvet. I had gripped my father tighter; his hand was reassuringly warm and soft. The only light in the caves was given off by beeswax candles, and I held mine so firmly that it melted in my sweaty palm. Great mysteries came with an element of fear.

I climbed the steep stairs to the lavra esplanade where I could see the city spreading around the Dnieper River, engulfing what only three decades ago used to be quaint villages. On both sides of the Dnieper, new villas and apartment complexes built by Kyiv's oligarchs broke through the summer greenery.

I leaned on the railing again and looked in the direction of the river. It flowed past the churches on the Right Bank and the brutalist apartment blocks, past the lush chestnut groves and the glass-and-chrome villas. It flowed and disappeared past the horizon where the white glare of the sun made the water blend into the skies. I thought about my father.

I felt only sadness and regret.

In our family, we often avoided talking about certain things. We pretended that the pain would go away if we didn't talk about it. Sergiy didn't talk about Nikodim. Asya didn't talk about the war. My mother didn't talk about her divorce. I didn't talk about my father's suicide. None of us were good at facing our fears.

I lingered at the entrance to the lavra caves. 'Do you want to go in?' a young monk selling candles at the entrance asked me. I remembered my first frightening visit and nodded. He handed me a candle and showed me the way to the necropolis. I followed the other pilgrims and descended slowly.

After the bright sunshine, the darkness of the underground chamber disoriented me. A drop of hot wax fell from my candle onto my hand, but instead of pain I felt panic. The humid air of the caves, smelling of incense, beeswax and sweat, made my head spin. I instinctively reached for a hand that was not there. The crowd was so dense that I couldn't move, so I let it carry me forth.

The further I went, the thinner the crowd became and the more my eyes adjusted to the murky darkness. As I entered the chapels branching out from the main pathway, the light from my candle made the shadows flutter like dove wings. The yellowish glow illuminated dark niches holding glass caskets with the relics of saints. In another alcove a monk intoned prayers. I heard the dry rustle of pages being turned. My panic subsided and the fear gave way to wonder. I moved closer to the casket and saw that it held Saint Nestor, the eleventh-century chronicler of Kyiv. 'When you pray, you can ask him for something, for yourself, but better for others,' I overheard a mother behind me instructing her son.

I whispered a prayer. I didn't know the correct Orthodox way to pray, but I asked for help to find Vladimir. I also prayed for

Valentina's garden to blossom. As I whispered, I could see my breath settling on the cold glass and then slowly evaporating. I lowered my head so close to the casket that my lips almost touched it. I didn't see the mummified hands of the saint. Reflected in the glass cover, I only saw my wide-open eyes.

'Namolenoe mesto,' someone whispered behind me. Namolenoe mesto literally meant a prayer-soaked place, a common phrase referring to Orthodox sites of pilgrimage. Previously, I would have thought of it as a cliché, but now I saw the whispered prayers as a patina that gave this place an emotional charge. Whispered prayers, whispered stories, settling in layers, invisible and yet present, waiting to be heard.

I left the lavra and returned to Grigori Goldberg's house. The doorbell reverberated in the silence. I even tried ringing the doorbell of Grigori's neighbours, but everyone was either at work or away on their summer vacations. The courtyard was suspiciously empty of children and other signs of life. I checked the addresses my mother had given me and felt relieved that the list included five more people. I pressed the doorbell one more time and then left a note for Grigori explaining who I was and why I needed his help.

For the next few days I pursued the leads from my mother's old address book, but despite my prayers at the lavra, my efforts were in vain. I could find nobody. People who knew my parents and Vladimir had either moved or emigrated. Many were dead. I feared that Vladimir's silence signified an irreversible separation.

Back at my aunt's apartment I looked through childhood photos Vladimir had taken of me. Before we had had our falling out, he had digitised photos and films from my early years. One of my favourites showed Daria resting her chin in her hand as she watched me write something in a thick notebook. The photograph was taken as we sat in our nook in the living room where a large wardrobe divided the space to create a small bedroom for me and my grandmother and a sitting room for the rest of the family.

Daria looked as I remembered her – wearing a black pinafore dress over a white shirt and a white headscarf. I could hardly recognise myself in the round-cheeked child with messy curls, but the notebook was instantly familiar. It was my childhood journal.

I must have been seven years old. Daria used to pick me up from school and take me to her office. After retirement, she worked part-time as a counsellor at a boys' boarding school – mostly her task was to make sure students didn't set fires in the dorm rooms. The building resembled a detention facility more than a school and smelled of wet chalk, stale sweat and chlorine. It was a depressing place, but it had a steady supply of colourful paper and stationery, the kind of loot I sought. One day, an eighth-grade student, Roman Yatsenko, dropped out of his Ukrainian literature class and had a temper tantrum in Daria's office, throwing his school bag against the wall. After Roman left sulking, I picked up one of his discarded notebooks and asked Daria if I could keep it. The notebook was new. She looked up while cleaning up the disorder that Roman had left in his wake and nodded. Mentoring teenagers with anger management issues exhausted her. I crossed out Roman's name and wrote in my own, '1 September. Author: Victoria.' Then, staring at the pristine white pages, I experienced my first case of writer's block. I asked Daria what I should write about. In preparation for first grade, my grandmother had been teaching me reading, writing and cursive. 'You can use the notebook to describe your days, like a diary,' she said. 'Because once something is written down, it's remembered.' Daria herself had stacks of black notebooks that she filled with poetry, notes and quotes from her favourite novels. After work, she sat down at the desk we shared and wrote in her notebooks. She disappeared into her own world, and I walked around her on tiptoes, anxious not to disturb her concentration.

My days were too uneventful to be consigned to a diary. From the memoirs that my mother and Valentina read I knew that people started their recollections by mentioning where they were born and what their families were like. In most cases, they were rich and important, and even the shabby gentry household of Bunin's *The Life of Arseniev* had a certain allure that my own didn't possess. Then, the writers were expected to share philosophical observations. I had none. I could barely spell the word 'philosophy'. Daria suggested that I draw or make a collage, because 'writing, like all arts, is about engaging your creativity'. She didn't treat me like a child.

I interpreted my grandmother's suggestion by cutting up a magazine that had pretty pictures of flowers and fruit. When Vladimir, who had no garden in Kyiv but subscribed to a gardening periodical, stormed into our corner of the apartment looking for the missing issue, he found it in shreds, with me pasting pictures into my journal. 'What have you done? That was the most important issue of the year, about planting potatoes, and I didn't have a chance to read it yet!' he cried, yanking the remaining pages from my hands. I tried to explain that the magazine was sacrificed for the sake of art, but he didn't listen and went to complain to my mother.

Discovering that artistic pursuits could have dramatic consequences, I left Vladimir's magazines intact and took to writing about things that I observed around me – the blossoming chestnut trees near the playground, the places Daria and I visited after school, my longing to leave Kyiv and visit Asya and

Sergiy in Bereh, or while in Bereh, my longing to return to Kyiv and go for a walk with Daria. Sometimes I wrote short stories, most of which were fiction, such as the one in which I walked through snowy woods on my own, running an errand for Daria. The only real elements were the scents of frozen bark and pine needles, the sound of snow crunching underfoot, and the delicate patterns of ice on frozen puddles. I was alone in the wintry wonderland, but armed with Daria's instinctive knowledge of secret paths, I wasn't afraid. Daria was the main character in my stories, my friend and accomplice.

I wrote in my journal until the age of eight. The notebook didn't end then, but my parents' marriage did. My mother and I left the apartment, and my father moved to a different part of town. I was separated from Daria by the Dnieper River and too many metro and bus stops. I occasionally wrote in my journal, but without Daria, my muse, its entries dwindled. I missed her reading Bunin's dark love stories out loud and sitting by her side as she wrote poetry or graded school papers. I missed our forest walks and the taste of the buttery crepes that she made in the wood-burning oven. I missed her green coat, with its misshapen pockets filled with chestnuts and pinecones, and the powdery, medicinal scent of her white handkerchiefs.

The last time I saw Daria before leaving for the US, I left my journal with her, promising to return. I never kept my promise, because Daria passed away a few months later. I could never reconcile myself to her death. I talked of her for years using the present tense. It seemed as if she had slipped out of my gaze, but that if I tried hard enough, I could find her.

Suddenly I wanted to visit the apartment where I grew up. Until then the idea hadn't occurred to me. For one thing, it had been mired in a painful legal battle. In the early 1990s, when individuals received the right to own property, Daria and

Vladimir privatised their home that until then had belonged to the state. The apartment was too large for the two of them, and they decided to sell it and buy a smaller place. Vladimir's childhood best friend volunteered to gather the necessary documents, a daunting task in the early post-independence years, and he took advantage of the situation to make himself the new owner. The story as related by Vladimir was as complicated as the Soviet-era legal codex inherited by Ukraine, but the outcome was that Vladimir lost the apartment. He fought to prove his rightful ownership, but his main struggle was to not lose faith in people after being betrayed by his friend.

Having paid almost half of the apartment's value in legal fees, Vladimir won it back. He sold it while already living in Israel, and the only time he mentioned the place was to express his dismay over his best friend's venality.

'That place that brought your uncle so much heartache,' Valentina observed. Valentina and I talked daily while I was in Kyiv, and our chats gained a more intimate dimension when Valentina stepped into the twenty-first century by acquiring an iPad. She couldn't always adjust the camera angle correctly, and when we spoke, it pointed either at the wall or the glum portrait of Pasha above the dining room table. She, however, could see me, and it amused her that she could do so with a single click. 'Why is your room such a mess?' she would say, observing the clothes on the floor or my papers scattered all over the desk. Nothing escaped her attention.

I told Valentina that I wanted to visit our old apartment, but that I was apprehensive about it.

'I was also reluctant to visit Mykhailivka at first,' Valentina said. 'But these days when I can't fall asleep, I envision our house, the apple orchard, the creek at the bottom of the hill. I then fill my reminiscences with everyone I loved and cherished.

Remember that amazing lady, Aunt Maria, whom we met when we were looking for Platon Bylym's house? She said that at the end of the day, we're left with nothing but memories, and she was right. You were right too. It's important to remember.'

Valentina fumbled with the iPad, the camera spun around the room and then her flushed face came on screen. She looked directly at me and said, 'If you went to the Rooster House to look for Nikodim, you can go to your childhood home.'

~

I circled the courtyard a few times and then sat down on a bench near the playground. A group of girls took turns on a swing that made the same creaking noise as it did when I was their age. Their laughter echoed in a large yard overgrown with spirea shrubs and criss-crossed with clotheslines. Squat five-storey buildings huddled around it, their windows decorated with flowerboxes and bird cages. Grandmothers were calling children home for supper. It had been more than two decades since I was here last. The chestnut trees looked taller, the cars parked on the lawn newer and the roads more potholed, but otherwise the street of my childhood hadn't changed.

I got up and walked to the building where I once lived with my parents and Vladimir and Daria. The windows of our apartment faced the courtyard. The bedroom window was covered with a thin curtain through which I could see a flickering television screen and moving shadows. The only thing I had to do was to press the doorbell.

I stood frozen in place. As brazen as I had become over these past years, knocking on random doors and barging into the houses of strangers, I now hesitated. What would I say to these people? How could I explain my reason for wanting to look around their home when I couldn't articulate it to myself?

I leaned on a chestnut tree at the edge of the courtyard and reflected.

'Are you spying on someone?'

The hoarse voice over my shoulder made me jump. I swung around to face a short man in boxer shorts and a tank top that revealed a collage of blue tattoos on his muscular arms. His German shepherd pulled him in another direction, but the man stood firmly in front of me, frowning.

'I used to live here,' I said, feeling my cheeks flush crimson.

The man wasn't convinced. 'I've lived here longer than you've been alive,' he said, 'but I don't remember you.'

'It was a long time ago. Do you know Vladimir Tsebrev?' I asked. The man broke into a big smile and slapped his thighs. The dog took advantage of the loose leash to dash into the bushes. 'Of course, I know Tsebrev,' the man said. 'Are you his daughter?'

I said that I was his niece. 'You must have moved away a long time ago. I'm Mishka, your third-floor neighbour.' Mishka shook his head and went in search of his dog. 'He must have sniffed an intruder. A cat, I mean,' he said, waving goodbye to me. I wished him good luck and headed towards the arch leading out of the courtyard. I felt like an intruder myself.

'Wait, but where are you going?' Mishka called out after me. 'Won't you go up to say hello? They are nice people, the folks that bought your place.'

Mishka pointed towards the entrance. 'Let me open the door for you. The intercom doesn't work well in these accursed khrushchevkas, and hell will freeze over before anyone fixes it,' he continued, not noticing that I was still standing in the middle of the street. What was I afraid of? Determined, I approached the front door.

The hallway still smelled of burnt biscuits and mildew. The

light bulb was still broken. I walked up the stairs and on the second floor I turned right instinctively, reaching for the door of our old apartment. Mishka remained downstairs. 'Goodbye and good luck! I need to find the dog before he slaughters all the cats in the neighbourhood,' he yelled out.

The rusty sound of the bell echoed for a few seconds behind the door and then silence fell. I stood in the darkness, not knowing whether I should leave or wait longer.

I started when the door opened without a noise. A young woman in a blue summer dress stood on the threshold, wiping flour-covered hands on her apron. She leaned forwards, trying to make out her visitor in the darkness of the hallway, before moving aside to let me step into a narrow corridor that smelled of freshly baked bread.

The woman had a pink, dimpled face and slightly slanted grey eyes that crinkled in the corners. Her blonde hair was tied into a heavy knot at the nape of her neck. She radiated health and the kind of ripe beauty that Daria often compared to a sugar bun. 'Pretty like a bulochka,' she would say admiringly whenever we passed tall, plump, blonde women. Daria and I were dark-haired, skinny and petite. The dusting of flour on the exposed arms of the woman standing in front of me only enhanced the comparison to a pastry. 'My name is Vika, and I'm Vladimir Tsebrev's niece. I used to live here,' I began. 'My name is Sonia and I'm your cousin,' the woman said as she took my hands into hers, turning me towards the light so that she could see my face better. We smiled at each other. My initial awkwardness was wearing off in the warmth of Sonia's welcome, but I was still dazed. I had just found a cousin.

A tall, dark-haired man walked into the hallway holding a toddler who looked like his mirror image. 'Khosh umadid, welcome,' he said in Farsi.

'My husband Keywan likes to use Persian phrases. He is determined to bring the etiquette of his native Iran to Ukraine,' Sonia explained, giving her husband an indulgent smile. 'But I'm afraid that it runs counter to our Slavic directness.' I assured Keywan that Ukrainian culture would benefit from Persian traditions of politeness.

'And this is my son Roman,' Sonia said, pointing at the boy. Roman stared at me with the same surprised expression I must have had looking at Sonia and then hid his face in his father's chest.

'Please take a seat and tell me everything,' my cousin said, leading me into the living room.

'Don't you think that it is you who needs to start with the story?' Keywan said to his wife. He spoke Russian fluently, and only his deep, sonorous 'a' gave away his Iranian roots.

'I have seen pictures of you,' Sonia said. 'And you look so much like Aunt Daria that there could be no mistake about you being my cousin.'

'Didn't Vladimir tell you that he sold his apartment to his niece?' Keywan asked.

'Grandniece, to be exact,' Sonia said. 'Daria's older sister, Sonia, was my grandmother. I'm named after her. I confess that I didn't keep in touch with either Daria or Vladimir. It was Vladimir who reached out to me when he decided to move to Israel. He knew that we were looking for an apartment. And so here we are.'

'Actually, Vladimir and I lost touch, and I came here because I didn't know where else to go,' I said. My head was spinning. I had spent the past two years looking for relatives, for clues about the past, and here was a cousin, however distant, sitting in front of me in the room that was once mine. I needed time to process it, and I asked Sonia's permission to walk around the apartment.

The geography of the place remained the same, but the atmosphere had changed. Everything looked fresher, brighter and happier. Only the sounds of the city knocking against the windows reminded me of the apartment as it used to be. I stood in my parents' old bedroom listening to the screech of trams, children's laughter in the courtyard and the gentle rustling of chestnut trees.

'Keywan is going to look up Vladimir's telephone number,' Sonia said, walking into the room. 'Come have tea and tell us about yourself.'

She set the table with pear-shaped Iranian glasses and a porcelain teapot featuring a bearded Qajar shah. A small cabinet in the living room held an Orthodox icon of the Virgin Mary, a Koran and a book of Hafez poetry.

Keywan returned with a pad of paper. 'Here is Vladimir's contact information. We will call him now,' he said.

However, the numbers were the same ones I had been trying daily for the past few weeks without success. And sure enough one number after another rang endlessly without anyone picking up.

'They moved,' Sonia said, replacing the untouched cold tea in my cup with a fresh batch. 'I remember Vladimir mentioning that they were changing apartments. Let me check the last time he sent me a message.'

Sonia logged into her email account and found that their last correspondence was six months ago. 'We should make more effort to stay in touch,' she said, visibly embarrassed.

'Modern life,' Keywan started and dropped his hand. 'Modern families.'

We drank tea, distracting ourselves from gloomy thoughts by talking about Roman and his charming way of mixing Persian and Russian into a language of his own. Anguish grew inside of me, cold and wordless. I thanked the couple for their hospitality and left my old home. The door closed behind me. I stood on the threshold for a moment, illuminated by the yellow street lamp, and stepped tentatively into the thickening dusk.

Fifteen

I had no choice but to return to Bereh and hope that my mother would find another connection to Vladimir or that Sonia and Keywan would write to him and ask him to contact me – if he still wanted to do so. Yet I delayed my departure from Kyiv. I had no energy to explore the city and sat on the balcony of my aunt's apartment pretending to write in my notebook. The sour smell of poplars, the muffled laughter of children playing in the courtyard below and the dry heat radiating from the brick wall brought my childhood back to me. On stuffy days like these, Daria, Vladimir and I used to escape to Hlibivka.

Hlibivka was a village near Kyiv where Vladimir had bought a cottage and fashioned it into a traditional Russian hut reminiscent of his grandparents' house. It had an enormous masonry oven, bench-lined walls and earthen floors. Hlibivka was the same size as Bereh, but the traditional oven, the dark forest around our house and the horse carriages that locals still used in the 1980s made it seem like an illustration from a fairy-tale book. Daria and I made bread and pancakes in the magical oven and foraged for herbs and mushrooms in the forests nearby.

Daria was Asya's contemporary, and she was also a teacher, but these were the only similarities between them. She was as soft-spoken and restrained as Asya was gregarious and extroverted, but in the forest, Daria became a different person. She talked about plants, their medicinal properties, and the magnificent woods of her Russian childhood. She sang songs about lovers wishing to transform themselves into birds and recited romantic Persian poems she knew by heart.

Hlibivka was where I first became aware of the Chernobyl disaster. The village is about fifty miles away from the nuclear plant. The twenty-sixth of April 1986 was a Saturday, and my mother and I had arrived in Hlibivka the night before to spend the weekend with Daria and Vladimir, who were already there planting potatoes. The morning was cool and sunny, and my mother took me for a walk along the Kyiv Sea, an artificial reservoir. The sand was damp and covered with shiny mussel shells and aquatic plants that resembled pine trees in miniature. I picked up a stick and drew a line in the sand. A wave splashed onto my feet and erased my drawing.

'Doesn't that shape look like a bear?' my mother asked, pointing at the slowly moving fog in the distance. I climbed onto a large piece of driftwood and peered at the glowing line separating the water from the sky. I wasn't thinking about the bear-shaped cloud. Daria told me that when the Kyiv Sea was built, it swallowed many villages, and I imagined that one day the houses, churches and gardens would re-emerge.

'What a strange fog,' my mother said, sitting down on the sand and opening her book. She was bored. She didn't like Hlibivka and only came because my father insisted.

We heard someone yelling our names. Both of us turned and saw my father running towards us, gesticulating.

'Get into the car. Right now,' he said, as he picked up my mother's book and lurched in my direction. 'I heard from a passing driver that something happened in Chernobyl.' A normally calm and placid person, he looked so agitated that my legs started shaking and I jumped off the driftwood. As I did, my tights were caught on a sharp branch and for a moment I was suspended in the air, held back by the piece of an ancient tree from a drowned village. My father picked me up and ran with me towards the car, where Daria and Vladimir were already waiting for us.

At first the accident at Chernobyl didn't mean anything to me, other than that I didn't have to return to school for the rest of the semester. A day after we returned to Kyiv, my father drove my mother and me to Bereh. We learned of the true nature of the disaster because my aunt's mother-in-law worked in the Ministry of Health, and she warned us to leave the city immediately and head east, in the opposite direction of the radioactive cloud. My mother called all of her friends and implored them to leave, but because the Soviet government denied the news, they laughed and told her to stop believing capitalist conspiracy theories. 'I have gas masks from my volunteer-nurse days,' her best friend Lana joked. 'If this radioactive cloud comes here, we will be well equipped.' A few years later Lana died of breast cancer and my mother paid for her funeral because Lana's family had spent everything on medical care.

Daria and Vladimir returned to Hlibivka after the Chernobyl explosion, accepting the risks and not willing to part with their charming cottage. I, on the other hand, no longer went with them. My parents were divorced, and while I visited Daria and Vladimir on the weekends, my mother forbade me from going to Hlibivka. That day in April 1986 was the last time I was there. Chernobyl became enshrined in my memory as the smell of dry pine resin, the musky taste of wild strawberries and grandmother's songs. It embodied my first loss and my first inchoate longing.

I typed Hlibivka into the search bar of my browser and the first page that popped up was an advertisement for a hotel. 'If you're tired of city bustle and want to spend unforgettable holidays near Kyiv, Hlibivka Holiday Hotel is the right choice.' I didn't know the address of our cottage, but it was hard to imagine that a place advertising a spa, corporate team-building events and five swimming pools was located in the Hlibivka that I had known. There was only one way to find out.

At the bus station, the routes towards Hlibivka advertised tours of Chernobyl. 'Unique, mysterious and extraordinary,' said one poster about the Chernobyl Exclusion Zone, making it seem like a safari trip. I took my seat on a bus to Hlibivka and scrolled through Vladimir's photos of our cottage on my phone.

The countryside around Kyiv looked so different from the meadows and steppes of Poltava that I turned my attention to the landscape beyond the window. The pine forests ran past, the dark mass of treetops striped with the bright red of their slender trunks. After the Chernobyl accident, the government ordered soldiers to raze the forest near the atomic station, and in the sudden heat of May, shirtless young men cut down the trees only to be cut down themselves by radiation sickness.

Daria and I had travelled to Hlibivka by bus so often that the moment it turned the corner, my hand shot up into the air, urging the driver to stop. It was the same road, the same boulder, the same hill up ahead. But as the bus sped off, leaving me in a cloud of dust, I doubted my memory. The dark, moss-festooned forest of my childhood was now so thin that I could see through it all the way to the next highway. A pile of beer cans and other litter sat near the main path where I had once picked wild raspberries and startled a bear. (Daria said that it was a drunkard, but in my mind the roaring figure with the mane of black hair always retained the form of a bear.)

Wincing, I turned away from the pile of rubbish, but wherever I glanced, I saw that Hlibivka had changed. The roads were newer and so were the houses. Some buildings looked like fancy villas, with satellite dishes perched on their roofs and imported cars in the driveways. Other houses were abandoned and decaying, and among these wrecks, I found the fairy-tale hut of my childhood.

Surrounded by overgrown apple trees laden with hard green fruit, the whitewashed house was at first difficult to see. I opened the rickety gate and walked in. The door stood wide open and a cat dashed out and startled me. Nobody had lived here for years. The roof was crumbling and young seedlings sprouted through the floor in what used to be our main room. I rubbed the white plaster and it crumbled under my fingers. The roof looked like it could collapse at any moment.

When Daria and I visited Hlibivka together, she would get up early to buy milk from a neighbour for our breakfast. I would wake up to the rustle of reeds on the riverbank and the clutter of firewood. Groggy and disoriented from the sudden awakening, I would stare absently through a small window with warped glass. My grandmother's green coat would flash past and I would feel so much comfort that my whole being seemed weightless. I would fall asleep again, pressing my face against a woollen quilt that smelled of Daria's calendula oil and herbal soap.

Miraculously, the small window was completely intact, as was the masonry oven. It still looked solid and majestic, imbued with the same mystery that I felt emanating from it as a child.

Both Daria and Asya often said that you couldn't step into the same river twice, waving away regrets and accepting the changes wrought by the passage of time. I resisted nonetheless, and the mismatch between my memory and reality often pained me. But now, standing in the middle of a wrecked house, piecing together the shards of my memories, I realised my grandmothers were wise. You could only control so much in your life. I was living through a war. I had lost friends and loved ones in tragic circumstances. I knew better than anyone that staring into the past could turn you into a pillar of salt.

I rushed out of the yard without turning back to look at the house. I crossed the road and walked into the forest, hastening my step past the pile of garbage. Deeper into the forest, the trees were sparse, but the groves looked clean. Sunlight filtered through the pine branches, falling into the golden confetti on the ground. The tiny purple flowers grew in a thick mass underfoot and when I stepped on them, they released a camphorous scent with a lingering sweetness. I recognised wild thyme, the same herb Daria brewed in her tisanes. I bent down and picked a few sprigs. I no longer had Daria with me and I didn't remember which way to go to find the wild strawberries or the lake with pristine water. Perhaps they no longer existed. I stuffed the thyme in my pocket. On the stifling-hot bus ride to Kyiv, I held it to my face and breathed it in deeply; in every flash of green behind the window, I saw Daria's coat.

When I returned home, I saw that I had missed a call from an unknown number. The voicemail notification beeped. 'Is this the right number? Grigori Goldberg here. Vladimir moved and his phone number has changed. Here is the last number I have ...'

The number was different from the one I had from Sonia and Keywan. I dialled it immediately. It rang and rang. I could not bear another loss. The phone continued ringing without anyone picking up.

Sixteen

I stayed in Kyiv. Days went by, but Vladimir didn't return my call and neither did he pick up when I rang again. I redialled his number several times a day, but I reached only the answering machine with its factory-recorded automatic message.

I thought about it and then called another number I knew by heart, despite not having used it for years. Nobody was picking up. Dejected, I was about to hang up when I heard a click and a familiar voice on the other end of the line.

'This is Vika,' I said simply.

Alyona squealed and then broke into her usual high-pitched laughter. I laughed too, giddy and excited.

'What a surprise! What a lovely surprise!' Alyona said, once she'd caught her breath and I had explained I was in Kyiv.

'What about meeting for a cup of coffee?' I asked.

'Wonderful! Let's meet on Maidan? How about four p.m.?'

'I'll see you near the pink chestnuts then.'

Light headed and anxious, I walked around the apartment,

pulling myself together. What should I wear? Should I bring a gift? If so, what kind of gift do you give a long-lost and then suddenly found friend? I scrutinised myself in the mirror, imagining how Alyona would find me after twenty years. We had met in the third grade when our classroom teacher assigned us to the same desk and we stayed friends till I left for the United States. Alyona and I made plans for her to come to Chicago to study English, but of course, those childish fantasies never materialised. Though I returned to Kyiv to visit Valentina, I never saw my schoolfriend because she spent most summers with her boyfriend's family in the south of Ukraine and seemed to have little time for me. I didn't begrudge her those absences, especially since my visits to Kyiv were rare and my letters to her were brief. Eventually we both stopped reaching out.

I grabbed my bag and ran out of the house, worried that I would be late.

I arrived before Alyona did and staked out a spot on the stone embankment under the chestnut trees. It was too late for their pink blossoms, but I liked the soft shade their branches cast on the square. The campsites and piles of tyres had long been cleared away. The memorial site to those who perished on Maidan was decorated with red carnations and blue and yellow ribbons. I stared at the ground and didn't notice when Alyona approached me.

When I raised my eyes and saw my friend, so surprisingly unchanged after many years, I believed that you really could go back in time, contrary to what my grandmothers would have said. Alyona wore a white trouser suit that made her look taller and slimmer than I remembered, and her dark hair hung loose below her waist. She was innocently unaware of her beauty, and it made her even more striking. She was carrying chocolate ice creams and a big bouquet of purple dahlias. She rewound the clock and returned Maidan to what it once used to be – the place where we came to share secrets and plan big adventures.

We ate our ice creams walking down Khreshchatyk. 'Were you here during the protests?' I asked, aware that I might be entering dangerous terrain. Some people rightly perceived this question as an enquiry about their political stance and became defensive, and Alyona and I hadn't been in touch for years. I didn't know how she had changed or what she thought. Yet I somehow didn't feel any reticence around her.

'I was here with my father in November, but when the situation turned more violent, he told me not to come. I still don't know whether it was the right decision in the end, given how terrible everything turned out.'

'You mean, the decision to support the revolution?'

'The decision to start the revolution. We're in the backyard of a country that still thinks it's an empire. Until Russia lets go of its imperial aspirations, we will be pulled back and forth. It's so exhausting that sometimes I think of emigrating.'

I didn't think that anyone had really directed the events of Maidan, or that the revolution was avoidable. People were so tired of corruption and dysfunctionality that they sought any way to voice their concerns. The reason Maidan attracted so many different groups was its promise of a new start, and such promises were needed in 2014.

I told Alyona so and she said, 'What happened, happened. Now we just need to wait and see what the future will bring. But we are resilient. Do you know how willing people were to volunteer and provide basic aid or food? This alone gives me hope.'

Alyona told me that she was single and still living with her parents in the same apartment near our school. She worked for an oil firm doing technical translation and tutored English in her spare time. Nikita, her boyfriend of many years, became a friend and married another woman.

'He lost patience waiting for me to accept his proposal,' Alyona said. 'Do you know that I actually introduced him to his future wife?'

I stared at Alyona, puzzled. 'I thought that you and Nikita loved each other. You spent so much time together. Even when I came to Kyiv, you preferred the company of your beloved Nikita to mine. And now you're telling me that you played a match-maker between him and another woman?'

Alyona looked away and sighed. She told me about an illness that upset her life and explained that Nikita was always by her side, but when he proposed, she felt that he was doing it more out of a sense of duty than real love. She decided to break off the relationship.

The people walking towards us blended into a variegated, blurry mess. I only saw Alyona's profile and a small blue vein pulsating on her temple. She was calm and collected, telling me this heartbreaking story as if relating an anecdote about some-one we both knew but barely cared about.

'But I don't regret my decision to stay single. I relish my freedom. I can do whatever I want. See whoever I want. Buy whatever I want.'

I took her arm and wrapped it around mine.

'And these days I don't regret not having children,' she said. 'Seeing what's going on here, I am worried.'

'The war . . .'

'I mean the war that's coming. The conflict now is mostly frozen, but it won't stay this way for ever. But enough about this. Tell me about yourself. How is your family?'

Hearing Alyona voice her fears gave me courage to speak of my own.

'My father is dead,' I said, letting go of her hand.

My words hung in air polluted with car fumes, making it even more difficult to breathe. I said what had been spinning around in my mind to someone who had been absent from my life for many years and yet I didn't need to fill in the gaps. Alyona hugged me and her thick, glossy hair swept around me like a curtain, shutting out the city and its clamour. I cried, and the tears I had held back poured out in a flood. We stood in the middle of Khreshchatyk, oblivious to people staring at us curiously but giving us space.

We found an ornate courtyard and sat on a bench. I still held the dahlias Alyona had given me, feeling the waxy chill of their petals under my fingers. The linden trees cast a deep shade, and the only sounds were of the murmur of traffic on the main street and the cooing of doves.

'I found out when my stepmother called me and blurted out the news. I've been replaying that conversation in my mind, but it makes no sense to me. My father was always a cool-headed person, rarely depressed.

'I know that he got into real estate and he was so busy with it that on the few occasions when we talked, he spoke of nothing else. It bored me to tears. I don't even remember the name of his business.' I looked at Alyona and my eyes welled up again.

'And what happened to the business?' Alyona asked.

'Karina says that it failed and he went bankrupt. I imagine that loan sharks were after him, but talking about it then was so painful that I preferred to avoid it altogether.' After the funeral Karina and I stayed in touch, but then talking to her became difficult. I knew that she suffered from her own burden of guilt, but our conversations drained me completely. She also stopped calling me.

'Now I want to understand what happened and I want to

speak with my father's older brother,' I said. 'And I can't even get in touch with him because we argued about Crimea and Ukrainian politics and haven't spoken since.'

'Oh, dear! Are you sure that there is no other reason why Vladimir isn't calling? Nobody holds grudges over Ukrainian politics for that long!' Alyona shook her head.

'The other explanation might be that he passed away,' I said, no longer holding back. 'But my mother says that she would have found out about it via her own network.'

'Then he will show up,' Alyona said. 'In the meantime, you have to take care of yourself and be kind to yourself. Everything else is out of your hands.'

I returned to my aunt's apartment and made a cup of tea. I opened the bookshelf and aimlessly leafed through a few art albums. The books were mostly Valentina's, collected during an era when illustrated volumes on art were rare and much desired. A small note fell from one book. It had our Bereh address written in Valentina's hand, though oddly enough our house number was listed as seven, instead of one. I looked closer and realised that Valentina wrote '1' in a peculiar way, with a long hook that made it look like '7'. I put the note back into the album and continued flipping through pages showing reproductions of Renaissance paintings. Something bothered me, but I wasn't sure what it was. I washed the dishes and went to sleep.

I woke up at dawn and bolted out of bed in search of my phone. I listened to Grigori Goldberg's message and compared the number he gave to the one I had written down. It all became clear then. The first time I heard it, I was so agitated that my scrawl for seven made it look like a one. This whole time I had been calling the wrong number.

I pressed the numbers with trembling fingers. The phone rang hollow, echoing in my temples.

'Allo!' Vladimir's bright, resolute voice sounded so close that I involuntarily looked around me.

'Diadia Volodia, this is Vika,' I said.

'At last! Do you know how worried I was? First of all, you blocked me on Skype and I figured that I would give you space. When you are my age, you know that space and time are the best remedies for many things. Then, not long ago, Grisha Goldberg sent me a message telling me that my niece was looking for me all over Kyiv. He told me that he gave you my number, but you never called.'

Vladimir spoke so rapidly that I couldn't keep up with his story. '... and stupid Grisha threw away your note before I had a chance to ask him for your number. I lost my mobile and all of my contacts, including yours. I'm getting old and forgetful, and even the technology is failing me.'

'I only want to say that I'm sorry,' I said. I wanted to say that I didn't block him and that he was the one who blocked me, but now I wasn't sure who had done what. It no longer mattered.

'Forget about that. I said idiotic things to you too. Let's not dwell on that. Are you still doing yoga every day?'

I stood at the window listening to Vladimir describe his daily routine and favourite exercises. Then I explained how I had uncovered the mysterious disappearance of Nikodim and how that search was important for me to understand my roots and my relationship to my family and even to Ukraine itself.

'You said that we should be grateful to the Soviet Union, but with a story like Nikodim's in our family, I can't feel this way,' I said.

'We had family members who also suffered during Stalin's era,' Vladimir said. 'My niece died by suicide after she lost faith in the system. She was in charge of a meteorological station. Some say that she was too principled and that she was killed, and her death was made to look like suicide.'

I told Vladimir about Nikodim's tragic end. Then I hesitated, but recalling my conversation with Alyona, I made up my mind.

'I want to ask you about Dad.'

I heard Vladimir take a sharp intake of breath and clear his throat. 'I also want to tell you something. Can I start?'

I said yes, still looking out of the window. In the courtyard below, the janitor was watering the wilting flower beds, and Petr Ivanovich was feeding his troupe of cats. People were crowding around a kiosk selling coffee and newspapers. The banality made my conversation with Vladimir surreal.

'Go ahead,' I said and closed the curtain. I sat down at the dinner table and put the phone in front of me, turning on the speaker function. Vladimir's voice filled the small room and echoed under its tall ceilings.

'We wanted to design the ultimate sound-recording machine. My brothers and I loved music, but in the Soviet Union, good-quality record players were difficult to find, to say nothing of Western music. When I wasn't accepted into the engineering programme, I decided to study at whatever school would accept me and learn engineering on my own. It was ambitious, but I wasn't daunted. I survived polio.

'Grisha Goldberg was also denied a place at the engineering university because he was Jewish. So we created our own engineering study group called "Invalid+Kosmopolit", poking fun at the reasons the university gave us to dismiss our applications. We went through the first-year engineering course textbooks, tutoring each other. Grisha gave it up and started dealing on the black market, but I finished the course on my own. After a couple of years of studies, building a sound recorder was a piece of cake, especially since Grisha could obtain the necessary tools for me.

'That's how our period of sound recording started. I built

recorders and copied music tapes. At first it was for fun, but then your father suggested selling my devices. He found clients through his university connections and we made money. A lot of money! I never cared about money, because I never had it, but suddenly I could see why people become fixated on it. Money gives you power. People don't care if you are a cripple if they smell money on you.

'The clients your father found for us were either music aficionados or black-market dealers themselves and it was seedy company to keep. What we were doing was highly illegal, and it was inevitable that someone would report us to the authorities. That's exactly what happened. Police raided our apartment, confiscated all of my recorders and tools and accused us of "speculation" and "parasitism". It was a felony offence under the Soviet law. I took the blame for everything.'

'Did you do that to protect Dad?'

'I was responsible. I wasn't going to deny it, but your father had his future in front of him. If he ended up in prison, he would have been ruined for ever.'

'You protected your brother!' My voice was so low and raspy that it sounded foreign. I thought of Nikodim, who tried to protect his brother Sergiy by not mentioning him during the interrogations. And, before Ivan and Asya interfered, Sergiy was willing to put himself at risk by investigating Nikodim's disappearance.

'I know that you don't believe me, but prison was the best life lesson. I saw things that most people don't see. I understood things about people that I wouldn't have learned otherwise. I never regretted it.'

Vladimir fell silent for a moment and then added, 'But of course, every decision we make has consequences. My wife left me, and I wasn't there to see my daughter grow up. Then your father lost his best friend Danil who was mobilised for Afghanistan and so destroyed by the experience that he died by suicide. Your father was a student, so he evaded the draft. Danil's suicide devastated him.'

I stood up and pushed my chair so abruptly that it fell to the floor with a loud thud. I struggled with latches that hadn't been touched in years and threw open the window. I needed air. I inhaled deeply.

The sun turned its full attention onto our side of the building and flooded the room with oppressive heat. 'Did he kill himself or was he killed?' As I formed the words, I thought of Nikodim's file and the same question I had reading the note about his suicide. 'Was he pushed to suicide?'

'He was goaded into a bankrupting scheme. He might as well have been killed.'

We were both silent. My attention was focused on the poplars in front of the window. The trees were tall enough to reach our floor, and lit by the sun, their leaves appeared almost transparent. The black hole inside me was swallowing all of my thoughts. I felt nothing and I had to bite my hand to see if I could still feel pain.

'You said before that American capitalism killed him,' I said, struggling to enunciate words. 'What did you mean by that?'

'He was roped into a project to build affordable green-energy housing. He who knew nothing about construction but imagined himself as the next great real estate developer. When we were young, he often started grand projects and then passed them off to me, but in America, he started believing that he could do it himself. "American dream," he called it. "Anything is possible here." Perhaps it was possible, statistically speaking, but the probability of success was too low. The whole endeavour was foolish.

'He wouldn't listen to me. He invested money. He borrowed more than he could afford. And the banks were eager to give him money, knowing full well that he was heading towards disaster. The whole system was set up to take advantage of gullible people like your father.

'And he failed. It didn't take long for the project to reveal itself as a mirage. The amount of money he would have needed to bring it to fruition was astronomical. But he kept hoping. He kept going to the banks. He kept knocking on doors. He found all doors shut. He was a loser. And nobody in America likes a loser.'

I stumbled backwards and leaned against the wall.

'I kept telling him to come and visit me in Israel, to take time off work and explore the world. But he kept putting it off, saying that he had enough time to travel and that now was his chance to do something big.

'And then it all collapsed. And I was too far away ...' Vladimir's voice frayed into sobs.

I slid down the wall slowly and sat on the kitchen floor covered with dust. I buried my face in my hands. I knew some of the details of my father's unsuccessful business venture from speaking to his friends in California, but hearing the story from Vladimir was still searing. I couldn't blame American capitalism the way my uncle did; I couldn't blame America. I just felt the heart-wrenching ache permeating my whole being. I thought that after three years the pain would be dulled, but it overwhelmed me.

Yet as Vladimir and I talked, I knew that it was the right time to have this conversation and to grieve without concealing anything or pretending that the pain wasn't there. I needed to get out of my Rooster Trap.

'I'm going to send you something at Sonia's address,' Vladimir said after a long silence. Then he hung up.

I sat on the dirty floor till the sun left the kitchen. The oppressive heat vanished, replaced by the musty dampness of summer dusk. I wanted to fall asleep and wake up to my life as it used to be before. But I couldn't identify the 'before' for which I yearned.

A few days later, Sonia called me to say that she had received a package from Vladimir. As soon as I arrived, she handed it to me. I pulled off the tape and saw a brown shoebox inside. There was no note, but I saw that it was unnecessary when I prised open the lid. By sending me his treasured collection of family photographs, along with my childhood journal, Vladimir wanted me to focus on what connected us despite the distance, departures and disagreements.

I already recognised some of the photographs from his digital archive, but holding the glossy paper that he had developed himself as a child moved me. Vladimir's early images were mostly of himself and the apartment, skewed and blurry, but as he grew strong enough to move around unaided, he took photographs in the streets of Kyiv – girls jumping rope, boys teasing girls, girls taunting boys, boys doing naughty things, soldiers marching, women queuing, kids having fun. These snapshots dappled with patches of overexposure captured unvarnished life in a place still marked by war. One of my favourite images was of Vladimir standing in front of a billboard advertising the 1953/54 performance season. One poster above his head announced the circus programme. Another featured a bill of concerts and plays. The Ukrainian Theatre of Opera and Ballet was staging *Lakme*, *Don Quixote*, *The Humpbacked Horse*, *Prince Igor*, and to finish off this eclectic selection, *Faust*. Vladimir's clothes looked too big for his thin body, but he struck a confident pose, with one hand tucked into a pocket, another into the front of his jacket – a tough-guy stance that masked his lifeless right arm. He had been ill and had suffered, but he refused to be a victim. 'Life goes on,' he seemed to say, as he cocked his head confidently to one side.

'I like Vladimir's pictures of Daria,' Sonia said as we sat on the sofa and spread the photos around us. Vladimir captured my paternal grandmother in a variety of moods – posing against a white wall and looking stiff and awkward, preparing a meal while throwing a furtive glance at the camera, darning socks, writing in her notebook and looking into the distance dreamily.

One of the most touching photographs in the collection was of Daria holding my father as an infant. When she returned to Kyiv after the war ended, she discovered that her husband had started an affair with another woman and moved her into the family's apartment. Daria endured it for the sake of Vladimir, because he needed help. Her husband relented and broke off with his lover, but for a few months Daria had to share her home with another woman whose husband was killed during the war and who herself had no place to go. Daria took Vladimir for his doctor's appointments and cared for him after his operations. Later, when she discovered that she was pregnant with my father, the family seemed to have reconciled. Vladimir was walking with a stick. The couple had their second honeymoon, and my father embodied their hopes for peace and happiness.

Vladimir captured Daria haggard and tired, with deep lines on her face and bags under her eyes. The familiar shapeless coat concealed her thin body, and her well-worn shoes appeared several sizes too big. I recognised the carelessly chosen clothes, recalling how my grandmother spent all of her money on her family, begrudging herself even a ball of new yarn for stockings. Much to my mother's shock, she collected our poodle's fur and knitted socks with it.

Yet despite the signs of age and the unflattering clothes, my grandmother beamed with happiness as she hugged her baby boy. I couldn't stop staring at her, and the longer I did, the more I felt something shifting inside of me.

'Her smile lights up her face,' Sonia exclaimed. The woman in the photograph was the Daria who loved forest walks, Persian poetry and wildflowers. The woman who despite hardships and suffering never became bitter or resentful and found the world around her full of wonder. I wished I could share this photograph with my father to remind him where he came from and why he needed to stay.

Sitting in my old bedroom surrounded by images of people I loved, I recognised that the past could hold pain and beauty and that though some pain never goes away, I could learn to accept it. I resolved to embrace the past in its complexity just as I embraced the future in its uncertainty. I gave myself the freedom to grieve.

Seventeen

The garden was silent in the limpid light of early morning, and the sounds of my rake and the leaves rustling in my footsteps echoed in the cool air. The cherry trees that I had whitewashed in the spring looked naked and forlorn. Their golden finery edged in frost lay on the ground. Earlier that week, Valentina, Uncle Tolya, Dmytro and I had trimmed the roses and piled wet earth around their stubby branches. Uncle Tolya's gravedigging gave him certain hard-to-break habits, and the neat, tapered piles of earth covering the roses looked funereal. 'For heaven's sake survive the winter,' Uncle Tolya said, waving his rake over the roses. 'These are not graves, they hold the roots of the future,' he told us solemnly, when my grandmother complained that our garden looked like a graveyard. Valentina rolled her eyes, and when her friend left, she asked me to sweep leaves over the buried roses to hide their sepulchral mounds.

I travelled back to Brussels not long after Vladimir and I had reconciled. Before I left, I promised Valentina and Dmytro to return in the autumn. Pani Olga joked that I was a modern-day Persephone, confined to Hades in winter and released into the gardens of Elysium in spring. I countered that Brussels was far from hell and Ukraine was hardly paradise, yet my friend's teasing had a grain of truth. I always assumed that unlike the rest of my mother's family, I wasn't desperately nostalgic for Bereh, but I was wrong. I longed for Valentina and Bereh while in Brussels and missed my husband and the idiosyncratic Belgian capital while in Ukraine. When I was a child, I oscillated between Kyiv and Bereh, my father's and my mother's sides, and now the familiar longing returned with force. It was different this time, however. I felt more at ease with my split loyalties and I found it comforting to know that I had more than one home that was ready to welcome me. Both shores were mine.

When I returned to Bereh in September, the conversations among our neighbours revolved around the coming winter. Sasha finished selling chrysanthemums in the Poltava market and no longer brought us a fresh dose of gossip at the end of the day. Instead, she was busy planting flower bulbs for the next year and had no time to worry about either the state of our garden or my wardrobe. Our neighbour Antonina complained that the woman hadn't whispered correctly to her cucumbers in the spring because her yield this year was meagre. Uncle Tolya said that all of it was nonsense because the world was coming to an end sooner or later. 'Mark my words, the Earth has shifted off its axis,' he said. Uncle Tolya harvested several sacks of potatoes and bought a cartload of cheap wood from the family of a man he had recently buried, and thus having ensured a warm and plentiful winter, he had no cares, even if the world was off-kilter.

Valentina looked more fragile than she had in the summer, and she relegated most of the garden work to Dmytro and Uncle

Tolya. But she didn't complain. She was anxious to finish ready-ing the orchard for its winter slumber, and it became my job to remind her to take her medicine. For her part, she encouraged me to see my friends. 'There will be time to talk when the snow comes,' she often said, rushing outdoors to pick apples or to check whether the cabbages were ready to be harvested.

Since I had been visiting Ukraine every year since 2014, my circle of acquaintances had grown so large that I could spend every day seeing a different person. Whenever I called my friends, they made plans and expected to see me the moment I arrived. Pani Olga needed my help to photograph her new rushnyky and classify different regional patterns. Nadia invited me to Reshetylivka for the opening of her embroidery exhibit. She had made a beautiful white-on-white shirt for me and regretted that I was already married because she wanted to sew a traditional wedding dress. 'You could always have a second wedding in Ukraine, like a renewal of vows,' she mused. Sonia and Keywan insisted that I stay with them in Kyiv, and Alyona invited me to spend a long weekend with her family in Odesa.

As much as I appreciated my friends' offers, I went nowhere and stayed with Valentina. I kept in touch with Vladimir via Skype, and I put a camera in our dining room so that he could join us for a virtual teatime. He never recanted his admiration of Putin and criticism of Ukrainian nationalists, but I accepted that the two of us wouldn't agree on everything. I also accepted both my grandmother's relentless drive for perfection and the importance of the orchard. 'Are we all fated to become slaves to the land?' I teased her, but I learned the rhythms of the garden so well that Valentina no longer needed to give me special tasks. In the morning I took a rake and swept the fallen leaves. Some days I could smell winter in the air and it made me anxious. The cycle of decay and rebirth was unrelenting, and to keep melancholy thoughts at bay, I reminded myself that I was preparing the garden for spring.

I heard Valentina call my name. My grandmother was leaning over the garden gate. She was pointing at my mobile phone and holding it away from her as if it carried a contagious disease. 'Organy,' she mouthed. It meant 'the organs', the popular name for the KGB. I wiped my dirty hands on dew-covered burdock leaves and hurried over to Valentina.

'This is Elena Ivanovna, the SBU archives director. I was going through some of my paperwork and am calling with regard to your visit to examine the file of Nikodim Berezko. Do you have a minute?' I recognised the voice of the archivist from the Rooster House. I didn't have Valentina's dread of the organisation, but receiving a call in such an unexpected fashion put me on edge.

'Yes, Elena Ivanovna, I'm listening.' I sat down on a bench under the lilac shrub and waved to Valentina to go inside. The air was frigid and she wasn't wearing a jacket. Uncertain, she lingered behind the wooden fence and then walked slowly towards the house.

'Can you please confirm your residence? I need to update the information on the file, since you've requested it twice.'

I felt my shoulders relax and explained my situation.

'But you spend a lot of time in Ukraine,' she said.

'Is this information needed for the official records?' I asked, crushing dried lilac leaves with the heel of my boot.

'No, not at all. You don't need to explain anything. I was merely curious.'

'May I ask you something, also unofficially? And you also don't have to respond if you don't want. The file on my great-uncle says that he died by suicide—'

Elena Ivanovna didn't let me continue. 'Nikodim Berezko didn't die by suicide,' she said. 'He was shot. Shot along with thousands of other people. In 1937, the KGB killed people to fill their quotas and later made up their cases to give the impression that they had followed due process to the letter. They also issued fake death certificates for suicides or heart disease to absolve the state of any responsibility. Berezko's death notice doesn't look right. The original has no date, no time, no signature, apart from whatever was written in later, in a different hand and different ink.'

Elena Ivanovna paused and then said, 'The people who wrote these documents were themselves shot. The chief interrogator, Zdykhovsky, was accused of being the mastermind behind the same rightist Trotskyist organisation that was the pretext for Berezko's execution.'

I was silent. I was tracing the veins of a yellow leaf that landed in my lap.

'Of course, we don't know for sure what happened. We will never know for sure. We can only see the patterns,' Elena Ivanovna said. 'But your uncle was innocent—'

'If Nikodim was innocent, why did you not issue the bloody rehabilitation notice to his son, instead of making him write dozens of letters and lose out on his pension?' I asked, interrupting her.

'I can't apologise for the entire organisation, but I'm sorry. I'm genuinely very sorry,' Elena Ivanovna said calmly. 'Even those of us working in the Rooster House have a conscience and our own fears,' she added.

'I have another question. My great-grandmother Asya was summoned by the KGB in 1945 over the question of her wartime employment but was released. Was she released on a condition, like a condition of collaboration, perhaps?' It pained me to say it, but if I came all this way, I needed to know the truth.

'May I check and call you back?'

I said yes and gave Elena Ivanovna Asya's full name and date of birth.

Long after we hung up, I sat staring at my silent phone and then slipped it into the pocket of my jacket and picked up the rake. The russet leaves smelled pungently of walnut shells and wine lees. Elena Ivanovna hadn't revealed anything earth-shattering about Nikodim's fate. I had read dozens of books about the Stalinist terror, about the extent of its reach and the random nature of the arrests and executions. At the height of the Great Terror, the arrested were first killed and their dossiers were compiled later to maintain the semblance of legal propri-ety. Totalitarian regimes, from Nazi Germany to the Khmer Rouge, have had a morbid attachment to documenting their deeds. Reading Nikodim's file, I had been aware that I risked entangling myself in a web of lies. Nikodim, however, wasn't a mere statistic to me, and his death was more than a case file. My hand was shaking while gripping the rake. I bit my lower lip and raked as hard as I could, as if along with decaying leaves, I could sweep away the pain, sorrow and disgust that I felt.

I stumbled into the house drenched in sweat and discarded my soil-smeared jacket in the hallway. Valentina sat at the dining room table holding the newspaper. She glanced at me with concern. 'Your cheeks are burning. Are you sure you haven't caught a chill? I told you not to do any garden work in this cold weather,' she said and touched my forehead. 'Anyway, what did the KGB want?' Whoever occupied the Rooster House remained the KGB to Valentina.

I replied that the archivist called to tell me that Nikodim didn't die by suicide and that his death was senseless and tragic. 'You and I always knew this, did we not?' she said gently.

'I was rude to the officer, as if she were responsible for everything. For Nikodim's fate, for his wife's suffering, for the cruel rigmarole that his son experienced as he tried to prove his father's innocence,' I told Valentina.

I recalled Nikodim's file with a shudder. It was harrowing to see that truth could vanish with the stroke of a pen. A story could be manufactured and then the facts could be made to fit it. Reality could be remade on demand. An innocent person could be made guilty. Black could become white or any shade in between.

'The truth always comes out,' the optimists might say. Perhaps, but by the time the fog clears and the outlines of the truth become obvious, it is too late. What did the officer say? 'He was shot. Shot along with thousands of other people.' One had to be even more of an optimist to assume that people learned from the mistakes of history.

Many times during my search for Nikodim I wondered what exactly was the truth that I wanted to find. I now knew what happened to Nikodim. He was dead. His family was dispersed. And this knowledge added nothing to my understanding of Nikodim or his past.

'What is the truth in this story?' I asked.

Valentina removed her reading glasses, pushed them away from her impatiently, and switched on the morning news. 'It depends on what you mean by "the truth",' she said. 'You were looking for Nikodim, but you were really looking for the explanation behind your father's . . .'

She didn't say 'suicide'. She cut herself off, turned to the TV, and increased the volume. She knew about my conversation with Vladimir.

'And I think that if that's your truth, then you found it.'

As usual, my down-to-earth grandmother delivered her philosophical statements in the matter-of-fact tone of the weather forecaster, to whom her attention was now riveted. She wanted to know whether today would be warm enough to plant flowers for next spring.

The phone rang as I was about to prepare dinner.

'Hello, this is Elena Ivanovna. I have found no records of Asya Berezko as being in our system, apart from her personal dossier. Perhaps the KGB found nothing suspicious in her record and had no reason to hold her.'

'In the copy of the dossier we have at home, I found the most positive statements about her were written by her neighbours and colleagues,' I said. 'I always expected that people took such opportunities to air grievances, either to curry favour with the KGB or for their own ulterior motives.'

'People are both worse and better than we think,' Elena Ivanovna said. 'I learned it on this job.'

'The best letter is from Sergiy Berezko,' she then said. 'It describes Asya in the most glowing terms.'

'Sergiy Berezko was her husband.'

'He said that he would stake everything on Asya being a loyal and patriotic citizen of the Soviet Union. Perhaps this too played its role in protecting her.' Elena Ivanovna sighed and added, 'He must have loved her immensely.'

'He did,' I said. 'He would give his life for her.'

'He almost did. Thank God, the KGB released her and didn't pursue the matter further.'

I set the kettle to boil and prepared a tea tray, piling it with our best porcelain cups, several types of jam and chocolates.

'What is all this?' Valentina exclaimed. 'Are we expecting the Queen of England for tea?'

'We deserve a treat after all of this garden work,' I said. 'It's a pity that we don't keep any wine in the house, or else we could have a drink.'

'I have a bottle of wine,' Valentina said. 'The last time we went to Crimea, your mother and I toured the Massandra vineyards and bought a bottle of Cabernet. It was years ago, so I hope that it's still fine.'

Valentina went into the pantry and returned with a bottle dusty enough to look like a grand cru and two even dustier cut-crystal wine glasses. I struggled with a rusted corkscrew to open the bottle and after a few attempts, I succeeded. The wine gave off a musty, sour scent, but it was passable and we filled our glasses.

'What shall we drink to?' Valentina asked.

'Let's drink to love,' I said. 'To love and family.'

Epilogue

Il faut cultiver notre jardin.

VOLTAIRE, *Candide*

Thauma is the Greek word for miracle. Not a miracle in the supernatural sense like walking on water or feeding five thousand people with five loaves of bread and two fish. Thauma is an everyday marvel, a brief glimpse of the divine through the veil separating the world of the mortals from the celestial realm. In the Orthodox tradition, the line between the two worlds is fluid and every moment could be a portal and a crossing.

The last time I saw the garden it stood covered in snow. 'Look, you can already see buds,' Valentina said, pointing at the cherry branches. Under the layer of ice, I spotted the violet tinge of the shells encasing future blossoms. The winter orchard should be a desolate sight, barren and frozen, but I saw reminders of life in every swollen bud and in every blade of grass pushing through the snow. The promise of summer in the winter orchard seemed like the best illustration of thauma to me, but when I said so to Valentina, she didn't listen. She contemplated the next planting season, with its new projects, excitements and anxieties. 'Would Uncle Tolya be able to build us a small greenhouse over there?' she asked me, pointing at the empty corner of the garden. 'I was reading about a new early-fruiting tomato hybrid.' Valentina blew into her hands to warm them up. Her cheeks were the colour of her favourite nightshade, but she was too deep into her reverie to care about the biting wind and dark clouds moving in from the east. 'I would so love to learn how to grow good tomatoes,' she said, as we trod back to the house through the snowdrifts.

Upon returning to Ukraine, I had assumed that I was searching for Nikodim. Even after realising that finding Nikodim was no simple matter, I still didn't understand that I was looking less for my great-uncle than for pieces of myself. I was filling the void. I was trying to find the equilibrium that had been upended when I left Ukraine and again when I realised in 2014 that I had never severed my ties. I was mourning my father. I needed to go on journeys, to sift through the archives and my memories. My great-grandparents' voices could be heard again as long as I knew how to listen.

I listened and searched, but in the way that only Valentina – or an Orthodox mystic – could explain, it was Nikodim who was guiding my quest. He was a catalyst that precipitated my journey and a mirror in which I could see my past reflected. I found this past to be a repository of loss and pain, but also a fount of resilience and hope. I saw that despite the trauma and suffering, the people who came before me found happiness and maintained their dignity. Even in the darkest times, they could embroider a rushnyk and grow a cherry orchard. I began to take my belief in thauma for granted.

Miracles abounded during my search. Hearing Sergiy's voice as I searched for Nikodim, I put together one puzzle. Talking to Vladimir about my father, I solved another. As difficult as these searches and conversations have been, they also helped me regain control over my fears. I wondered sometimes what it was exactly that I'd found, but at its simplest it had been my sense of self and my belonging. Ukraine remained my home.

Up until 2019, I visited Ukraine whenever I could, spending as much time with Valentina as possible to make up for the years we'd been separated. I also kept in closer touch with Vladimir, my cousin in Israel and the other members of my extended family. Valentina and Vladimir's wisdom and fortitude impressed me, and even if their stubbornness exasperated me, I held my tongue. We're from the same rootstock. When Valentina and I prepared our Easter breads, we set aside two loaves for Nikodim and my father. After decades of oblivion, Nikodim returned to the family stories. We remember him not as a victim or a hero, but as Sergiy's older brother who inspired him to study and become a teacher. We don't know where Nikodim is buried, and my father's resting place is far away in California, but in a gesture of remembrance, we followed tradition and left the breads in the local Bereh cemetery.

Pani Olga found a new job, settled into her own apartment, and continues to catalogue embroideries and collect rushnyky. Nadia's beloved white-on-white patterns from Reshetylivka earned a UNESCO intangible heritage nomination, and she now works to turn this nomination into a full status. She's employed at an arts centre dedicated to the preservation of embroidery. When the Covid-19 pandemic forced her to stop travelling around the world to promote Reshetylivka-style arts, she took her project online. She continues to teach and create exquisite garments. Whenever I observe Nadia at work, her fingers so deft and graceful, it strikes me as incredible that despite the maelstrom of Ukrainian history, art and beauty endure. 'We've survived Communism,' Nadia says. 'Let's hope that we can survive this war too.'

Nikodim always remains young. He has no grave. He has no face. He is the man who vanished but who escaped oblivion. Sometimes I think that Nikodim's odyssey – my odyssey – isn't over, and that there remains much more to discover. I sometimes pass by the Rooster House and stand across the street gazing upon its magnificent crimson facade. The place still makes me uneasy, but it no longer frightens me. I could visit more archives and search for more stories. Perhaps one day I will. Until then, I would stay in the cherry orchard. I walk between the trees and rub their rough bark. 'But thy eternal summer shall not fade,' I whisper to the garden. I became my own version of a cucumber whisperer after all the years in Bereh. Sometimes I even entertain the idea of settling here and growing my own orchard.

～

The last time I saw Valentina was in the final months of 2019. We prepared the orchard for winter and planned the planting for next spring. However, the following year the pandemic and an ongoing health issue made travelling to Ukraine impossible for me. In late 2021 Valentina fell ill with Covid. The last time we talked on Skype my grandmother breathed with difficulty but dismissed her illness. 'I can move about and do some work,' she said. 'I dried a tray of apples for you. Do you know how many apples we had this year?' She then added, 'Sasha is sick too, but she cannot even get out of bed.' The next day Valentina was taken to hospital where she passed away in her sleep at the age of eighty-seven. Sasha survived her illness and helped Dmytro with the funeral arrangements. Uncle Tolya took care of the burial. Flights to Ukraine were being cancelled owing to a new wave of Covid, and my mother and I followed the funeral via Skype. It made me feel that the whole thing was a stage play, somehow unreal.

On 24 February 2022, Russia invaded Ukraine and started a war that at the time of writing is still ongoing. The war was played out on social media in videos showing bombardments, destroyed buildings and blood-splattered bodies. I lost my ability to sleep and came to a breaking point. I couldn't go to Ukraine, but my connection with it was now so deep that every day was filled with immense pain to the extent that it was no longer possible to cope. What made 2022 different from 2014 was that I could share my distress and anger with many other people, my friends and acquaintances in Brussels as well as my blog readers around the world. The war was so senseless and the destruction was so indiscriminate that I no longer had to explain the catastrophe to anyone. We all shared the pain and suffering of Ukraine as we sought ways to help.

I opened my customary hoard of flour and rice and worked with the local Ukrainian community in Brussels to distribute food to the newly arrived refugees. They were mostly families with young children and elderly people who had escaped the occupation of eastern Ukraine and were beginning to remake their lives in Belgium. Yet every conversation with them was about their yearning for Ukraine and a desire to return home as soon as possible. This longing for a homeland in peril echoed my own and became amplified by my long absence from Ukraine. I sometimes wondered bitterly if we would be in this situation in 2022 had the world cared about my country more in 2014. Either way, I lived in Ukraine while being outside of it.

Dmytro stayed in Bereh. Losing Valentina made all of us feel that nothing could ever be the same, but his refusal to leave had a deeper meaning. He stayed because he wanted to continue tending our grandmother's garden. He cleaned up the land, pruned the trees and whitewashed them even as the sirens announced another air raid. Poltava was largely spared the destruction suffered by other eastern and central regions, but the situation remained tense. Still, what I received from my cousin were photos of new saplings and the orchard in bloom. During harvest time, he told me that he picked two buckets of cherries. 'I froze them so that we can make varenyky when you come,' he said. 'When we win this war.'

I envisioned us rolling out the dough on Valentina's oakwood table and filling dumplings with sugared fruit. I imagined the scent of flour and cherry juices and the feel of the heavy rolling pin in my hands. The scene was so poignant that I cried, but I hid my tears from Dmytro and joked that two buckets of cherries would make enough varenyky to feed the whole of Poltava. 'That sounds like a good idea, doesn't it?' he said.

Now I better understand why Asya and Sergiy grew their cherry orchard and how they survived the many calamities of the twentieth century in the borderlands. We carry on living and we tend to our garden one day at a time, one tree at a time. The orchard still stands full of sunlight and birdsong, and its bounty is a refusal to submit to despair and fear. Every bud and every branch is a reminder of the irrepressible vivere memento that illuminates the darkest of days with hope.

Brussels, August 2022

Acknowledgements

Writing a book is a journey, and in my case, it was a pilgrimage. Many people made it possible, and I will start by mentioning the most serendipitous of encounters with Pani Olga and the volunteers at the Saint Nicolas Ukrainian Orthodox Church. As I became their unofficial archivist, the church staff welcomed me warmly and taught me about Ukrainian art, history and religion. My pilgrimage would not have taken its fascinating route without their help.

Nadia Vakulenko and the staff of the Reshetylivka Arts College were my teachers when it came to embroideries and other Ukrainian crafts. I took lessons with Nadia and learned why the white-on-white technique deserved UNESCO Intangible Heritage Status.

Kateryna Ivanyvna and Volodymyr Mykolaevych Nakaznenko kept the doors of their house in Poltava open for me and shared their own family stories as I searched for mine. The artist Natalia Satsyk in Lviv helped me understand what made Ukrainian culture so vibrant and gave me inspiration to research the arts scene. The icon artists at the Kyivo-Pecherska Lavra Natalya Gladovska and Mykhailo Haiovy further expanded my knowledge of Ukrainian arts and initiated me into the mysterious world of icon painting. Since the resilience of art and culture is an important leitmotif in the Rooster House, their lessons were invaluable.

Although the Rooster House, the former KGB headquarters, initially frightened me, its archivists went above and beyond their duties to help me track down Nikodim's file and obtain any other necessary information. For privacy reasons, their names were changed, but I remain grateful for their assistance.

I thank my agents Charlie Campbell and Sam Edenborough for their help throughout this book's journey. They were invariably patient and supportive at every step of turning the manuscript into a book. A big thank you to my American agent Beniamino Ambrosi. I thank my Virago editors Anna Kelly and Rose Tomaszewska, and my Abrams Press editor Jamison Stoltz, for their guidance and help. The talented teams at Virago and Abrams Press deserve a special mention for their hard work on this book. Their passion and dedication made our collaboration thrilling.

I also thank Markku Aalto of Tammi, Dorotea Bromberg and Casia Bromberg of Brombergs Forlag, Ana Luísa Calmeiro of Porto, Raïssa Castro of BestSeller, María Fasce of Lumén, Iago Fernández of Grupo Enciclopedia, Camilla Rohde Søndergaard of Klim, Monika Rossiter of Mova/Kobiece, Friederike Schilbach of Aufbau, Elisabetta Sgarbi of La Nave di Teseo, Jan Swensson and Marie Kleve of Aschehoug, Michel van der Waart of De Arbeiderspers, the editorial teams of Faces, Könyvmolyképző, Moonhak Soochup, and my other international editors and their teams.

I also can't fail to mention the long conversations with my friend Farran Smith Nehme about the painting *Landscape with the Fall of Icarus* that inspired me to reconsider how I thought about loss and mourning. I'm grateful to Katherine Foshko Tsan for reading the first drafts of the story and sharing her feedback.

My husband Paru deserves special mention for reading every version of the manuscript and tolerating my long absences as I travelled around Ukraine. This book would not have been possible without the help of my family who read the different versions of the book and helped me establish dates and fact-check stories. I thank them for their support and love.

The book is written in the memory of my grandmother Valentina, who passed away in autumn 2021. She was a formidable person who cultivated her cherry orchard until her last day.